The Life Insurance Buyer's Guide

William D. Brownlie CLU, ChFC, CIP, LIA

With **Jeffrey L. Seglin**

McGraw-Hill Publishing Company

New York St. Louis San Francisco Auckland Bogotá
Caracas Hamburg Lisbon London Madrid Mexico
Milan Montreal New Delhi Oklahoma City
Paris San Juan São Paulo Singapore
Sydney Tokyo Toronto

Library of Congress Cataloging-in-Publication Data

Brownlie, William D.
  The life insurance buyer's guide / William D. Brownlie with
  Jeffrey L. Seglin.
      p.   cm.
      Bibliography: p.
      Includes index.
      ISBN 0-07-008512-9 :   . — ISBN 0-07-008513-7 (pbk.) :
      1. Insurance, Life—United States.   2. Insurance, Disability—
  United States. I. Seglin, Jeffrey L., date.   II. Title.
  HG8951.B68   1989
  368.3'2'0029—dc19   89-2364
                                                          CIP

1234567890   DOC/DOC   895432109

ISBN 0-07-008512-9
ISBN 0-07-008513-7 {PBK}

*The editors for this book were Martha Jewett and Georgia Kornbluth, the
designer was Naomi Auerbach, and the production supervisor was Suzanne W.
Babeuf. This book was set in Baskerville. It was composed by the McGraw-Hill
Publishing Company Professional & Reference Division composition unit.*

Printed and bound by R. R. Donnelley & Sons Company.

*For more information about other McGraw-Hill materials,
call 1-800-2-MCGRAW in the United States. In other
countries, call your nearest McGraw-Hill office.*

To John Marks Templeton,
whose beliefs have been inspirational fuel
for my mind, body, soul, and spirit.

About the Authors

WILLIAM D. BROWNLIE, CLU, ChFC, CIP, LIA, is a life and disability insurance salesperson in Chelmsford, Massachusetts, a life member of the Million Dollar Round Table, and a renowned consumer advocate who has appeared before Congress as an expert on life insurance. He is lecturer in continuing education at the Insurance and Financial Services Institute of Northeastern University in Boston, and a member of the external faculty of the American College in Bryn Mawr, Pennsylvania. He has been featured on the cover of *Financial Planning* magazine.

JEFFREY L. SEGLIN is a regular contributor to *Venture, Inc., Personal Investing, Financial Planning,* and other publications. He is also the author or coauthor of 10 business books. He runs Seglin Associates in Boston, a consulting group specializing in writing, editing, and marketing projects.

Contents

Part 3. Getting Down to Choices: Types of Life Insurance

Part 4. Who Should Write the Check to Pay the Premium?

Part 5. The Economic Need for Present-Value Living Money

Preface

My work over the past 30 years has shown me that most people don't get down to the basics of life and disability insurance. In *The Life Insurance Buyer's Guide,* I do get down to the basics. I give you straight talk, telling you what it is that you're buying when you purchase life insurance and disability insurance.

My goal is to cut through the confusion caused by lack of plain talk and to give you full disclosure, telling you what esoteric terms such as "cash value," "present value," and "tax-free buildup" *really* mean. *The Life Insurance Buyer's Guide* provides you with clear, concise nontechnical straight talk for all the important aspects of life insurance and disability insurance.

I discuss the areas of life insurance, disability insurance, and retirement issues that are most frequently talked about. I give you my hard-earned insights, without using any form of sensationalism. The book is essential reading for those who purchase, advise about, recommend, sell, teach, criticize, and study life insurance.

The Life Insurance Buyer's Guide covers all areas of life insurance in depth and is written in layperson language. My style is designed to influence you, the reader, to make a decision about your life and disability insurance needs and to take action to satisfy them.

Remember, the book is written by a salesperson who is also a consumer advocate. I give you total disclosure and up-to-date information. I meet all objections head-on, and I tell it like it is. I take you behind the assembly line and show you how the product is manufactured.

The Life Insurance Buyer's Guide shows you how to tackle life and disability insurance issues head-on. I'll show you how to determine how much life insurance is enough, whether or not you should own your own life insurance, how to understand various methods of life insurance cost disclosure, how to pick a life insurance company and agent, how to determine when you should replace your existing life insurance, and how to sort out differences between group and individual disability insurance.

In Chapter 18, "The Perfect Payment Scenario," I give you—most likely for the first time—the essential criteria to keep in mind when you are considering how to pay for life insurance. Not only will consumers learn how to calculate and design a perfect payment progam, but also agents will be able to ensure that they provide full disclosure to prospective customers.

Life insurance ledger statements are the sales tools of the industry. But by themselves, ledger statements do not tell all. By working through examples of annotated ledger statements for various types of life insurance policies, I'll show you how to navigate your way through the specific ones that interest you.

With all this coverage, the book should be valuable for everyone involved in the buying and selling of life and disability insurance, including individual customers, advisers, brokers, salespeople, agents, financial planners, estate planners, lawyers, and accountants.

In essence, life and disability insurance aren't about getting rich, they're about not getting poor. *The Life Insurance Buyer's Guide* tells you the truth about a difficult subject that most people don't understand and don't want to think about. If you follow my advice, you'll never leave your family or yourself vulnerable, you'll never pay too much for your life and disability insurance, and you'll know what you're getting when you sign on the dotted line of a life or disability insurance application.

There are several people who provided valuable insight and assistance in the preparation of *The Life Insurance Buyer's Guide*. While this book reflects my own original work, judgments, and opinions, these people must not go unmentioned.

My collaborator, Jeffrey L. Seglin, expertly organized my thoughts and feelings about life insurance, disability insurance, and retirement issues. Martha Jewett, senior editor at McGraw-Hill, became an advocate for this book and saw it through to production. The technical help and encouragement of Jerold Bischoff, CLU, and Bradford D. Haseltine, CLU, ChFC, has not gone without notice. Stephen Frankel, FSA, Robert Piatelli, and Warren C. Sylvester, CLU, furnished me with life insurance ledger statements I needed. Carragher, Fox, and Lampert, P.C., Attorneys at Law, and Sprague, Cain, and Cullen, P.C., Certified Public Accountants, furnished me with federal and state tax forms.

Finally, Reverend Father Emery Tang, OFM, helped me to realize what it really means to be human: that my ministry of selling life and disability insurance is my opportunity to serve, to be the best that I can be.

WILLIAM D. BROWNLIE

PART 1
First Things First: Life Insurance Fundamentals

1
What Is Life Insurance?
(Capital Formation)

The Life Insurance Buyer's Guide will not help you lower your cholesterol, stop smoking, lose weight, lower your blood pressure, or learn how to calculate why the gross premium for a $100,000 traditional whole life insurance policy paying dividends as declared for a 45-year-old nonsmoker, nonunisex rate (see Chapter 5 for a discussion of unisex rates) is $2001. It will, however, give you straight talk on three important areas of your life, all of them affected by money: death, disability, and retirement.

Reading this book from cover to cover and putting what you learn into practice will help you to make sure that:

- Your family will continue to live in the fashion to which they have become accustomed (if that is what you want) when you die.

- Your business interests will not go down the drain because of some misunderstanding or lack of money.

- If you become disabled, you will be able to continue to live in the fashion to which you have become accustomed.

- You will be able to retire or slow down with dignity, because you will have enough *present-value money.*

Nuts and Bolts

You, as a consumer, have every right to ask the questions: "Whom can I trust?" and "Who can tell me 'how the watch works' versus only 'what time it is'?" I assure you that after reading this book you will know 'how the watch works' when it comes to life insurance, disability insurance, and how to work the numbers now for your retirement, before it's too late.

This book provides total disclosure. It talks about the *design* of specific life and disability insurance products; the *service* you should expect from the person you entrust with the responsibility for making life, disability, and retirement recommendations; and the *trust* that's needed between consumers and professionals. Total disclosure, design, service, and trust are more essential in today's marketplace than cost. To base your decisions strictly on cost is to make life insurance, disability insurance, and retirement financial services products solely into commodities, which they are not.

Life insurance is not a commodity, and decisions about its purchase should not be determined solely by price. Every life insurance decision should be analyzed by a qualified life insurance agent or a person selling life insurance as a financial services product. This person should be particularly skilled in the area of life insurance cost disclosure and in ownership and beneficiary arrangements. This book is not filled with a lot of figures; rather it is nuts-and-bolts information about what you should know, what you should ask yourself, and when necessary, what you should ask the person responsible for your life insurance and financial planning.

Life insurance and related financial matters are very complex subjects. Each situation must be examined and studied separately, and no generalization—whether you read it in this book or hear it elsewhere—should be construed as applicable to all cases. My task in this book is to help you acquire a better understanding of life insurance, disability insurance, and some retirement issues. The publisher's task is to market the book to its designated audiences. Though the book mentions specific legal, accounting, insurance, and financial terms, it is not my intention nor the publisher's to offer any specific professional advice. If such professional assistance is required by you after reading this book, the services of a competent professional should be sought.

Language

Life insurance, disability insurance, and other aspects of personal finance have a language all their own. To help you understand the concepts, a variety of terms, expressions, and statements will be defined throughout the book. The definitions that I will give are based on my experience in life insurance and financial services, beginning in 1958. As such, these definitions reflect none of the textbook complexity or professional doubletalk all too common in today's marketplace. What you will read here is commonsense straight talk about financial subjects—straight talk that will help you to understand financial matters that have become extremely complicated with the growth of financial services industries through the years.

Capital Formation

The objective of life insurance is not to make you rich, but rather to make sure that you and those important to you never become poor. The time-honored definition of life insurance is that it provides for a stipulated sum to be paid to a designated beneficiary upon the death of the insured. In a very real sense, life insurance is *capital formation*.

Capital is usually defined as the value of accumulated goods which are devoted to the production of other goods, and accumulated possessions calculated to bring in income. *Formation* is defined as an act of giving form or shape to something, or of taking form.

After an insured person dies, capital is formed when the death benefit (the face amount of the life insurance policy) is paid to the beneficiary. The initial value is the death benefit. The value can be used to produce other goods or to bring in income depending upon how the beneficiary decides to use it.

Unlike other ways to create capital (e.g., regular savings, investing in a mutual fund, or investing in a business), life insurance chiefly forms capital when the insured dies. But, depending upon the type of life insurance, capital may be formed without the insured having to die—e.g., by borrowing against the cash reserve (cash-surrender value) of an insurance policy, or by using paid-up dividends (paid by an insurance company on a policy that is fully paid up) to provide a capital stream of income.

Looking upon life insurance as a vehicle for capital formation will allow you to determine whether it is the proper vehicle for you to use to create capital for your own specific needs—needs which could take the form of protection for your family, protection for a business obligation, or provision of supplemental retirement income to yourself, just to name a few of many possibilities.

Living Benefits from Life Insurance

Chapters 10 to 16 discuss in depth the various types of life insurance that are available. In this chapter we simply address the issue of whether or not these various types of insurance can be used as a vehicle for capital formation while the insured is still alive.

Term Insurance

When you buy term insurance, you buy only protection. There are no living benefits from term life insurance because there often is no cash reserve building up. As a result, there usually is no cash-surrender value, and capital cannot be formed before the insured dies.

Traditional Whole Life and Graded Premium Life Paying Dividends as Declared

With a traditional whole life and graded premium life policy paying dividends as declared, you can borrow from the policy's reserve (its cash-surrender value). No taxes become due on such a borrowing because it is considered a loan, provided that, for all types of nonterm life insurance issued on or after June 21, 1988, the seven-annual-premium-payments test is met. The death benefit, however, is reduced by the amount you borrow. This reduction is made because the reserve is the amount of money the insurance company has set aside to meet death claims. The insurance company carries the reserve as a liability, *not* as an asset on its balance sheet. When the reserve is borrowed out, the insured has received (as a loan of money) a portion of the death benefit in *advance*. Interest is charged on the loan because when the insurance company calculates the premium to charge and projects dividends, it must take into consideration:

- Mortality expenses
- Business overhead expenses
- Interest the company can earn on money coming into the store (premium payments)

Because the reserve is borrowed out, the insurance company can no longer earn interest on it. As a result, it must charge interest to make up the difference.

Money can also be received as a living benefit without borrowing if the policy is put on a paid-up basis. For example, it takes X dollars of reserve at each age to pay up $1000 of insurance. Once paid up, the reserve increases each year, and in addition, the insurance company may pay a paid-up dividend (though this is not guaranteed). The paid-up dividend, in addition to the reserve increase, represents the interest the insurance company is paying to the insured on the money used to pay up the insurance. The paid-up dividends are tax-free until they exceed what the policy cost, which is the cumulative sum of the premiums paid. The reserve increases on a tax-exempt basis because it is part of the paid-up death benefit.

As a life insurance purist, I believe it is best never to borrow indiscriminately against the cash reserve of an insurance policy, because:

- Borrowing destroys all the equity within the policy; borrowing on a life insurance policy is similar to refinancing the mortgage on a house.

- Borrowing forces you to pay interest which is nondeductible for federal tax purposes, according to the Tax Reform Act of 1986.

What you have just read about the effects of borrowing and interest for traditional whole life and graded premium life paying dividends as declared also pertains to all other nonterm life insurance policies—i.e., interest-sensitive whole life, universal life, variable life, and universal-variable life. Ask the person responsible for your life insurance for a detailed explanation of the seven-annual-premium-payments test, as mandated by the 1988 Technical Corrections Act, and its effect on living benefits via loans or withdrawals.

Interest-Sensitive Whole Life

Since an interest-sensitive whole life policy pays no dividends, the only way to get living capital formation benefits from interest-sensitive whole life is to borrow against the reserve, i.e., the cash-surrender value.

Universal Life

Any withdrawal from a universal life policy should be tax-free unless it is in excess of premiums paid. A withdrawal is not a loan. You can also take a loan against the reserve, i.e., the cash-surrender value, of the policy to get living capital formation benefits from universal life.

Variable Life

Since most variable life policies pay no dividends, the only way to get living capital formation benefits from variable life is to borrow against the separate investment account, i.e., the cash-surrender value of the policy.

The True Value of Life and Disability Insurance

Historically, the life insurance company from which I purchased my life and disability income insurance is not number 1 in terms of lowest costs. The contractual ingredients within its policies are, however, excellent. These provisions, combined with the company's proven track record of treating all policyholders the same (i.e., making new benefits retroactive to existing policyholders) and its fairness, common sense, and compassion when a claim arises, make the company attractive to continue to do business with.

But, you may well ask, when it comes to choosing life and disability insurance, how does this author know that design, trust, and service are more important than price? The answer is that I know because on January 18, 1986, I almost died. Since that date, I have had seven hospital admissions, two surgical operations, and one medical-surgical procedure. My "brand-name" life and disability insurance policies have done and will continue to do their job. Even though I had sold these policies for many years and had believed myself to be highly knowledgeable on the subject of life and disability insurance, I did not fully appreciate what my policies could and would do for me and my family, nor how truly valuable they are, until I myself almost died and did become disabled. Here is what they have done:

- My disability insurance has enabled me to go on living in the fashion to which I had become accustomed, and I will continue to be able to live in financial comfort if I remain either totally or residually disabled. (Refer to Chapter 19 for discussion of the importance of disability insurance.)

- My disability insurance has enabled, and will continue to enable, my family to go on living in the fashion to which they had become accustomed. If I should die, my life insurance will enable them to continue to live as comfortably as they do now.

- When I am ready, my disability insurance will allow me to retire with dignity. It is sufficient so that my retirement plans (i.e., Keogh, IRA, and a pension plan through a life insurance company) can remain untouched and continue to grow, tax-deferred. In addition, the premiums on my life and disability insurance are waived (refer to Chapter 17 for an explanation of waiver of premium), thus not creating a current cash-flow problem. Finally, my type of life insurance—traditional whole life paying dividends as declared (refer to Chapter 13)—in addition to providing a constant paid-up death benefit starting at age 65 and continuing for the rest of my life, also provides supplemental income in the form of paid-up dividends, also starting at age 65.

Summary

You should investigate whether or not your insurance company has a complete menu of insurance products available. If it does, you should consider exchanging interest-sensitive whole life, universal life, and variable life for paid-up whole life so that you can have a policy that features paid-up dividends—in the event that your own specific circumstances may require supplemental retirement income.

2

How to Pick a Life Insurance Company

(Look for a Brand Name)

Before you decide which company you should buy your insurance from, it's essential that you know what a life insurance company is.

What Is a Life Insurance Company?

Life insurance companies are financial intermediaries. They deal in *finance* and act as *go-betweens*. They receive payments in the form of premiums from a large number of people, invest the premium payments to earn interest, and pay money to the beneficiaries of insureds who have died. Strictly speaking, none of the insurance company's money is ever at risk. The payment of a claim is made from money received from all who are insured, plus interest earned. In essence, at any point in time, those who have not died are paying for those who have died.

How Does a Life Insurance Company Distribute Its Products?

Generally speaking, what distinguishes one life insurance company from another—besides expense ratios, rate of return (ROR) on investments, and mortality experience—is how each distributes its life insurance products.

In the current marketplace, life insurance is distributed in a number of ways. Two of the more common methods of distribution are described below.

- Life insurance may be distributed on a *direct basis* to buyers, using the media (television, radio, newspapers and magazines, and direct mail). When insurance is sold on a direct basis to the buyer, the attraction is its alleged low cost, because no agents are involved and no commissions are paid.

- Life insurance may be sold through a *general agency system,* where the general agent is authorized by the life insurance company to distribute its product(s) within a specific geographical area. It is the responsibility of the general agent to hire and train agents in cooperation with the life insurance company. Companies that use the general agency system believe that consumers are better served by dealing with highly educated people in the life insurance business: experienced agents, chartered life underwriters (CLUs), chartered financial consultants (ChFCs), certified financial planners (CFPs), and licensed insurance advisers (LIAs).

Every life insurance distribution system has a cost element to consider: e.g., mail, television, or radio advertising; salaries; fees paid to well-known personalities to promote the product; and commissions. You will have to decide which system you prefer.

The "Niche" Concept

In addition to differences in how they distribute life insurance, companies also employ the niche concept, both in product design and in market emphasis. The implications of the *niche concept* are that the life insurance company feels it is qualified (i.e., well suited) to sell insurance in specific scenarios.

Product Design Scenario

When a life insurance company chooses to have a complete menu of insurance, it is saying to the buyer, "The whole 'waterfront' is covered. You decide which specific product *best fits* your own specific circumstances."

However, not all life insurance companies believe in the "waterfront" approach. For reasons of *economics* (it is extremely expensive to retool and come out with a new product) and *philosophy* (a specific product may very well be a result of a short-term trend; for example, universal life came into being because of high interest rates in the early 1980s), some life insurance companies feel that they cannot be all things to all people and therefore prefer to *specialize* in a limited number of products.

The niche concept as it applies to product design means that a company focuses on offering one, some, or all of the following products:

- Term insurance
- Traditional whole life and graded premium life paying dividends as declared
- Interest-sensitive whole life
- Universal life
- Variable life
- Universal variable life
- Disability income insurance

Market Emphasis Scenario

A specific life insurance company may *target* one, some, or all of the following market segments:

- All levels of the salaried income market (low-, middle-, and high-income via individual product sales and payroll deductions)
- Self-employed professionals
- Business owners
- Publicly owned companies (Fortune 500 companies)
- Closely held companies (not publicly owned)

In so doing, it is saying to the buyer, "We have the necessary *products* and *personnel* (qualified life insurance agents) and *home office support systems* (the corporate office of a life insurance company is referred to as the 'home office') to get our fair share of a respective market."

Rating the Life Insurance Companies

Life insurance companies receive ratings from outside objective sources. The best-known source is A. M. Best Company, Inc., in Oldwick, New Jersey. In its publication *Best's Agents Guide to Life Insurance Companies* (Life/Health Edition), Best rates life insurance companies as follows:

A+   Superior

A   Excellent

B+   Very good

B   Good

C+   Fairly good

C   Fair

You should purchase life insurance only from a company that has achieved an A+ rating from Best for a prolonged period of time. You can ask your agent to provide you with information on the historical Best ratings of a company you are being advised to buy from.

Insurance Forum,[1] a four-page monthly periodical focusing on insurance, publishes a list of life insurance companies that have achieved an A+ Best rating for 10 consecutive years. The charge for a copy of this report is $3.

Insurance Forum also publishes a list of life-health and property-casualty companies designated by the National Association of Insurance Commissioners (NAIC) through its Insurance Regulatory Information System (IRIS) for immediate or targeted regulatory attention in at least 1 of the past 3 years. The charge for a copy of this report is $5.

Insurance Forum, which is edited by Joseph M. Belth, Ph.D., insurance professor at the school of business at Indiana University in Bloomington, also discussed two other sources of ratings for life insurance—*Moody's Investors Service* and *Duff & Phelps*—in its November 1988 issue. This issue is available for $3.

---

[1]Insurance Forum, Inc., P.O. Box 245, Ellettsville, IN 47429.

The Four Givens—What People Want

Bruce Bare, Jr., CLU, ChFC, is a well-respected insurance professional in Pasadena, California. In a satellite educational network conference given by the American Society of CLU and ChFC, he reported that recent studies by a large advertising research group revealed the following:

1. People are looking to restore the social bonds of the past. People today are asking the question: "Is it right?" in a wide variety of contexts.
2. When looking at products, people are deciding that value is more important than price.
3. People like to buy a brand name because it saves them time.
4. People want control of their lives. They want to spend their time doing what interests them, and therefore they value authority. They want someone to tell them what to do.

Purchasing life insurance from a company that has been rated A+ by A. M. Best for 10 consecutive years and has not been subject to or targeted for regulatory attention is, in my judgment, buying a brand name.

Conclusion

Although it is always best to buy life insurance from companies rated highly by authorities in the field—e.g., *Insurance Forum, Best's Agents Guide to Life Insurance Companies, Moody's Investors Service,* and *Duff & Phelps*—remember that evaluations of life insurance companies deal always with the concept of a moving target, in that results reported are based on a "snapshot in time." There is no guarantee that change either positive or negative will not take place.

3

How to Pick a Life Insurance Agent

(Straight Talk versus Sales Talk)

It is a given fact that your life insurance agent should be a professional. But in order to be a professional, does a life insurance agent have to be a CLU—a chartered life underwriter? Not necessarily, although it certainly may help. Many years ago, I asked a physician what in his opinion is the essential attribute of a good doctor. His immediate response was, "Judgment." Briefly stated, a person who has judgment knows what he or she is doing and talking about.

Look for a Professional

How does someone earn the right to be referred to as a "professional"? A *professional* is a person engaged in work in a professional field that requires specialized knowledge and often long and intensive academic preparation. The professional person conforms to the technical and business standards of his or her profession.

In plain talk, professionals are people who protect the unrealized interests of those seeking their authoritative judgment. Examples of protecting unrealized interests are:

14

- The physician who knows that some recovering heart attack patients must take medication in the form of a calcium blocker to slow down the heart rate and reduce the risk of heart spasms
- The accountant who knows that the alternative minimum tax must be considered since, if it is not taken into account, the taxpayer may get an unexpectedly large tax bill
- The attorney who provides total disclosure about legal terminology when analyzing a contract a client is asked to sign
- The financial planner who spells out the pros and cons of a specific financial services product
- The life insurance agent who makes a recommendation based not on the fad of the moment, but rather on the client's way of thinking, comfort zone (financial philosophy), and immediate and long-range capital formation requirements

When you choose a life insurance agent, you should use the same techniques you use to select a physician, dentist, lawyer, accountant, or any other professional you depend on. Listed below are some time-proven techniques.

- Get a recommendation from a person whose judgment you trust.
- When reading publications such as newspapers or magazines featuring articles on life insurance, look for names of people in your area who are favorably written about or quoted by their peers.
- When you meet or speak to a professional whose services you are considering using, ask direct questions about his or her background, experience, and references. Such questions can reveal the person's educational credentials and length of time in the profession, as well as evidence that other people are satisfied.
- Look for evidence of how the person keeps current in his or her professional field.
- Trust your own gut feelings about whether or not you can trust and have faith in the person.

In addition to the general standards used in selecting any professional, there are a variety of specific factors you should be aware of when you choose a life insurance agent. Becoming knowledgeable about these factors will not only help you during the selection process but also will enable you to better understand the agent you eventually choose and thus to develop a mutually trusting relationship.

The Difficult and Demanding Nature of the Life Insurance Business

Success in selling life insurance requires a great deal of a person, including the ability to discuss death in an empathic manner with people who would prefer not to discuss it, the ability to take rejection, and credibility in the eyes of clients. In percentage terms, very few can succeed. Many enter the field of life insurance; few stay.

One of Boston's foremost estate-planning attorneys once asked me, "Do you realize that the practice of probate law is very similar to the selling of life insurance? We both must talk about a very unpleasant subject—death." He was right on target.

Life insurance is a very difficult and extremely stressful business. Here is an example: One night, more than 20 years ago, I was in Framingham, Massachusetts, trying to sell life insurance to a physician. It has always been my style to say, "*When* you die...," not "*If* you die...." After I had used this phrase a few times during the interview, the physician's wife said, "Mr. Brownlie, I want you to leave our home immediately. I am sure our children have heard what you have said regarding George's death. This, I know, will make them very apprehensive. Please leave."

Life insurance industry statistics reveal that in order to make 1 sale, a life insurance agent must make 10 phone calls, which will result in 3 interviews. This fact of sales life is called the "10:3:1 ratio."

It seems that the more someone has suffered, the more credible he or she becomes. People who have been required to submit to investigation, whose life circumstances have forced them to feel keenly about issues, who have "paid their dues" by acquiring experience, who are able and willing to put up with the inevitable distress involved in making others think and talk about subjects they don't want to discuss, who are willing to sustain damage to their ego (e.g., rejection), or who have experienced a disability are often able to empathize. Empathic people make the best life insurance agents.

Life insurance agents are always mindful that people do not particularly object to owning life insurance. They simply object to paying for it.

Regulations

There are specific laws (state laws, not federal) governing the life insurance industry. An agent must be licensed to sell or offer a life insurance product in the particular state in which the buyer resides. In order for the agent to possess a specific license, he or she must pass an examination. Agents must conform to state law both in selling new life insurance policies and in making recommendations about the replacement of existing life insurance.

Professional Designations

Life insurance is a financial services product. As such it has been affected by the deregulation of the financial services industry, which has resulted in everybody getting involved in everybody else's business. Stockbrokers sell life insurance. Life insurance agents sell mutual funds and real estate limited partnerships. Accountants and lawyers actively engage in the financial services industry. The advantages and disadvantages of financial services deregulation are beyond the purview of this book.

The following list will enable you to be aware of the meaning of a professional designation after the name of someone who is talking to you about life insurance:

Designation	Meaning
JD	Juris Doctor, law school graduate
LLB	Bachelor of Laws, law school graduate
LLM	Master of Laws, holder of a master's degree in law
CPA	Certified public accountant
CIP	Holder of a certificate in investment planning, given by many colleges and universities which have financial planning programs
CFP	Certified financial planner, a designation awarded by the College for Financial Planning in Denver, Colorado
CLU	Chartered life underwriter, a designation awarded by the American College, Bryn Mawr, Pennsylvania
ChFC	Chartered financial consultant, a designation awarded by the American College
MSFS	Master of science in financial services, a degree awarded by the American College
MBA	Holder of a masters degree in business administration

PhD	Holder of a postgraduate doctorate degree in a specific area (In order for the person to be qualified to work in the financial services, the area in which the degree was awarded should be related to finance, economics, business, or accounting.)
FSA	Fellow of the Society of Actuaries
LIA	Licensed insurance adviser (This designation is awarded on the basis of a specific examination, different from the standard agent's examination, given by an individual state. In most states only a licensed insurance adviser can charge fees for advice on insurance matters.)
CFA	Chartered financial analyst
CPCU	Chartered property and casualty underwriter
RHU	Registered health underwriter
CEBS	Certified employee benefits specialist
EA	Enrolled agent (Designates a person permitted to practice before the Internal Revenue Service.)
CFM	Certified financial manager
CMC	Certified management consultant
CA	Chartered accountant; the Canadian equivalent to a CPA
CMA	Certificate in management accounting
BBA	Bachelor of business administration

Degrees and professional designations are important, but people are more important. Remember that we cannot legislate honesty and ethics; people either have these qualities or they don't.

Compensation

The life insurance business is a commission-based business. The present value of the commission to the agent is dependent upon the premium paid, not the face amount of life insurance purchased. Typically, depending upon the type of life insurance purchased, the agent's commission in the first year ranges from 35 to 55 percent of the premium paid.

The agent also receives a percentage of the premium paid in subsequent years, as long as the policy stays in force. The compensation system is structured so that the agent will not be forced to charge you a fee (if allowed) for yearly ongoing service work and professional expertise. State laws differ, but usually only licensed insurance advisers can charge fees.

Because the agent's commission is dependent upon the premium, not the face amount of life insurance, there are some who believe that agents are biased against term insurance (because it has a lower premium) in favor of other types of insurance that have a higher premium.

The *profit* concept (compensation) is concisely stated by Adam Smith in Books I and IV, Chapter II, of *The Wealth of Nations.* Today, more than 200 years after the passage below was written, this concept is referred to by some as the "invisible hand concept."[1]

> It is not from the benevolence of the butcher, the brewer, or the baker that we expect our dinner but from their regard to their own interest....Every individual who employs his capital in support of domestic industry, necessarily endeavors so to direct the industry, that its produce may be of the greatest possible value....He generally, indeed, neither intends to promote the public interest, nor knows how much he is promoting it. By preferring the support of domestic to that of foreign industry,...he intends only his own gain, and he is in this, as in many other cases, led by an invisible hand to promote an end which was no part of his intention.

Simply stated, the invisible hand is the profit motive that exists in all of us. No one should be expected to work or provide a service for nothing. Usually, something that costs nothing is worth nothing.

It is the invisible hand, the intention to make a profit, that always puts the best interests of the profit maker first—the life insurance agent no less so than the butcher, the brewer, or the baker. One cannot succeed in the arena of commerce, however, without providing a legitimate service worthy of the price. When life insurance agents put their own best interests first in order to succeed, they are, in essence, also putting the best interests of their clients first.

Life insurance agents are no different from any other businesspeople. They will not stay in business unless they are competitive. They become competitive by earning a sufficient profit to sustain their lifestyles and to pay for the necessary business overhead that helps them serve their clients.

In life insurance, as in any business, there are the minority who become greedy and seek to make an excessive profit by making improper recommendations. But the way of life of the successful agent (one who can stay in business and make a profit) is best described by Edwin Nadel, CLU, of New York City, as "offering the *right* product or service

---

[1]Modern Library Edition, Random House, New York, 1937, 1965.

to the *right* audience, with the *right* message, at the *right* price, at the *right* time, to meet the *right* needs."[2]

Characteristics of a Good Life Insurance Agent

Life insurance agents are entrepreneurs. They organize, manage, and assume the risk of a business or enterprise—namely, the selling of life insurance. Talk to any successful person in any field and ask for the one attribute that is necessary for success, and the answer usually is "hard work." Hard work in the life insurance business means knocking on doors, making cold calls, and asking people to talk about a reality that is extremely unpleasant—death. Again we can learn from Edwin Nadel:

> Failure happens to the agents who thought they worked hard, but didn't. They kept busy with details, worked long hours, but still didn't work smart. Agents don't work hard in this business until they are face to face with prospects, giving sales presentations and asking them to sign the application and pay the premium.

The professional, competitive, successful life insurance agent will:

1. *Listen when a client talks.*   A good life insurance agent develops a manner of listening that encourages clients to tell their "life stories"—their fears, dreams, and aspirations. Knowing these things about a client enables the agent to custom-design life and disability recommendations based upon the revealed feelings.

2. *Answer a client's questions.*   The agent should take the time to ask whether the client has any questions, and whether he or she is talking in clear, understandable terms.

3. *Take a complete financial history of the client.*

4. *Help to educate the client about life insurance.*   The agent should explain all recommendations and put them in writing when necessary or when asked.

5. *Provide the client with total disclosure regarding specific, relevant issues.*   For example: How was the amount of life insurance being recommended arrived at? How were the recommendations for the owner of the policy and beneficiary terminology determined?

---

[2]"Formula for a Successful Future: The Key Ingredients," *The Massachusetts Life Underwriter,* November–December 1987. Published by the Massachusetts Association of Life Underwriters, Boston.

6. *Respect the client's financial comfort zone.*

7. *Return the client's telephone calls promptly.*

8. *Tell the client, when asked, what professional associations he or she is a member of.*

9. *Not be rigid or arbitrary.*

10. *Not get uptight when the client expresses an intention of asking for a second opinion.*

11. *When taking a financial history, ask the necessary questions with discretion, in order to bring to the surface any hidden, unstated objections that the client may be harboring.*   For example, when I was selling life insurance, it was standard procedure to ask questions like "How is your relationship with your spouse?" and "What kind of car do you drive?" I wanted to know not only clients' lifestyles but, more important, their attitudes about their families. It has been stated many times that life insurance is a "character" sale and purchase, meaning that clients buy policies not for themselves but rather for others. It is as appropriate for a life insurance agent to ask such personal questions as for a cardiologist to ask whether a patient smokes.

12. *Never ask the client to make a check payable to anyone other than the specific life insurance company.*   The agent should never offer to finance or pay the life insurance premium for the client, but should only recommend a specific life insurance policy that the client can afford. As soon as the agent has received the policy issued by the life insurance company, he or she should immediately either deliver it to the client in person or mail it with explanations. Most state insurance laws provide for a 10-day free look. If the policy is not acceptable to the client within 10 days after receipt, he or she can return it and get the money back in full.

The Relationship between Insurance Companies and Their Agents

Life insurance agents are the best police force an insurance company has. An insurance company depends upon its agents to present all the facts in a straightforward manner so that the proper price can be charged for the risk assumed. For example, an agent is obligated to indicate honestly on the application that a smoker is in fact a smoker—not to hide the fact so that the buyer will get an unjustified lower price.

I do not agree with the marketing concept of an *independent agent.*

Most successful life insurance agents, regardless of how they market themselves, have one main company they represent.

When I was selling life insurance, I never accepted the concept of spreading my insurance business around, except under rare circumstances. All my business was placed with one specific company. The realities of life are such that loyalty usually gets loyalty. Over the years, this principle has had many positive benefits for me and for my policyholders.

On the basis of both my professional and my personal experience, I strongly recommend that you purchase your life and disability insurance from an agent known and respected by the insurance company and from a company whose name and reputation you know and respect.

4
How Much Life Insurance Is Enough?

(Four Methods, and Form 706 and the "Other Form" Approach)

Life insurance is purchased to provide an immediate creation of capital. It overcomes the problem of time. Once the insurance is in force—issued and paid for—X dollars are payable upon the death of the insured. Life insurance is purchased primarily for the following reasons:

- As income replacement for the benefit of the insured's family
- To create capital (i.e., money available in cash upon the death of the insured) for the payment of final expenses, including federal estate and state inheritance taxes, so that the survivors will not be forced to sell nonliquid assets in order to raise cash
- To form capital to fund an obligation that arises upon death, such as a partnership buyout, purchase of stock in a business, or payment of deferred compensation

Also keep in mind that people nowadays do tend to live longer than in former times. The result is that serious medical expenses without adequate insurance reimbursement could be a future possibility for any of us. Life insurance with all premiums vanished can be used as collateral to borrow money (at the death benefit value, not cash value) to meet these costs and, as a result, not place a financial burden on those important to you (e.g., your children). Do not assume that the longer you live, the more your need for life insurance will disappear.

Thomas A. FitzGerald, JD, LLM, of White Plains, New York, feels that in many cases the reason for buying the insurance will determine the amount needed. When the amount is not readily ascertainable, however, a variety of approaches can help, such as: X times gross earnings, multiples of salary, insurance needs analysis, the present-value concept, form 706 and the "other form" approach. In my opinion, of these five methods, the present-value concept is the most useful (in that it requires the practice of present value, future value, and time span in determining the time value of money), reliable (in that it requires use of the client's tax return), and practical (in that it is easily understood by clients, once explained) method available for use in determining the amount of life insurance required for income-replacement purposes.

X Times Gross Earnings Approach

Edward Dana, CLU, of Wayland, Massachusetts, is an advocate of the X times gross earnings approach for determining an amount of life insurance for income replacement. It is his contention that principal should not be spent; rather, it should be preserved for the surviving spouse and then passed on to children, regardless of their ages. He readily admits that this financial philosophy is a result of his own family background.

The X times gross earnings method does not require a computer or a financial decisions calculator. Dana bases all his calculations on pretax dollars and does not consider the residence an offset against assets.

The pretax investment yield on the safest of investments (e.g., treasury obligations, annuities, and various money market investments) should provide the necessary after-tax yield to allow the breadwinner's family to maintain their accustomed lifestyle. (See the definition of "money market investment" later in this chapter.) Dana feels that ideally the goal should be 10 times earnings, but the figure decided upon is usually between 5 and 7. He also acknowledges that all assets *except* the residence can be used as an offset against the amount of life insurance needed. ("People have to live someplace," he says.)

Multiples-of-Salary Approach

The multiples-of-salary approach is used to determine the amount of life insurance required as income replacement. The reasoning behind this method is that, if the breadwinner dies, the family will need 75 percent of his or her after-tax income. This approach was developed by First National City Bank (Citibank) of New York City, which recommends that insurance provide at least 60 percent and preferably 75 percent of after-tax income replacement.

When this approach was first developed in 1976 (as reported in *The Wall Street Journal* on Monday, December 6, of that year), it was assumed that the life insurance proceeds would produce a before-tax yield of 5 percent above the inflation rate (e.g., for an inflation rate of 4 percent, the pretax yield should be 9 percent; this may well be too aggressive an assumption). Another assumption is that principal will be exhausted during the surviving spouse's life expectancy. (See Table 4-1.)

According to the multiples-of-salary chart (Table 4-1), if your spouse is 45 and your gross earnings total $65,000, the amount of life insurance you need to replace 75 percent of your after-tax income is $487,500 ($65,000 times 7.5). For a 60 percent replacement, $390,000 is needed ($65,000 times 6.0).

The multiples-of-salary factors were developed with the assumption that the family will be receiving social security benefits. In addition, other assets in excess of 1 year's income (e.g., savings, retirement plans, or potential inherited money), to the extent that they are in excess of 1 year's gross earnings, can be used to reduce the amount of insurance

Table 4-1. The Multiples-of-Salary Chart

Your present gross earnings	Present age of spouse							
	25 years		35 years		45 years		55 years	
	75%	60%	75%	60%	75%	60%	75%	60%
$ 7,500	4.0	3.0	5.5	4.0	7.5	5.5	6.5	4.5
9,000	4.0	3.0	5.5	4.0	7.5	5.5	6.5	4.5
15,000	4.5	3.0	6.5	4.5	8.0	6.0	7.0	5.5
23,500	6.5	4.5	8.0	5.5	8.5	6.5	7.5	5.5
30,000	7.5	5.0	8.0	6.0	8.5	6.5	7.0	5.5
40,000	7.5	5.0	8.0	6.0	8.0	6.0	7.0	5.5
65,000	7.5	5.5	7.5	6.0	7.5	6.0	6.5	5.0

needed. In the example cited above, if your other assets add up to $130,000, you may reduce the $487,500 by $65,000.

The X times earnings and the multiples-of-salary methods for determining how much life insurance is enough to replace income can be calculated without using a computer or a financial decisions calculator, provided that the life insurance agent has the necessary experience, economic background, and analytical powers to custom-design these approaches to suit your specific situation. These characteristics are necessary because these two methods fall into the classification of "rules of thumb."

Insurance Needs Analysis, or Programming Approach

Use of the *insurance needs analysis* to determine the amount of life insurance needed for income replacement requires a computer and the necessary financial decisions software. Before the day of the computer, this approach was referred to as the *programming approach,* as it still is by some today. Those using the approach today, however, commonly refer to it as "insurance needs analysis." One advocate of this method is Robert J. Glovsky, JD, LLM, CLU, ChFC, of Boston.

The analysis is done by first measuring current needs (e.g., funeral costs, federal estate taxes, state inheritance taxes, settlement of nonmortgage debt, settlement of mortgage debt if desired, an emergency fund, a college fund, and expected living expenses). Glovsky believes that survivors' income needs can be divided into time periods. For instance, a surviving spouse may need a certain amount of income until the children leave home, and then the needed amount may drop to some lower number.

Once all the needs are measured, the calculation is made, using an inflation factor, and then all monies are discounted back to current time (today).

The amount of money needed today is the amount of life insurance required. The amount calculated is reduced, however, by any existing life insurance or other assets already in place. The net figure is the amount of life insurance that the individual should buy. The calculation assumes that principal will be exhausted. The calculation uses as a point in time the life expectancy of the surviving spouse.

Present-Value Approach

Recently Mike, a client of mine, came to my office in Chelmsford, Massachusetts, for a financial discussion. Before we got down to particulars, the subject of sports salaries and the state lottery came up.

Mike said he'd like to know how lottery payments are guaranteed by the commonwealth of Massachusetts. I answered that it is my understanding that the state purchases an annuity to guarantee the payments and that the purchase price of the annuity is based upon the concept of present value. (The present-value concept as used in this chapter and as shown in Table 4-4 exhausts the present-value amount of money at the end of the time period desired. It does not keep the principal—the amount of present-value money—intact forever.)

For example, if someone hits the lottery for $3 million, Massachusetts pays that person $150,000 each year for 20 years. In order to guarantee those payments, the state negotiates with an insurance company to purchase an annuity. Assuming that the insurance company guarantees a 10 percent interest rate for 20 years, in reality that 10 percent interest rate becomes what is called the "discount rate." A present-value amount of money, in this instance $1,404,738, is required to guarantee 20 annual payments of $150,000.

If the state can negotiate a higher interest rate (which in essence means a higher discount rate), the present-value amount of money required is less. Conversely, the lower the discount rate, the higher the present-value amount of money required.

It is good to be conservative in the use of an assumed interest rate for present-value calculation purposes. If you are too aggressive in your interest-rate assumption and it is not realized, you will not provide enough present-value money. The lower the interest rate (which becomes the discount rate), the higher the present-value amount of money. The higher the interest rate, the lower the present-value amount of money.

Sports salaries work the same way. Take a recent example. A young man signs with a professional sports team and is guaranteed $7 million over the next 5 years. Again using 10 percent as a discount rate, the team will have to put up only $5,837,811 in order to guarantee the player a yearly payment of $1.4 million for each of the next 5 years. And if the team is able to negotiate a discount rate in excess of 10 percent, it will have to put up less than the amount required at 10 percent.

Once we had settled the question of lottery payments and professional sports, Mike asked, "But how can the concept of present value be used by me, personally?" I told him that the concept can be used on a personal level to analyze whether one should lease or buy a car, or to decide whether to purchase a bond at a premium or at a discount—and I told him also that the concept of present value can be used to determine how much life insurance a family needs, which is more important in the context of this book. Furthermore, the present-value calculation of life insurance needed should be redone at least every 2 years.

Financial Base, Net After-Tax Income, Inflation, and Other Variables

On the assumption that his family would need 75 percent of his after-tax income if he were to die, Mike's situation would be as follows. His taxable income, increased by allowable deductions and personal exemptions, minus federal income tax, and minus state income tax (if any), equals a financial base of $86,730. His family would need 75 percent, which is $65,047, if he died right now. If inflation were factored in, the amount would increase year by year; that is, the $65,047 would have to increase year by year compounded at an assumed inflation rate.

When he heard this, Mike's ears perked up. "What is a reasonable inflation rate?" he asked. I told him that for the past 10 years inflation has averaged approximately 6.5 percent compounded.

I showed Mike a table of compounded annual rates of return (see Table 4-2), in which the Consumer Price Index is taken as the measure of inflation. Approximately 43 percent of the inflation rate is for housing. I also showed him a table entitled "Market Baskets, Old and New" (see Table 4-3). If we assume that inflation will continue on average to compound at 6.5 percent and that a family's housing costs will not increase over what they are today, then 3.71 percent compounded should be the inflation factor used in calculating life insurance needs.

Table 4-2. Compounded Annual Rates of Return

	15 years	Rank	10 years	Rank	5 years	Rank
U.S. coins	18.8%	1	16.3%	1	11.4%	3
Oil	13.9	2	3.0	13	−11.8	14
U.S. stamps	13.6	3	11.8	3	−1.3	12
Gold	11.9	4	9.2	8	6.8	7
Silver	10.3	5	9.7	6	4.0	9
Treasury bills	9.2	6	10.2	5	8.5	6
Old Masters	9.2	7	9.7	6	9.5	5
Stocks	8.6	8	13.9	2	24.1	1
Bonds	8.7	9	9.7	7	19.1	2
Chinese ceramics	8.3	10	11.3	4	3.4	11
Housing	8.2	11	7.4	10	4.8	8
Consumer Price Index	6.9	12	6.5	11	3.5	10
U.S. farmland	6.3	13	1.5	14	−7.8	13
Foreign exchange	4.6	14	4.1	12	6.8	7
Diamonds	4.1	15	8.9	9	10.2	4

SOURCE: *Barron's*, June 15, 1987, page 15. The table as published is the twelfth annual survey prepared by Salomon Brothers. Reprinted with written permission of both *Barron's* and Salomon Brothers.

Table 4-3. Market Baskets, Old and New

	Previous		Revised	
Expenditure category	Average expend- iture*	Relative impor- tance	Average expend- iture*	Relative impor- tance
All items	$22,065.00	100.000	$19,362.65	100.000
Food and beverages	4,380.12	19.851	8,454.36	17.840
Food at home	2,776.44	12.583	1,962.94	10.138
Food away from home	1,352.14	6.128	1,189.82	6.145
Alcoholic beverages	239.85	1.087	301.60	1.558
Housing	8,318.95	37.702	8,255.57	42.637
Residential rent	1,367.95	6.198	1,099.66	5.679
Homeowners' rent	3,029.08	13.728	3,519.20	18.175
Apparel and upkeep	1,116.71	5.061	1,263.23	6.524
Transportation	4,772.88	21.631	3,620.03	18.696
New vehicles	851.49	3.859	1,064.36	5.497
Used vehicles	1,014.77	4.599	246.08	1.271
Motor fuel	1,215.34	5.508	929.49	4.800
Public transportation	347.97	1.577	269.67	1.393
Medical care	1,383.25	6.269	928.58	4.796
Entertainment	931.58	4.222	848.02	4.380
Other goods and services	1,173.64	5.319	992.85	5.128

*By urban consumer risk.

SOURCE: Bureau of Labor Statistics. *Barron's*, March 2, 1987, p. 24. Reprinted with permission of *Barron's*.

Calculations of how long an income of $65,047 would be needed if Mike died are based on the current age of Mike's wife, which is 38. At her present age, Lauren's life expectancy is 40 more years. Therefore, she will need income for the next 40 years.

Mike must provide answers for other variables. Are payments to be guaranteed for the next 40 years? Will Lauren work? If so, will her net income after taxes and expenses be offset against the yearly required payments? Do Mike and Lauren want the yearly payments to increase according to the assumed inflation rate of 3.71 percent compounded?

In Table 4-4, the present-value method has been used to estimate how much life insurance families need. The figures vary according to the length of time the family will need financial support and according to the family's financial base income. The present-value amount of life insurance needed is arrived at by discounting the stream of yearly payments required through the surviving spouse's life. (See the definition of "stream of payments" at the end of this chapter.) For the purposes of this table, 5.6 percent was used as the discount rate. Expressed another way, the present-value amount of life insurance, if invested at 5.6 per

Table 4-4. Calculating the Amount of Life Insurance Needed

Net after-tax income of breadwinner	Yearly amount required for family	Present-value amount of life insurance needed
Present Age of Spouse, 25 Years—Life Expectancy, 52 Years		
$ 15,000	$11,250	$ 199,666
18,000	13,500	239,599
30,000	22,500	399,332
47,000	35,250	625,620
60,000	45,000	798,664
80,000	60,000	1,064,885
130,000	97,500	1,730,438
Present Age of Spouse, 35 Years—Life Expectancy, 43 Years		
$ 15,000	$11,250	$ 191,768
18,000	13,500	230,122
30,000	22,500	383,537
47,000	35,250	600,875
60,000	45,000	767,074
80,000	60,000	1,022,766
130,000	97,500	1,661,995
Present Age of Spouse, 45 Years—Life Expectancy, 34 Years		
$ 15,000	$11,250	$ 178,872
18,000	13,500	214,647
30,000	22,500	357,745
47,000	35,250	560,467
60,000	45,000	715,490
80,000	60,000	953,987
130,000	97,500	1,550,29
Present Age of Spouse, 55 Years—Life Expectancy, 25 Years		
$ 15,000	$11,250	$ 157,814
18,000	13,500	189,814
30,000	22,500	315,628
47,000	35,250	494,483
60,000	45,000	631,256
80,000	60,000	841,674
130,000	97,500	1,367,721

cent, will produce the yearly required payments at the beginning of each year throughout the spouse's remaining life expectancy.

The present-value amount of life insurance needed can be reduced in direct ratio to existing net after-tax current assets within the family, e.g., cash, bonds, liquid stocks, and liquid real estate, but not restricted stock and tax shelter investments.

Tax-deferred plans—e.g., deferred compensation, 403(b) tax-sheltered annuities, corporate and unincorporated retirement plans, and IRAs on the life of the breadwinner can also reduce the present-value amount of life insurance needed, but only after the taxes due are taken into account.

Social security payments, if any, should not be used to reduce the present-value amount of life insurance needed, if it is arrived at on a constant dollar basis (unadjusted for inflation). If it is arrived at on a real dollar basis (adjusted for inflation), however, social security payments can be used to reduce the present-value amount of life insurance needed. (See the definitions of "constant dollars" and "real dollars" at the end of this chapter.)

The values shown in Table 4-4 are figured on a constant dollar basis. For example, 5.6 percent net after taxes is the average result of a 7.5 percent before-tax yield in a money market investment taxed at 15, 25, and 33 percent marginal ordinary federal income tax brackets. In today's economic environment, 5.6 percent net after taxes is a reasonable opportunity cost or discount rate representing the annual rate of return that could be earned currently on similar investments (e.g., treasury bills, money market funds), assuming a before-tax yield of 7.5 percent. A discount rate of 5.6 percent net after taxes may not always be reasonable, however, depending upon economic conditions.

Marginal Ordinary Federal Income Tax

Before passage of the Tax Reform Act of 1986, there were 14 marginal tax brackets, ranging from a low of 11 percent to a high of 50 percent. Marginal tax bracketing means that the federal income tax system is progressive; the more money we make, the more tax we pay. The marginal bracket means that the individual's last dollar subject to tax is taxed at that individual's ultimate marginal tax bracket. Marginal tax brackets effective in 1988 are shown in Table 4-5.

Table 4-5. 1988 Marginal Ordinary Income Tax Brackets

	Taxable income	
Rate	Joint returns	Single return
15%	$0–$29,750	$0–$17,850
28	$29,750–$71,900	$17,850–$43,150
33	$71,900–$171,090	$43,150–$100,480
28	Over $171,090	$100,480

For example, a married person filing jointly with a taxable income of $50,000 will face the following tax situation:

First $20,750 taxed at 15%   = $ 4,462.50

$29,750–50,000 taxed at 28% = $ 5,670.00 ($20,250 at 28%)

Total tax paid $10,132.50

The total tax paid is not much higher than a 20 percent effective tax rate paid on $50,000 taxable income. However, this person's ultimate marginal tax bracket is 28 percent, because the last dollar subject to tax is taxed at 28 percent.

Capital market investments have not been considered in determining the present-value amount of life insurance required in Table 4-4, because of their higher risk factor. (See the definition of "capital market investment" later in this chapter.) In considering these investments, however, keep in mind that an individual decision must be made about certain factors, including the ones listed below.

1. The interest rate to be assumed

2. The type of investment, i.e., money market or capital market

Also keep in mind that, regardless of the type of investment, interest, dividends, and gains are all taxed the same, as mandated by the 1986 Tax Reform Act, i.e., at marginal federal ordinary income tax rates. The favorable effect of the long-term capital gains tax is no longer available.

Constant Dollar versus Real Dollar Calculations

There is a substantial difference between calculating the present-value amount of life insurance needed on a constant dollar basis and calculating it on a real dollar basis. As a constant dollar payment, each and every year for 40 years, using 5.6 percent as the interest rate (discount rate), $65,047.38 requires $1,087,878 in present-value life insurance (capital formation in the form of money).

When the same amount is calculated on a real dollar basis, the stream of continuous payments, using 3.71 percent as the assumed inflation rate, increases year by year as shown in Table 4-6 (assuming beginning-of-the-year withdrawal of the annual stream of income). Discounting (to arrive at present value) the 40 separate cash-flow payments at 5.6 percent (discount interest rate) requires $1,869,408 in present-value life in-

Table 4-6

Year	Payment	Year	Payment	Year	Payment
1	$ 65,047	15	$108,313	28	$173,913
2	67,460	16	112,331	29	180,365
3	69,962	17	116,498	30	187,056
4	72,557	18	120,820	31	193,995
5	75,248	19	125,302	32	201,192
6	78,039	20	129,950	33	208,656
7	80,934	21	134,771	34	216,397
8	83,936	22	139,771	35	224,425
9	87,050	23	144,956	36	232,751
10	90,279	24	150,333	37	241,386
11	93,628	25	155,910	38	250,341
12	97,101	26	161,694	39	259,628
13	100,703	27	167,692	40	269,260
14	104,439				

surance versus $1,087,878 on a constant dollar basis, a difference of $781,530.

The constant dollar calculation is executed as follows in my hand-held calculator (the Hewlett-Packard 41C Series with the financial decisions module):

1. Payments are entered as $65,047.

2. Interest is entered as 5.6 percent.

3. Time is entered as 40 years.

4. The calculator is asked to solve for present value.

5. The answer is $1,087,878.

The real dollar calculation is executed as follows in my hand-held calculator:

1. The 40 separate cash-flow payments are entered.

2. The discount rate is entered as 5.6 percent.

3. The calculator is asked to solve for net present value.

4. The answer is $1,869,408.

Terms Defined

Constant Dollars. A *constant dollar* is the buying power of a dollar unadjusted for inflation. A dollar today has a greater value than a dollar 2 years from now because you can do something with it (spend it, save it, invest it). A dollar 2 years from now, with an assumed inflation rate of 3.71 percent compound, is worth only 93 cents on a present-value basis (meaning today). In determining the present-value amount of life insurance required on a constant dollar basis, the stream of income payments required for X years has not been adjusted for inflation. This means that when the yearly payment is first established it does not increase.

Real Dollars.   A *real dollar* is the buying power of a dollar adjusted for inflation. For example, $1 invested at 3.71 percent compound net after taxes will be worth $1.08 at the end of 2 years. This $1.08 discounted at 3.71 percent and compounded for 2 years has a present value of $1, versus 93 cents for a dollar adjusted for inflation. If you do not want your life insurance death benefit to become outdated because of inflation, then you should calculate your present-value money needs on a real dollar basis rather than a constant dollar basis. This means that when the first yearly required payment is established, it is increased each year on a compound basis at the assumed inflation rate (which is the interest rate), for the number of years that the stream of payments is required.

Stream of Payments.   *Stream of payments* is an expression used mainly by financial people to indicate a constant and continuous flow. When used in finance it means X dollars per year for X years.

Money Market Investment.   *Money market investments* are investments which by definition usually mature in 1 year or less (e.g., commercial paper, certificates of deposit, and certain treasury obligations). Generally speaking, the rate of return for money market investments is less than that for capital market investments; the reason is that there is less risk involved because of the shorter maturity date of 1 year or less.

Capital Market Investment.   *Capital market investments* are investments which by definition mature for longer than 1 year (e.g., bonds). Generally speaking, the rate of return for capital market investments is greater than that of money market investments because of the risk involved in the longer maturity date.

Form 706 and the "Other Form" Approach

While writing this book, I received a telephone call from Edmund Cocco, LIA, of Lynnfield, Massachusetts, one of the nation's foremost experts in travel insurance and my boyhood chum, with whom I grew up in Everett, Massachusetts. Ed wanted to know what, in my opinion, is the best method to use to establish the need for life insurance not as income replacement but for paying federal estate and state inheritance taxes. My response was swift: "Form 706 and the 'other form'!"

Form 706 is the United States Estate Tax return, which consists of 16 pages, each accompanied by a blank, for a total potential of 32 pages. (Figure 4-1 shows the front page of form 706.) This form must be filled

Form **706**	**United States Estate Tax Return**
(Rev. Jan. 1979) Department of the Treasury Internal Revenue Service	Estate of citizen or resident of the United States (see separate instructions)

Decedent's first name and middle initial	Decedent's last name	Date of death
Domicile at time of death	Year domicile established	Decedent's social security number
Name of personal representative	Address (Number and street including apartment number or rural route, city, town or post office, State and ZIP code)	

Name and location of court where will was probated or estate administered	Case number

If decedent died testate check here ▶ ☐ and attach a certified copy of the will.

Authorization to receive confidential tax information under 26 C.F.R. 601.502(c)(3)(ii) if return prepared by an attorney for the personal representative:

I declare that I am the attorney of record for the personal representative before the above court and prepared this return for the personal representative. I am not under suspension or disbarment from practice before the Internal Revenue Service and am qualified to practice in the State shown below—

* Name of attorney	State	Address (Number and street, city, State and ZIP code)

Computation of Tax

1 Total gross estate (from Recapitulation, page 3, line 10)	1	
2 Total allowable deductions (from Recapitulation, page 3, line 29)	2	
3 Taxable estate (subtract the amount on line 2 from the amount on line 1)	3	
4 Adjusted taxable gifts (total amount of taxable gifts (within the meaning of section 2503) made by decedent after December 31, 1976, other than gifts which are includible in decedent's gross estate (section 2001(b))). See instructions	4	
5 Add the amount on line 3 and the amount on line 4	5	
6 Tentative tax on the amount on line 5 from Table A in the separate instructions	6	
7 Aggregate gift taxes payable with respect to gifts by decedent after December 31, 1976, including gift taxes paid by decedent's spouse for split gifts (section 2513) if decedent was the donor of such gifts and they are includible in decedent's gross estate. See instructions	7	
8 Gross estate tax. Subtract the amount on line 7 from the amount on line 6	8	
9 Unified credit against estate tax from Table B in the separate instructions . . .	9	
10 Adjustment to unified credit. See instructions	10	
11 Allowable unified credit (subtract the amount on line 10 from the amount on line 9)	11	
12 Subtract the amount on line 11 from the amount on line 8 (but not less than zero)	12	
13 Credit for State death taxes not to exceed the amount on line 12; see Table C in the separate instructions and attach credit evidence	13	
14 Subtract the amount on line 13 from the amount on line 12	14	
15 Credit for Federal gift taxes (see section 2012 and attach computation) . . .	15	
16 Credit for foreign death taxes (from Schedule P). (Form 706CE is required) . .	16	
17 Credit for tax on prior transfers (from Schedule Q)	17	
18 Total (add the amounts on lines 15, 16, and 17)	18	
19 Net estate tax. Subtract the amount on line 18 from the amount on line 14	19	
20 Prior payments. Explain in attached statement; see instruction 5	20	
21 United States Treasury bonds redeemed in payment of estate tax	21	
22 Total (add the amount on line 20 and the amount on line 21).	22	
23 Balance due (subtract the amount on line 22 from the amount on line 19)	23	

Note: Please attach the necessary supplemental documents; see instruction 6.

Under penalties of perjury, I declare that I have examined this return, including accompanying schedules and statements, and to the best of my knowledge and belief, it is true, correct, and complete. Declaration of preparer other than the personal representative is based on all information of which preparer has any knowledge.

Signature of personal representative		Date
Signature of preparer other than personal representative	Address (and ZIP code)	Date

Figure 4-1. Form 706—U.S. Estate Tax Return

out and filed along with the amount of money due for federal estate taxes, if any, 9 months from the date of death.

The *other form* is the particular state form used for payment of state inheritance taxes, if any. (See Figure 4-2 for an example of the "other form.")

Form M-706

MASSACHUSETTS DEPARTMENT OF REVENUE

ESTATE TAX RETURN

For every estate with date of death on or after January 1, 1986

Filing Fee $10

For Department Use Only

GENERAL INFORMATION

DECEDENT'S FIRST NAME AND MIDDLE INITIAL | DECEDENT'S LAST NAME | DATE OF DEATH

RESIDENCE (DOMICILE) AT TIME OF DEATH | YEAR DOMICILE ESTABLISHED | PROBATE COURT | DECEDENT'S SOCIAL SECURITY NUMBER

DOCKET NUMBER | DATE BOND APPROVED

EXECUTOR(S), ADMINISTRATOR(S) OR PERSON(S) IN POSSESSION OF PROPERTY: NAME | DESIGNATION | ADDRESS (INCLUDE ZIP CODE)

ATTORNEY(S) REPRESENTING THE ESTATE, IF ANY: NAME | ADDRESS (INCLUDE ZIP CODE) | TELEPHONE NUMBER

POWER OF ATTORNEY

AUTHORIZATION TO RECEIVE CONFIDENTIAL INFORMATION UNDER M.G.L., Ch. 62C, Sec. 21 and POWER OF ATTORNEY.
I (we) hereby appoint the undersigned nominee, subject to written revocation, as attorney(s)-in-fact to represent the taxpayer before any office of the Massachusetts Department of Revenue, to receive confidential information and to perform on my (our) behalf the following acts for this estate: **(Strike any of the following that were not granted).**

TO receive, but not to endorse and collect, checks in payment of any refund of Massachusetts taxes, penalties, or interest.
TO execute waivers (including offers of waivers of restrictions on assessment or collection of deficiencies in tax and waivers of notice of disallowance of a claim for credit or refund).
TO execute consents extending the statutory period for assessment or collection of taxes.
TO execute closing agreements.
TO delegate authority or to substitute another representative.
Other acts (specify)_____

Send copies of notices and other written communications addressed to the taxpayer(s) in proceedings involving the above matters to:
Name_____ Telephone No._____
Address (Include ZIP code)_____

Signature of Nominee | Date | Signature of Executor, Administrator, etc. | Date

TAX COMPUTATION

1. Massachusetts Taxable Estate (from Reconciliation Schedule, page 16, Item 5)......................1
2. Tax on Massachusetts Taxable Estate (from Estate Tax Table on page 16).......2
3. Enter Item 2 or $1,500, whichever is less...................................3
4. *Subtract Item 3 from Item 2*...4
5. Enter 20% of the amount in excess of $200,000 of Net Estate, (from Reconciliation Schedule, page 16, Item 3)...................................5
6. Massachusetts Estate Tax. Enter the smaller of Items 4 or 5.................6
7. Maximum credit for state death taxes allowable against Federal Estate Tax (see Instructions)..7
8. Enter the larger of Items 6 or 7...8
9. Amount previously paid (do not include filing fees).........................9
10. Balance Due.* *Subtract Item 9 from Item 8. Make check payable to the Commonwealth of Massachusetts* 10
11. Refund. *Subtract Item 8 from Item 9*....................................11
*Add to the total in Item 10, if applicable: Interest $_____, Penalty $_____.

SIGNATURE(S)

Under penalties of perjury, I declare that I have examined this return, including all accompanying statements, and to the best of my knowledge and belief it is true, correct and complete. I further declare that the copy of U.S. Form 706 and all copies of documents filed with the Internal Revenue Service, Estate Tax Division are exact duplicates (without alteration). Declaration of preparer (other than executor(s), administrator(s) or person(s) in possession of property) is based on all information of which he has any knowledge.

SIGNATURE(S) OF EXECUTOR(S), ADMINISTRATOR(S) OR PERSON(S) IN POSSESSION OF PROPERTY | DATE

SIGNATURE AND ADDRESS OF PREPARER OTHER THAN EXECUTOR(S), ETC. | EMP. IDENT. OR SOC. SEC. NO. | DATE

Mail to: Mass. DOR, Estate Tax Bureau, P.O. Box 7023, Boston, MA 02204

Figure 4-2. "The other form"—state estate tax return

In my opinion, when considering the purchase of life insurance to pay taxes, the individual's attorney and accountant should be consulted and asked to fill out form 706 and the state form. (These forms are professionally handled by an attorney or an accountant, not a life insurance agent.) Only by doing this is it possible to find out what may be left after Uncle Sam and the individual's state of residence take what is legally theirs.

Summary

1. There are four methods for determining how much life insurance is needed: X times gross earnings, multiples of salary, insurance needs analysis, and the present-value concept. There is also form 706 and the "other form" approach.

2. Of these, in my opinion, the present-value concept is the most useful, reliable, and practical for use in determination of income-replacement needs. Without a present-value calculation based on 75 percent of your financial base (taxable income plus deductions and exemptions minus federal and state taxes, if any), you will have no idea how much life insurance is enough. This calculation should be redone at least every 2 years.

3. Opportunity cost or discount rate is a moving target. Assumption of a specific rate will depend upon the current economic environment.

4. Life insurance with all premiums vanished can be used as collateral to pay for serious medical expenses.

5. Be conservative in the use of an assumed interest rate when determining how to invest your money.

6. Be ever mindful that there is a substantial difference between calculating the present-value amount of money required on a real dollar basis and calculating it on a constant dollar basis.

7. Life insurance agents skilled in use of a hand-held calculator can calculate present-value requirements on a constant or real dollar basis right in front of you. If asked, they can also take you step by step through the procedure.

PART 2

How to Buy
Life Insurance

5
Methods of Life Insurance Cost Disclosure

(What Are You Getting for Your Money?)

The next step after determining how much life insurance you need is to ask the cost, i.e., the premium. When you buy life insurance, it is important to know what you are getting for your money. There are three methods that may be used to find the answer: (1) cash-flow analysis, referred to by the life insurance industry as the "traditional method"; (2) the numerical figures, called the "interest-adjusted index method"; and (3) the compound interest, or rate-of-return method, which the industry has not adopted as a cost-disclosure method. All three are discussed in this chapter, but in my opinion, the rate-of-return method is superior to the others.

Cash-Flow Analysis— Traditional Method

Prior to the late 1960s, the accepted method of life insurance cost disclosure was to simply subtract from the gross premium the dividends paid, in order to determine the net payment. Both dividends paid and cash value were subtracted from the gross premium to determine net cost. *Gross premium* is the charge for life insurance, not taking dividends into consideration.

The serious flaw in this approach is that it does not take into account the time value of money.

Time Value of Money

Money has a value: the rate of return that can be realized on the safest of investments (e.g., U.S. Treasury obligations). Some financial commentators refer to this value as the "opportunity cost of money." When money is used for a specific purpose (e.g., paying for life insurance, buying a car, investing in a mutual fund, paying a college tuition bill), the question of time cannot be ignored. To ignore it would be to assume that there was no prevailing force at work providing an opportunity for the money to earn interest.

What this means is that, for example, the true cost of the tuition bill I just paid for my son's college education includes the interest I could have earned on the money if I had not spent it for that purpose. The actual interest earned will depend upon the length of time that the money is invested.

The time value of money in relation to life insurance is illustrated in the examples below.

Traditional Net Payment Example

45-Year-Old Male
Policy: $100,000 traditional whole life
Age: 45
Smoker: No
Unisex rate[1]:   No
Dividends: Yes; dividends declared and paid are used in reduction of the gross premium. Projected dividends are based on the current scale, where *current* means the year the policy is being considered for purchase.

Total net payments (gross premiums minus projected dividends declared and paid from age 45 to age 65) come to $13,325.

To state the average net payment as $666.25 ($13,325 divided by 20 years) would be incorrect because the time value of money would not have been considered.

[1]See the discussion of unisex rates later in this chapter.

Traditional Net Cost Example

45-Year-Old Male
  Policy: $100,000 traditional whole life
  Age: 45
  Smoker: No
  Unisex rate: No
  Dividends: Yes; dividends declared and paid are used in reduction of the gross premium. Projected dividends are based on the current dividend scale, where *current* means the year the policy is being considered for purchase.

Total net payments from age 45 to age 65 come to $13,325. Guaranteed cash value at age 65 is $38,580.

To state that the total net premiums less the guaranteed cash value would produce a gain of $25,255, resulting in the insurance costing nothing, would be incorrect because the time value of money would not have been considered.

What Is Allowed?

The states (not the federal government) regulate life insurance. When the traditional method is used as a sales illustration today, state regulations generally allow use of only a version of the traditional method of cost disclosure, in the form of a cash-flow analysis with a footnote stating that the time value of money has not been considered.

Numerical Figures— Interest-Adjusted Index Method

Historical Background

In the late 1960s, after years of debate, the *interest-adjusted index* method of cost disclosure arrived on the scene, recommended by the National Association of Insurance Commissioners (NAIC) as a model. This method, which *does* take into consideration the time value of money, has been adopted by more than 40 states.

The interest-adjusted index for both net payment and net surrender appears on all ledger statements. (See the Appendix for sample ledger statements.) Unfortunately, this method is extremely complicated to explain. It uses an interest-rate assumption about the rate at which money can be invested and is worthless when you are attempting to find out the rates of return upon death and upon surrendering a policy, as measured and expressed in terms of compound interest.

Ledger Statement

A *ledger statement* is provided by the insurance company for a policy being considered for purchase. The ledger statement is only a "current snapshot," based upon the company's investment strategy for the life insurance plan under consideration for purchase. It is extremely important to find out from your agent whether or not the dividend projections or current interest rate and mortality charges are realistic as reflected in the ledger statement. The financial strength of the life insurance company is also of great importance; to determine it, ask for an A. M. Best Company report, as discussed in Chapter 2.

Interest-Adjusted Index

The *interest-adjusted index* found on a ledger statement provides numerical figures that result from the cash flows within the policy (which consist of gross premiums; dividends projected, if any; and cash value interrelated with a specific interest rate).

The index is used to compare like-kind policies issued by different companies. *Like-kind* means an oranges-to-oranges comparison—say, comparing one company's traditional whole life policy using dividends as declared and paid in reduction of the gross premium with another company's policy on the same basis. It is not an oranges-to-apples comparison, which might be, for example, comparing one company's whole life policy with another company's universal life policy. The index takes into consideration the time value of money and what you could earn on your sum of money if it were not being used to purchase life insurance.

In comparisons of like-kind policies, as in golf, *the lower numerical figure wins.* As with any other method (e.g., the traditional which you just read about, and the rate-of-return method, discussed later in this chapter), the interest-adjusted index method is not foolproof because whether or not the financial figures shown on a current ledger statement will be realized is impossible to predict.

Use of the interest-adjusted index method is shown in the examples below.

Net Payment Example

45-Year-Old Male
  Policy: $100,000-traditional whole life
  Age: 45
  Smoker: No
  Unisex rate: No
  Dividends: Yes; dividends declared and paid are used in reduction of the
               gross premium. Projected dividends are based on the current
               dividend scale, where *current* means the year the policy is being
               considered for purchase.

The index expressed as a numerical figure represents the index figure you are presumed to have paid for life insurance for a specific time
period. It would appear on the ledger statement in the following form:

Example

Life insurance net payment cost index for 10 years: $16.24; for 20
years: $9.89
Age 65: $9.89

In order to understand the numerical figure index, you must know how
it is calculated.

Calculation Steps

Step 1. Select the time period (e.g., 10 years, 20 years, years to age 65).

Step 2. Compound the gross premium, as indicated on the ledger state-
        ment, for each and every year of the time period selected, at 5
        percent (the interest assumption used). The calculation is based
        on the beginning of the year, not the end of the year. The pre-
        mium is compounded at 5 percent to determine its value if not
        used to purchase life insurance.

Step 3. Compound the stream of yearly projected dividends, if any, as
        indicated on the ledger statement, at 5 percent for the time pe-
        riod selected. The calculation is based on the end of the year,
        not the beginning of the year, because dividends are normally
        paid at the end of the year. Dividends are compounded at 5
        percent because they represent cash flows to the policyholder as
        a result of purchasing life insurance.

Step 4. Subtract the result of step 3 from step 2, and divide by the value of
        $1 compounded at 5 percent to be paid each and every year for
        the time period selected. For example, in 10 years the value is
        $13.21; in 20 years it is $34.72; etc. Dividing by the value of $1
        paid each and every year compounded at 5 percent for the time

period used (e.g., 10 years, 20 years, years to age 65) means that the time value of money has been taken into consideration.

Step 5. Divide the result of step 4 by the amount of life insurance, i.e., $100,000. The result is the numerical index.

Net Cost Example

45-Year-Old Male
  Policy: $100,000 traditional whole life
  Age: 45
  Smoker: No
  Unisex rate: No
  Dividends: Yes; dividends declared and paid are used in reduction of the gross premium. Projected dividends are based on the current dividend scale, where *current* means the year the policy is being considered for purchase.

The index expressed as a numerical figure represents the amount you are presumed to have paid for life insurance for a specific time period, taking into consideration the cash-surrender value. It would appear on the ledger statement in the following manner:

Example

Life insurance surrender cost index for 10 years: $3.09; for 20 years: $1.95 –
Age 65: $1.95 –

Calculation Steps

Step 1. Select the time period (e.g., 10 years, 20 years, years to age 65).

Step 2. Compound the gross premium, as indicated on the ledger statement, for each and every year of the time period selected, at 5 percent (the interest assumption used). The calculation is based on the beginning of the year, not the end of the year. The premium is compounded at 5 percent to determine its value if not used to purchase life insurance.

Step 3. Compound the stream of yearly projected dividends, if any, as indicated on the ledger statement at 5 percent for the time period selected. The calculation is based on the end of the year, not the beginning of the year, because dividends are normally paid at the end of the year. Dividends are compounded at 5 percent because they represent cash flows to the policyholder as a result of purchasing life insurance.

Step 4. Add to the result of step 3 the guaranteed cash value and terminal dividend, if any, for the time period selected. These values are added because, in order to ascertain the net cost index, it is assumed that the policy is surrendered for its surrender value.

Step 5. Subtract the result of step 4 from step 2, and divide by the value of $1 to be paid each and every year compounded at 5 percent for the time period selected. For example, in 10 years the value is $13.21; in 20 years, $34.72; etc. Dividing by the value of $1 paid each and every year compounded at 5 percent for the time period used (e.g., 10 years, 20 years, years to age 65) means that the time value of money has been taken into consideration. A minus sign following a numerical figure indicates a lower number, which means a greater value, i.e., gain, not cost, to the consumer; and it also means a lower numerical figure.

Step 6. Divide the result of step 5 by the amount of life insurance, i.e., $100,000. The result is the numerical index.

Compound Interest— Rate-of-Return Method

Back in the days when my office was in Boston, I was a member of a nearby health club. One morning after my daily jog, Jack, a client of mine, asked me, "Bill, how could you have sold me that junk?" I knew that he was referring to the traditional whole life policy paying dividends as declared which I had sold him, but I didn't know what had prompted the question, and so I asked him, "Jack, what are you talking about?

What Jack was talking about was the 1979 Staff Report to the Federal Trade Commission (FTC) on Life Insurance Cost Disclosure, which concluded that life insurance provided a very unacceptable rate of return. This FTC study, in my opinion, was prepared by essentially anti–life insurance FTC staff members. Combined with my studies in the Boston University program for financial planners, this report sparked my interest in the subject of *rate of return for life insurance*—which, in my view, means the rate of return upon death. Let me now share with you my thoughts on rate of return as a method of cost disclosure.

There is much confusion and disagreement about the rate of return as it applies to life insurance. Some people believe that to apply the term "rate of return" to the death benefit, what I would call the "beneficiary's rate of return," is totally inappropriate. They believe it is not necessary to measure the beneficiary's rate of return, and to do so would cause life insurance to be considered an investment.

But if the beneficiary's rate of return is ignored, how can you determine which plan of life insurance and which method of premium payment provide the most cost-efficient death benefit for the number of years required? Is not the essential purpose of life insurance to provide a death benefit? I cannot believe you would buy life insurance if you did not need to provide a death benefit.

Others believe that the only valid rate of return on a life insurance policy is the rate of return which the insured receives if the policy is surrendered. After the cost for protection is taken into consideration, the method used for this calculation is an adaptation of the Linton yield method, discussed below.

Linton Yield Method

The FTC report on life insurance cost disclosure used the Linton yield method for purposes of arriving at rates of return on life insurance. In my opinion, this resulted in:

- An inaccurately reported (possibly inflated, but in any event, not a true, intrinsic) rate of return to the insured
- A complete disregard of the beneficiary's rate of return
- Confusion among the public concerning the purpose of life insurance (which is to provide a death benefit), caused by the FTC's disregard of the beneficiary's rate of return
- The public's being led to believe that they are not getting their money's worth out of life insurance
- Reaction from the life insurance industry involving a proliferation of interest-sensitive life insurance products, all concentrating and marketing themselves based upon the rate of return to the insured, not to the beneficiary, and using procedures not historically found within the industry such as questionable investment strategies, mortality charges (i.e., a term insurance charge for the amount of insurance for which the company is at risk), and foremost, the abuse of the concept of tax-free buildup of the reserve, i.e., the cash-surrender value, the separate investment account, or both

The late M. Albert Linton, a distinguished actuary, created the Linton yield method in 1919. This method provides a way of knowing what the rate of return is on the cash value or separate investment account component of a life insurance policy. It does not measure the rate of return to the beneficiary. It does not even measure the actual, true, intrinsic rate of return to the insured, net after taxes, if the policy is surrendered. The Linton yield method indicates what you would have to earn in interest if you bought term life insurance and invested the difference, in order to duplicate the same financial scenario as the nonterm life insurance policy (refer to Chapter 12).

The Linton yield method should be used only in discussions which involve the concept "Buy term, invest the difference."

Measuring Rate of Return

The rate of return is always measured in terms of compound interest. Separate measurements are used for the beneficiary and for the insured.

Compound interest is a measurement which is universally accepted. For example, the chief executive officer of a Fortune 500 company, or any firm for that matter, will always measure corporate goals in terms of compound growth. Mutual funds, tax shelters in real estate, oil and gas, common stocks, and the consumer price index are all measured in terms of compound interest. Life insurance should also be measured in terms of compound interest return both to the beneficiary and to the insured.

Compound interest is the interest paid on both the principal and the accumulated unpaid interest. If you put $1 in the bank, the interest paid each and every year is always added to the original $1 plus all previously paid interest. Therefore, $1 at 10 percent compound interest will grow to $2.59 in 10 years, $6.73 in 20 years, and $13,780.61 in 100 years. Compound interest is a basic element of the mathematics of finance when you are seeking to measure the return on your money or on money you have given someone else to manage for you.

Rate of Return upon Death

Life insurance provides an extremely acceptable rate of return for your beneficiary. The return is so significant, in fact, that duplicating it in any other financial services product might be impossible or at least extremely difficult. This is particularly true during the first 20 years of the life of the policy, or perhaps even longer, depending upon the particular plan of life insurance purchased.

The longer you live, the lower the rate of return to your beneficiary, because of the time value of money. Depending upon your individual tax bracket [and as long as the Congress of the United States allows life insurance proceeds to be exempt from federal income tax, as specified in section 101(a) of the Internal Revenue Code], however, it may continue to be difficult for you to duplicate in another financial services product the compound interest return which life insurance provides as a death benefit for your beneficiary. Here is an example.

Rate-of-Return Example

45-Year-Old Male

Policy: $100,000 traditional whole life

Age: 45

Smoker: No

Unisex rate: No

Dividends: Yes; dividends declared and paid are used to purchase additional paid-up life insurance. Projected dividends are based on the current dividend scale, where *current* means in the year the policy is being considered for purchase. A gross premium of $2001 is paid for the first 20 years; from year 21 on, the dividends pay the premiums. (See Table 5-1.)

Table 5-1

Years	Total death benefit	Rate of return upon death
1	$100,000	4897.50%
5	101,460	90.50
10	110,848	30.00
15	135,297	17.32
20	180,071	12.87
29 (life expectancy)	283,645	9.77

Once the rate of return upon death is known, it can be determined what would have to be earned before taxes (assuming that the death benefit is considered life insurance proceeds and as such is not subject to federal taxes) in other financial services products (e.g., mutual funds, certificates of deposit, real estate, commodities) to duplicate the tax-exempt rate of return provided by life insurance. The before-tax rate is determined by dividing the life insurance rate of return by the marginal tax bracket subtracted from 100 percent (e.g., for 15 percent, the factor is 0.85; for 28 percent, 0.72; for 33 percent, 0.67; and for 34 percent, 0.66). The result, as shown in Table 5-2, is affected by the following factors:

1. Marginal federal ordinary income tax brackets as mandated by the 1986 Tax Reform Act

2. Maximum corporate federal ordinary marginal income tax bracket as mandated by the 1986 Tax Reform Act

Table 5-2

Years	15%*	28%*	33%8*	34%†
1	5761.76%	6802.08%	7309.70%	7420.45%
5	106.47	126.69	135.07	137.12
10	35.29	41.67	44.78	45.45
15	20.38	24.06	25.85	26.24
20	15.14	17.88	17.27	19.50
29	11.49	13.57	14.58	14.80

*Marginal federal ordinary income tax brackets as mandated by the 1986 Tax Reform Act.

†Maximum corporate federal ordinary marginal income tax bracket as mandated by the 1986 Tax Reform Act.

According to the Tax Reform Act, interest-bearing investments, which are usually money market investments and capital market investments such as stocks, bonds, and real estate, are all taxed the same—at marginal federal ordinary tax rates. Long-term capital gain rates are no longer allowed.

Current Federal Corporate Income Tax Rates

After the 1988 act became effective, the corporate tax rates shown below began to apply for corporate taxable years beginning on or after July 1, 1987 (and they will continue to apply, provided it remains as enacted):

Taxable income	Tax rate
$0–50,000	15%
50,000–75,000	25
75,000–100,000	34
100,000–335,000	39
Over $335,000	34

The lower brackets are phased out between $100,000 and $335,000 because of an additional 5 percent surcharge for that income range.

Rate of Return upon Surrender

Life insurance does not offer a significant rate of return to the insured for any plan or method of premium payment in the early years of the policy. However, the longer the policy is in force, the more significant the increase in the rate of return to the insured because of the accumulation of reserve by the insurance company, which is represented by the cash value or the separate investment account. An example is shown below.

Example

45-Year-Old Male
    Policy: $100,000 traditional whole life
    Age: 45
    Smoker: No
    Unisex rate: No
    Dividends: Yes; dividends declared and paid are used to purchase additional paid-up life insurance. Projected dividends are based on the current dividend scale, where *current* means in the year the policy is being considered for purchase. A gross premium of $2001 is paid for 20 years; from year 21 on, dividends pay the premium. (See Table 5-3.)

Table 5-3

Reserve years	Total cash value including dividends	Rate of return upon surrender
1	$ 0	−100%
5	7,696	−8.62
10	23,069	2.57
15	47,945	5.66
20	89,420	7.16
29 (life expectancy)	174,946	7.40

When the rate of return upon surrender is positive, this means that taxes are assessed on the difference between the cash-surrender value and the premiums paid. The positive rates of return shown in Table 5-3 do not take income taxes into consideration.

How Can the Rate of Return Be Determined?

All life insurance companies have the capability to indicate, on their official ledger statements, the rate of return upon death or upon cashing in a policy. Currently, a few give this information to prospective purchasers; most do not.

But life insurance agents, or persons who sell life insurance as a financial services product and who are skilled in the area of present value, future value, and the time value of money, can use an official ledger statement to calculate the rate of return either on a hand-held calculator capable of doing financial decisions or on a personal computer with the proper software.

The rate of return is determined by the interrelationship of the present-value payment (the premium), the future value (death benefit to the beneficiary, cash value, total cash value, or net equity value to the insured), and the time span (number of years paid). This measurement takes into consideration the time value of money, as measured in terms of compound interest.

Rate of return, as a measurement, consists of dollars in (premiums paid to the life insurance company) and dollars out (money to be paid by the life insurance company to the beneficiary or to the owner if the policy is surrendered) for the time period the policy is in force. In measuring the rate of return upon surrender (upon cashing in the policy), the premium is not reduced for the cost of death protection.

The compound interest return, for your beneficiary and for you, is self-contained within the life insurance policy. This is very important. Many investment products deliver a return which then must be reinvested elsewhere in order to actually realize a given level of compound return.

Rule of Thumb for Rate of Return

The *unisex rate* is a blend of male and female rates, resulting in a lowering of rates for males and an increase for females. Generally speaking, the lower the premium, the greater the rate of return to the beneficiary upon the death of the insured. Conversely, the higher the premium, the greater the rate of return to the insured if the policy is surrendered. For this reason, a policy issued to a man aged 45, or to a man of any age, will have a greater cash value upon surrender than will a policy issued to a woman aged 45, or to a woman of any age, because the man's premium is higher. Conversely, the rate of return to the beneficiary, upon the death of the woman insured, will be greater because the woman's premium is lower. This fact should convince women that they are better off with specific rates for women than with a unisex rate.

Women who wish to have more reserve (cash value within their policies) should do one of the following:

1. Invest the difference between their own specific female rate and a specific rate for a man of the same age in the investment vehicle of their choice.
2. Invest the difference between their own specific female rate and

what the unisex rate would be in the investment vehicle of their choice.

Summary

1. The three possible methods that may be used to determine the actual cost of life insurance are cash-flow analysis, which is the traditional method; the numerical figures, or interest-adjusted index method; and the compound interest, or rate-of-return method.

2. Of these three, rate of return should be the method used to inform you about what you are getting for your money, as measured in terms of compound interest.

3. Make sure that your life insurance agent, or any person who offers to sell you life insurance as a financial services product, understands and, equally important, is able to calculate the rate of return. Such understanding and capability are as important for the seller of life insurance as anatomy is to a physician, as contract law is to an attorney, as the balance sheet is to an accountant, or as the Linton yield method is to an actuary.

4. In addition to being complicated to explain, the interest-adjusted index method is not able to do the job for which it was originally intended: providing an index for comparison of like-kind policies. This situation has come about because of the rapid proliferation of a variety of life insurance plans. The traditional method falls short because it fails to take into consideration the time value of money.

5. The rates of return given in this chapter (i.e., Tables 5-1 to 5-3), as well as all rates of return in the entire book, are calculated as of the beginning of the year, not the end of the year. When comparing policies issued by different companies on the basis of rate of return, make sure that the calculations are on the same basis—i.e., either beginning of year or end of year.

6
Should You Own Your Own Life Insurance?
(Complete Control versus Taxes)

So far, you have learned what life insurance is, how to pick a life insurance company, how to pick a life insurance agent, how much life insurance you need, and what you are getting for your life insurance money. Now you'll learn what you should be aware of when considering who should be the owner of your life insurance.

Complete Control

If you want to maintain complete control, then you should be the owner of your life insurance. Complete control means that all incidents of ownership reside with you. You have the absolute right to:

1. Change the beneficiary.
2. Surrender or cancel the policy and receive the reserve (the cash value or the separate investment account), if any.
3. Assign the policy.
4. Pledge the policy as collateral for a loan.

Why would you want to give up the control of all incidents of ownership? For only one reason: so that the face amount of life insurance payable at your death would not be included in your estate for federal estate and state inheritance tax purposes. You should make sure that you really understand what rights you will be giving up if you allow someone else to own your life insurance.

Tax Planning

By the same token, tax planning is important, but decisions should not be based on taxes alone.

The federal estate tax is an excise tax for the privilege of transferring property at death. In some states where state inheritance tax is imposed, it is a tax for the privilege of allowing others to inherit your property.

The federal estate tax return (form 706), if required, must be filed and the federal estate tax paid in cash within 9 months from the date of your death. Form 706 is required to be filed if the federal estate tax amount due is in excess of $192,800.

$192,800 in Plain Talk (Form 706, Estate Size, and Taxes)

An estate tax due of $192,800 translates to a tax base of $600,000. This means that if the federal estate tax due is not in excess of $192,800, you did not die with a taxable estate in excess of $600,000, there is no money due Uncle Sam, and form 706 is not required to be filed under current law. Be advised that all forms of property that you own, tangible and intangible, real and personal (e.g., stocks, bonds, gold coins, real estate, life insurance, and business interests), constitute property in your estate.

Your life insurance will be includable in your estate, for federal estate tax purposes, in the following situations:

1. When the death benefit is payable to your estate or is received for the benefit of your estate

2. When your life insurance is payable to a beneficiary other than your estate but you possess one or more of the rights listed under "Complete Control" above at the time of your death

3. When you have made a gift or sale[1] of your life insurance within 3 years of your death

---

[1]Unless "adequate consideration" is paid. IRS PLR 8806004 was issued by the Internal Revenue Service in November 1987 to clarify this issue. Even so, the issue remains very complicated. You should consult your tax professional for advice on determining whether or not adequate consideration has been paid.

Does $192,800 translate to a tax base of $600,000 for state inheritance tax purposes? Not automatically. It depends on the particular state. For instance, it does not apply in Massachusetts.

Other Taxes

Generally, most states follow the federal estate tax inclusion requirements. Each state is different, however. You should consult with your professional adviser about the rules for the state of which you are a legal resident. If you are a legal resident of a community-property state your planning will be different from that of residents of non-community-property states, and you should consult an attorney.

Life insurance death proceeds are not subject to federal income tax provided they are considered life insurance proceeds. In order for nonterm life insurance to meet the statutory definition of life insurance [section 7702(a) of the Internal Revenue Code] for policies issued after December 31, 1984, the following tests must be met:

1. *State law test.*   The policy must be considered life insurance under the applicable state law.

2. *Cash-value accumulation test.*   The reserve, i.e., the cash-surrender value, must not at any time (age is a moving target) exceed the amount of money required by the specific life insurance amount to fully pay up (so that no further premiums are required) X dollars of life insurance.

3. *Guideline premium test.*   The premium paid must not exceed the guideline for a one-time deposit (single-premium test) and the cumulative amount of premiums paid (level annual premiums) to fund (pay for) future benefits (death benefits) determined at the time the policy is issued.

4. *Cash-value corridor test.*   The death benefit payable at any time (age is a variable) must exceed the reserve (i.e., the cash value) by specific predetermined percentages.

Why then are life insurance death proceeds subject to federal estate tax? The federal income tax and the federal estate tax are two different and distinctly separate taxes. Life insurance is subject to the federal estate tax (1) if it is includable in your estate, (2) if your gross estate exceeds $600,000, or (3) if you do not qualify for the marital deduction.

Marital Deduction

The *marital deduction* is a provision in the federal tax code which permits the transfer of your estate assets during your life or at your death to your spouse without paying any federal estate tax.

Depending upon your own specific situation, the use of the marital deduction may not be in order. For example, you as a father or mother may wish your spouse to enjoy an income from your business but want your son or daughter to run the business. In this situation, planning outside the marital deduction must be done. Another example is a spouse who has substantial assets in his or her own right. Again, planning outside the marital deduction may be in order.

The *unlimited marital deduction* is a provision in the federal tax code which permits the transfer of your entire estate assets during your life or at your death to your spouse without the necessity of paying any federal gift or estate tax.

When I use the term *limited marital deduction*, however, I mean to suggest that there is a limit on how much of your estate assets qualify for the marital deduction. The limit is determined individually by you with the help of your legal counsel. It is not determined by the federal government.

The purpose of limiting the marital deduction is to reduce estate taxes at the second death—the death of the surviving spouse.

The marital deduction is not allowed unless you are married and survived by your spouse. Your life insurance will qualify for the marital deduction provided that:

1. The death benefit is payable in a lump sum to your surviving spouse regardless of whether a secondary beneficiary is named.
2. The death benefit is payable singularly to your surviving spouse or to the estate of the surviving spouse.
3. The death benefit is payable to your spouse under a settlement option with secondary beneficiaries named, and your surviving spouse is given a general power of appointment over the proceeds. If the executor of your estate elects to have the value of the death benefit qualify for the marital deduction (with the value of the death benefit held under the interest option for the surviving spouse for his or her lifetime), interest must be payable at least annually and no power may reside in any person to appoint any of the value of the death benefit to anyone other than your spouse during his or her lifetime.
4. The value of the death benefit is payable outright to your surviving spouse under your will, or is payable to a trust that qualifies for the marital deduction.

Types of Ownership

Owner at inception means that when a new life insurance policy is being purchased, an owner is named in the application. If you name an owner at inception other than yourself, you do not have to live longer than 3 years to make sure that the value of your death benefit is not includable in your estate for federal estate tax purposes.

Owner by transfer means that the ownership of your existing life insurance policy is being transferred from you as owner to a new owner, generally to avoid having the death benefit includable in your estate when you die.

Types of Transfers

In a *transfer by gift,* you transfer the ownership of your life insurance policy to your spouse. No money changes hands between you and your spouse. You transfer ownership of the policy, including the cash value, if any, by making a gift to your spouse, not by selling the policy for value. Because of the unlimited marital deduction, you and your spouse may make unlimited gifts between yourselves. After making the transfer of ownership by gift, you must live longer than 3 years to keep the policy out of your estate. When making a transfer by gift, the life insurance proceeds at your death still are not subject to the federal income tax.

In a *transfer by sale,* you transfer the ownership of your life insurance policy to your spouse in the form of a sale just like any other sale. A purchase takes place, and money does change hands between you and your spouse. You transfer the ownership of your policy with its cash value, if any, to your spouse for consideration—meaning you receive value in the form of money for making the transfer. After making the transfer of ownership by sale, you must live longer than 3 years to keep the policy out of your estate. When making a transfer by sale, some of the death benefit, though not all, will be subject to federal income tax. An example is shown below.

Example

Face amount of the policy: $100,000
Purchase price at sale: $10,000
Subsequent premiums paid from the date of the sale to date of death: $20,000
Income tax consequences at death: $30,000, which represents the sale purchase price and subsequent premiums paid not subject to federal income tax

The difference between $30,000 and $100,000, which is $70,000, is subject to federal income tax, under the current law based on existing transfer-for-value rules.

Transfer-for-Value Rules

The unfavorable result of having only the sale purchase price and subsequent premiums paid exempt from the federal income tax applies in all transfer-for-value situations except when the transfer for value is to:

1. The insured

2. A partner of the insured

3. A partnership in which the insured is a partner

4. A corporation in which the insured is a shareholder or officer

The example given previously of transfer for value between you and your spouse does not meet any of the transfer-for-value exceptions listed above.

Crummey Power of Appointment in an Irrevocable Trust

Once your taxable estate reaches a sizable amount, or under other specific circumstances (e.g., you become the owner of a business), your attorney may recommend the use of other transfer techniques, such as an irrevocable trust with a Crummey power of appointment.

An *irrevocable trust with a Crummey power of appointment* is a way to remove assets from both your estate and the estate of your spouse, which means that at your death and the death of your spouse, the assets will not be subject to the federal estate tax. When life insurance is involved, if at inception the irrevocable trust is named in the application as owner of the policy, for the insured living longer than 3 years estate tax is not a factor. (Internal Revenue Code section 2035 covers the 3-year consideration; section 2042 covers incidents of ownership.)

Whenever a trust is created, a Crummey power of appointment within the trust is a necessity, so that the premium will be considered a gift of present interest and thus will allow qualification for the present-interest gift tax exclusion. If the person named in the irrevocable trust is not named as owner in the application at inception but becomes owner later, through a transfer of an existing policy either by gift or by sale (for less than adequate consideration), then the insured must live longer than 3 years in order to make sure that the death benefit payable is not in the estate. Further, there may be no incidents of ownership during the 3 years before the insured dies. (It is assumed that at inception the owner of the policy is the insured.) The present-interest gift tax exclusion under current law is $10,000 per year per person. The present-interest gift tax exclusion under current law for marital gifts (gifts given by husband and wife together) is $20,000 per year per recipient. To draft an irrevocable trust with a Crummey power of appointment, you should consult an attorney.

Summary

1. Maintaining complete control of your life insurance means that you possess one or more incidents of ownership.

2. Life insurance decisions should not be made with taxes as the primary consideration.

3. Life insurance planning in relation to state taxes is different in each state; consult an attorney.

4. Depending upon your own specific situation, use of a limited or unlimited marital deduction, or an irrevocable trust with a Crummey power of appointment, may or may not be appropriate; again, consult an attorney.

7

Should You Replace Your Existing Life Insurance?

(Maybe, But Have an Examination First)

Perhaps you have read or been told that your existing life insurance is old-fashioned. It is tired and should be turned in. Do not be misled by glib talk about replacement of existing life insurance. Replacement of life insurance is a serious matter and should be done only after much study and careful consideration—not simply as a result of a snap decision to "update" or become more modern.

When you replace an existing life insurance policy, you terminate your existing policy with one company and initiate another life insurance policy, either with the same company or with a different company. If someone advises you to terminate an old policy and purchase a new one, and does not reveal to you the rate of return in both scenarios, it is as if a physician had written out a prescription without first examining you or asking specific questions.

Rate of Return

By now you should know that when it comes to life insurance cost disclosure, the method I advocate is the rate-of-return method. Not being aware of the rate of return on your life insurance is similar to not being aware of how much money you have in your savings and checking accounts, the current market value of your home, or the amount of your outstanding mortgage.

When dealing with an existing policy, rate of return is more important than other cost-disclosure measures for the following reasons:

1. The traditional method ignores the time value of money and therefore is not a valid method.

2. It has been my experience with most companies that the interest-adjusted index is not indicated on an in-force ledger statement. Even if it were, the numerical figures shown must be the same exact numerical figures shown on the original ledger statement used at the time of purchase. If, in fact, a particular company indicated the interest-adjusted index on an in-force ledger statement and the numerical figures were not the same, this would be misleading because it would be ignoring the time period for which the existing policy had been in force. Ignoring the time period would cause lower-than-accurate numerical figures to be shown.

Assessing Your Existing Policy

If you can have the same amount of life insurance for less money than you are currently spending, or more insurance for the same amount of money, then you should consider replacing your existing life insurance. An increase in the rate of return to the beneficiary, to you yourself (the insured), or to both is what you will probably be looking for. However, an increase in the rate of return to the beneficiary is generally what you can realistically expect to achieve. The rate of return to you personally cannot usually be increased because of acquisition costs involved in buying a new policy (e.g., commissions).

The increase should be at least 1 percent compound. If the rate of return to your beneficiary, upon your death, cannot be increased at least 1 percent compound, forget about replacing your existing life insurance.

In-Force Ledger Statement.   Where do you start, when you set out to determine the rate of return of an existing policy? The first thing you should do is request from the insurance company an in-force ledger statement for the policy currently in force. Once the in-force ledger statement has been obtained, then the rate of return, both for you and for your beneficiary, can be calculated. Other pertinent information can also be given. See the model worksheet in Figure 7-1 for information you should get from your insurance agent about an in-force policy.

Figure 7-1. Worksheet for an in-force existing policy. Copyright William D. Brownlie, CLU, ChFC, CIP, LIA, 1988. All rights reserved.

PLAN OF LIFE INSURANCE:　　　　　WORKSHEET FOR AN IN-FORCE
　　　　　　　　　　　　　　　　　　　EXISTING POLICY

_____

_____　　　INSURED:_____

Company:_____ Age at issue:_____ Sex:_____

Face amount:_____ Policy number:_____

Basic premium:_____ Waiver of premium included:_____

Dividends:　Yes_____ No_____ How used:_____

Existing loans:　Yes_____ No_____ If yes, amount:_____

Interest rate on loan:_____ Fixed_____ Variable_____

Current cash-surrender value:_____

Current status of dividends:_____

Q. When calculating the rate of return on an existing policy, how do you handle the current cash surrender value and dividend values?
A. The values must be entered as a present-value payment.
Q. What are the future present-value payments?
A. They are the future premiums to be paid—as indicated on the in-force ledger statement furnished by the insurance company.
Q. What is the future value to the beneficiary?
A. The death benefit as indicated in the in-force ledger statement furnished by the insurance company.
Q. What is the future value to the insured?
A. The cash-surrender value as indicated in the in-force ledger statement furnished by the insurance company.
Q. What is the time span?
A. (Number of years over which the rate of return is being measured.) Depends upon the information in the in-force ledger statement.

RATE OF RETURN MEASURED IN TERMS OF COMPOUND INTEREST

	Total death benefit	ROR	Reserve, i.e., cash-surrender value	ROR
Years: _____	$_____	___	$_____	___
_____	$_____	___	$_____	___
_____	_____	___	_____	___

(Continued)

What would_____ have to earn in compound interest before taxes to duplicate the rate of return upon death provided by life insurance? _____ Marginal federal ordinary income tax bracket:_____

Rate of return

Years:_____   _____

_____   _____

_____   _____

_____   _____

Is the life insurance information based upon the official in-force ledger statement of the insurance company? Yes _____ No _____ Death benefit as of the beginning of the year? Yes _____ No _____ End of year? Yes _____ No _____ Cash-surrender value as of the end of year? Yes _____ No _____ Any comments regarding the cash-surrender value: _____ _____ Is the official ledger statement of the insurance company enclosed? Yes _____No _____

Q. How were the rate-of-return calculations done?
A. On the Hewlett-Packard 41C series hand calculator with financial decisions module.

Read: *Life Insurance: Its Rate of Return* by William D. Brownlie, LIA, CIP, CLU, ChFC, published by the National Underwriter Company, 420 E. 4th Street, Cincinnati, Ohio 45202.

The rate of return is calculated from the present time to a future point in time based on the information from the in-force ledger statement. Only you, as the person considering replacing a life insurance policy, can choose the future point in time. You may choose to measure 5, 10, or 20 years, or your life expectancy. The length of time will depend on how long you wish the insurance to remain in force and how much information is shown on the ledger statement.

Investment Strategy. The next thing you should do is become aware that all plans of life insurance have a specific investment strategy. Find out what the investment strategy is for the policy you hold. Ask about:

- Capital market investments.
- Money market investments.
- Real estate.

- Old money, new money. Old money is money previously invested by the insurance company (e.g., 5 years ago); new money is money currently being invested by the insurance company.

- Pure portfolio rate. The yield in percentage terms, e.g., X percent, which the entire assets invested by the insurance company produces.

- Modified portfolio rate. A certain percentage, e.g., 20 percent, of invested money plus interest earned is rolled over each year into a new money note. Over a 6-year period (with of course no rollover in year 1), all money invested in year 1 is rolled over into new money.

- Weighted average portfolio rate. The yield in percentage terms on the entire invested assets of the insurance company as a result of given weight to old money and new money, e.g., X percent old money and X percent new money.

If your current policy pays dividends, also ask what the insurance company is assuming it must earn on money to warrant its dividend projections. This is referred to as the "dividend interest-assumption rate." The assumption is based upon the investment strategy employed by the insurance company, i.e., pure, modified, or weighted-average portfolio rate, and upon the company's treatment of old versus new money.

None of the information on investment strategy listed above will be on the ledger statement (nor will the dividend interest-assumption rate be listed for a dividend-paying policy). The person analyzing your policy will have to provide the answers, provided they can be obtained from the insurance company.

Do not listen to rhetoric, demand facts. The facts should be provided for you when you ask your agent to fill out the worksheets in Figures 7-1 and 7-2.

Calculating Rate of Return.   When calculating the rate of return on an existing policy other than term insurance, the current cash-surrender value and dividend cash value, if any, must be entered as a present-value payment. If the existing policy is term insurance, only the future premiums to be paid, as shown on the in-force ledger statement, are to be entered as present-value payments. The subsequent premiums to be entered as present-value payments are the premiums shown on the in-force ledger statement.

The future value to be paid to the beneficiary is the death benefit, as indicated on the in-force ledger statement. The reserve (the cash-surrender value) indicated on the in-force ledger statement is the future value to the insured, if the policy is surrendered.

Weighted Average.   When there is more than one existing life insurance policy in force, the rate-of-return calculation must be done on a weighted-average basis. Weighted average is more complex than simply the average result of a number of policies divided equally, and must be calculated properly in order to be meaningful.

For instance, suppose that a 47-year-old person has three separate life insurance policies in force—with face amounts of $13,117, $44,701, and $40,000—all purchased in prior years at different ages. The insured wants to know the rate of return upon death at age 65, as determined by the in-force ledger statement provided by each insurance company. The rate of return upon death for each policy would be as follows, 18 years from now:

Policy	Percent compound
$13,117	8
$44,701	12
$40,000	14
Total	34

The total, 34, divided by 3 equals 11.33 percent. But is 11.33 percent correct? No, because this calculation gives each policy equal weight, which is incorrect because the face amounts vary. The correct calculation follows:

Face amount	×	rate of return	= numerical result
$13,117	×	8%	= $ 1,049.36
44,701	×	12	= 5,364.12
40,000	×	14	= 5,600.00
$97,818			$12,013.48

The numerical result, $12,013.48, is divided by the face amount of life insurance, $97,818, resulting in a weighted-average rate of return of 12 percent compound.

Exactly the same procedure is used to determine the weighted-average rate of return upon surrender. Each policy's reserve is multiplied by its rate of return. The numerical result is then divided by the total of the reserve of all policies. The result is the weighted-average rate of return.

Assessing the Proposed
Replacement Policy

All the factors pertaining to an in-force existing policy apply also to the proposed policy. From the official ledger statement of the proposed policy, the rate of return for the insured and the beneficiary must be calculated. In addition, the investment strategy of the insurance company being recommended, and, if appropriate (as for a dividend-paying policy), the dividend interest-assumption rate, must be revealed to you.

Once these factors have been determined for the proposed replacement policy, you then compare the respective rates of return of your existing life insurance and the proposed policy. The ledger statement for the proposed policy will be based upon how the person recommending the new policy has used the existing reserve (the cash value) from the existing policy. The recommendation for where the reserve, i.e., the cash-surrender value, of the existing policy is to be invested must now be influenced by the seven-annual-premium-payments test. If your existing policy is replaced, the new policy must meet the state law, cash-value accumulation, guideline premium, and corridor tests in order to be considered life insurance. In order for a loan not to be considered a taxable event, the new policy must meet the seven-annual-premium-payments test. The model worksheet for the recommended new purchase to be used with the ledger statement is shown in Figure 7-2. (See the sample ledger statements in the Appendix.)

Additional Factors to Consider before Purchasing a New Life Insurance Policy

1. You should understand the financial facts relative to the proposed new policy. In addition, you will have to decide whether or not you are comfortable with the proposed recommendation. Only you can decide your comfort zone in financial matters.

2. Be aware that, whenever you replace an existing policy, a new period of contestability will start, to protect the insurance company against material misrepresentations or fraudulent statements. The period of contestability ranges from 1 to 2 years, depending on the life insurance company.

3. Ask about the underwriting requirements for the proposed policy. Depending upon your age and the amount of insurance, the underwriting requirements could vary anywhere from nonmedical to medical underwriting. In addition, other tests could be required—e.g., resting EKG, exercising EKG (stress test), chest x-ray, and now, because of acquired immune deficiency syndrome (AIDS), blood tests.

4. You should not replace or exchange an existing policy until the new policy has been issued, in the form in which it was applied for, and the premium has been paid, placing the new policy in force.

5. Be aware that if the cash-surrender value exceeds the premiums paid for your existing policy, there is an ordinary marginal income tax on the difference.

Figure 7-2. Worksheet for proposed purchase. Copyright William D. Brownlie, CLU, ChFC, CIP, LIA, 1988. All rights reserved.

PLAN OF LIFE INSURANCE: **WORKSHEET FOR PROPOSED PURCHASE**
TRADITIONAL WHOLE LIFE   <u>PROPOSED INSURED:</u> _____

Company:_____ Age:____ Sex:____
Face amount:_____ Basic premium:_____Waiver of premium
included:_____ Cost:_____
Dividends: Yes_____ No_____ How used:_____
Dividend direct recognition (projected dividends reduced if cash value bor-
rowed against): Yes_____ No_____ Fixed loan rate:_____ Variable loan
rate: Yes_____ No_____
Current variable loan rate:_____
Variable loan rate singularly or elected option: Singularly___ Elected option___
If variable loan rate used, will projected dividends be reduced if cash value
borrowed against? Yes_____ No_____
Interest currently being used to warrant dividend projections:_____
Is this a new money rate or a combination of old money and new money re-
ferred to as a blended rate or portfolio rate?_____
Guaranteed interest rate on cash value:_____
Describe in detail how the reserve i.e. cash surrender value from the existing
policy is being used:_____

RATE OF RETURN MEASURED IN TERMS OF COMPOUND INTEREST

	Total death benefit	ROR	Reserve, i.e., cash-surrender value	ROR
Years: _____	$ _____	___	$ _____	___
_____	$ _____	___	$ _____	___
_____	$ _____	___	$ _____	___
_____	$ _____	___	$ _____	___
_____	$ _____	___	$ _____	___

What would_____ have to earn in compound interest
before taxes to duplicate the rate of return upon death provided by life
insurance? _____ Marginal federal ordinary income tax bracket:_____
Years:_____   Rate of return:_____

_____   _____

_____   _____

_____   _____

Is the life insurance information based upon the official ledger statement of
the insurance company? Yes _____ No _____
Death benefit as of the beginning of the year? Yes _____ No _____
End of year? Yes _____ No _____
Total termination value as of end of year: Yes_____ No_____
Any comments regarding termination value:_____

Is the official ledger statement of the insurance company enclosed? Yes___
No___

Q. How were the rate-of-return calculations done?
A. On the Hewlett-Packard 41C series hand calculator with financial deci-
sions module
Read: *Life Insurance: Its Rate of Return* by William D. Brownlie, LIA,
CIP, CLU, ChFC, published by the National Underwriter Company, 420
E. 4th St., Cincinnati, Ohio 4520.

SOURCE: Model worksheet, William D. Brownlie, LIA, CIP, CLU, ChFC.

Section 1035 Exchange
Applied to Life Insurance

Section 1035 of the Internal Revenue Code provides for permissible
nontaxable life insurance exchanges in order to avoid having a gain
subject to tax. The essence of an exchange is a transfer of property between owners. If the replacement is to qualify as an exchange under
section 1035, the recommended procedure is an absolute assignment of
the existing contract to the new insurance company, which then surrenders the contract and issues a replacement contract.

Section 1035 of the Internal Revenue Code allows for like-kind
exchanges. When applied to a life insurance policy, one policy may be exchanged for another. The following are nontaxable like-kind exchanges:

1. *The exchange of a life insurance policy for another life insurance policy or for an endowment or annuity.*

2. *The exchange of an endowment contract for an annuity contract or an
   endowment contract under which payments will begin no later than
   payments would have begun under the contract exchanged.*

3. *The exchange of an annuity contract for another annuity contract.*

4. *The exchange of a life insurance policy, endowment contract, or fixed
   annuity contract for a variable annuity contract with the same company or a different company.* This qualifies as a tax-free exchange
   under section 1035(a).

Existing Policy with Loan
Outstanding

Be aware that a section 1035 like-kind exchange does not solve the
problem of deferring a gain on an existing policy with a loan outstanding. Consider the following hypothetical situation:

Examples of 1035 Exchanges

Hypothetical situation: Surrender value: $60,000
Cost-basis sum of premiums paid: $30,000
Taxable gain if policy surrendered: $30,000.

Watch for the tax consequences in the scenarios described below.

Scenario A.   A policy is exchanged for a permissible nontaxable exchange policy with either the same insurance company or a different company. No loan is outstanding. The exchange is executed according to the recommended procedure. The result is a nontaxable event, with a gain of $30,000 carried forward to the exchanged policy. Be aware that a section 1035 like-kind exchange does not solve the problem of deferring a gain on an existing policy with a loan outstanding.

Hypothetical Example

Surrender value: $60,000
Cost-basis sum of premiums paid: $30,000
Loan outstanding: $20,000
Taxable gain if policy surrendered: $30,000.

Scenario B.   A policy is exchanged for a permissible nontaxable exchange policy with either the same insurance company or a different company, with a $20,000 loan outstanding. The exchange is executed according to the recommended procedure. The result is a $20,000 taxable event because the existing policy has an inherent taxable gain of $30,000. A $20,000 loan outstanding means $20,000 was actually received. Therefore, $20,000 of the $30,000 gain is deemed to be realized and recognized upon exchange.

However, some commentators say that an existing policy with a loan outstanding can be exchanged and a taxable event can be avoided. The existing loan can be carried forward to a new policy. Is this true?

The Internal Revenue Service has issued a private letter ruling (letter 8604033) on this issue: the exchange of an existing policy with a loan for another permissible nontaxable exchange policy, with the same dollar amount of loan remaining outstanding with the new insurance company on the new policy. The private letter ruling stated that there was no taxable gain because the existing loan was not forgiven. The new policy was subject to the same dollar amount of loan as the existing policy.

Be mindful that a private letter ruling, even though it is issued by the Internal Revenue Service, is just that: a private letter to the taxpayer applying for the ruling. It does not apply to other taxpayers. It certainly is not a tax law. And in fact, most companies currently either will not issue a new policy subject to an original loan from an exchange policy or do not have a procedure in place for issuing such a policy.

Finally, even if a company will issue a new policy with the outstanding loan from the exchanged policy carried over (if, in fact, the exchanged policy has an inherent taxable gain), the original insurance company, by law, must issue a 1099 form to the policy owner, with a copy to the Internal Revenue Service. It then becomes the responsibility of the taxpayer, not the insurance company, to use private letter ruling 8604033 as evidence that the same procedure should apply in his or her arguments with the Internal Revenue Service.

Summary

1. Make sure you are provided with a rate-of-return study both for your existing policy or policies and for the recommended replacement policy.

2. If you have more than one existing policy, make sure that the rate-of-return study is on a weighted-average basis.

3. Be mindful that all newly issued policies must meet certain tests to be considered life insurance rather than loans subject to income tax and penalties.

4. If you are considering a replacement policy, first make sure that you understand the implications of any existing policy (or policies) with a loan (or loans) outstanding.

8
Vanishing Premium
(When Can You Stop Writing the Checks?)

The term *vanishing premium* describes a method of premium payment whereby premiums eventually stop without the insured having to borrow against the reserve (the cash value or separate investment account). Note that the vanishing premium is not a plan of life insurance but only an insurance trade expression describing a method of premium payment.

Chapters 10 to 16 discuss in depth the various types of life insurance that are available. Here, we simply address the issue of whether or not it is possible to have vanishing premiums with the various types of life insurance available.

Term Insurance

You cannot vanish premiums on term insurance unless you accumulate a sufficient amount of money in a separate investment from which to pay future premiums.

Traditional Whole Life and Graded Premium Paying Dividends as Declared

In traditional whole life and graded premium policies, dividends as declared and paid can be used to purchase additional paid-up life insurance. The duration of time for the payment of the gross premium depends on projected dividends for the policy. When the value of the newly paid dividend combined with the accrued dividend is sufficient, the premium will vanish. At this point, the yearly declared and paid dividend can be used to reduce the gross premium. Any balance due is taken from the accrued dividend value. When the yearly declared and paid dividend exceeds the gross premium, the dividend may be taken in cash or used to purchase additional paid-up life insurance. Keep in mind that the premium vanishes through the use of the dividends. There are no loans against the cash value of the policy.

What happens to the dividends in the event of a loan against the cash value? If the insurance company uses the concept of direct recognition, the dividends will be reduced only if the fixed-interest-rate loan is paid. If the variable-interest-rate loan is paid, dividends will not be reduced, provided the interest rate is at least equal to the assumed dividend interest rate. If the interest on the variable-rate loan is greater than the dividend interest-rate assumption, the dividends will increase. (See Chapter 13 for a detailed explanation of direct-recognition, fixed-interest, and variable-interest loan rates. The dividend interest-rate assumption is discussed in Chapters 7 and 13.)

Will the death benefit always be equal to the original face amount? No, it will be equal for the first year only. From the second year on, the original face amount is increased through the purchase of additional paid-up life insurance by the declared and paid dividend.

Interest-Sensitive Whole Life

The amount of the premium and the number of years required to pay for interest-sensitive whole life insurance is determined by the insurance company. The determining factors are:

1. Current interest rate as shown in the ledger statement will be realized and paid throughout the life of the policy.
2. Current mortality charges will not increase.

Refer to Chapter 14 for an explanation of current interest rate and current mortality charges.

Universal Life

In the universal life policy, you can decide the number of years you wish the death benefit to remain in force and the interest rate you wish to assume. Having set your own specifications for the face amount of insurance, you will be told the premium amount.

Conversely, you decide the amount of premium you wish to pay and to what age you want the death benefit to remain in force. After deciding the interest rate you wish to assume, you will be told the number of years you have to pay and the face amount of the insurance.

Keep in mind that your specifications will be met only if:

1. The interest-rate assumption is realized.
2. Current mortality charges are not increased.

Refer to Chapter 15 for an explanation of interest-rate assumption and current mortality charges.

Variable Life

Generally speaking, it is not possible to vanish premiums on most variable life products currently in the marketplace. Some variable life products are automatically paid up at age 65, however. In these products, all premiums vanish at age 65. In addition, some variable life products declare dividends. Through the use of these dividends it may be possible to vanish premiums.

When considering a specific variable life product, ask how and whether it is possible to vanish premium payments. Remember, making a loan against the separate investment account does not vanish the premiums.

9

Life Insurance Fads: Past and Most Recent

(What Congress Giveth Can Be Taken Away)

Past Fad: Tax-Qualified Minimum Deposit

Tax-qualified minimum deposit is an insurance trade expression for a method of paying for life insurance. This method involves borrowing against the reserve (the cash value of the policy or the separate investment account).

Tax-qualified means that if the policy qualifies, the interest charged for loans against the cash value is tax-deductible. For policies issued after August 6, 1963, the policy is considered qualified if any 4 of the first 7 premiums are paid without any direct or indirect method of borrowing. In other words, 4 out of the first 7 premiums must be paid.

The Appeal of the Tax-Qualified Minimum Deposit

Prior to passage of the 1986 Tax Reform Act, advocates of this method of premium payment believed that being able to deduct the interest made it possible to provide a death benefit less expensive than term insurance. They believed that this was true for two reasons: (1) interest was tax-deductible, and (2) high marginal federal ordinary tax brackets (maximum of 50 percent for individuals and 46 percent for corporations) existed. State income taxes, if any, increased these brackets to an overall higher level.

The Effect of the 1986 Tax Reform Act

Interest on loans on personal life insurance policies will no longer be tax-deductible by 1991. Sixty-five percent was deductible in 1987, 40 percent in 1988, 20 percent in 1989, 10 percent in 1990, and 0 percent thereafter.

Business-owned life insurance policies purchased prior to June 21, 1986, when interest is charged for loans against the reserve, is fully tax-deductible provided that, for policies purchased after August 6, 1963, any 4 out of the first 7 premiums were paid without any direct or indirect method of borrowing.

For policies purchased after June 20, 1986, and owned by a business, loan interest is deductible, provided the 4-out-of-7 test is met, only to the extent that policy loans in the aggregate do not exceed $50,000 per insured. Interest on loans exceeding $50,000 will not be tax-deductible.

Prior to passage of the 1986 Tax Reform Act, marginal federal ordinary income tax brackets ranged from a low of 11 percent to a maximum of 50 percent. The 1986 act has mandated the following marginal federal ordinary income tax brackets for individuals, for tax years 1988 and after: 15, 28, and 33 percent.

What You Should Do

First, do not panic. Second, do consult with your life insurance agent. Here are some things you will learn:

1. In some cases, you can use dividends to pay the interest.

2. If the loan is repaid, you can use dividends either to reduce the premium or to vanish the premium.

3. If your policy has a low fixed interest rate, your interest payments may not be a serious cash-flow problem. Lower income tax rates reduce the cost of nondeductible expenses.

4. Be aware that policy loans may be repaid and increased dividends

may be generated because of direct recognition. (Refer to Chapter 13 for a detailed explanation of direct recognition.) Loans may be repaid in full or in installments.

5. If your policy has been using dividends to purchase 1-year term insurance equal to the cash value, it can usually be converted to nonterm life insurance, without a medical examination and without regard to your present or past medical history. This will keep your death benefit at the desired level while your loan is being repaid.

6. Individually owned personal policies (i.e., non-business-owned policies) purchased prior to June 21, 1986, can be transferred to a business in which the insured is an owner (shareholder or officer) without incurring a transfer-for-value problem. The interest on those policies may be deducted by the business in full thereafter, regardless of when the loans are taken out.

Tax Implications

What are the federal income tax implications to you if you decide not to use any of the above six suggestions, and instead surrender your policy or allow it to lapse?

A loan against the reserve is an advance of that portion of the death benefit. As such, it is not a loan that must be paid back. When death occurs, the loan against the reserve is paid back by being deducted from the face amount of the policy. If you surrender your policy or allow it to lapse, however, and receive the reserve in the form of the cash-surrender value, then and only then are you considered to be in receipt of cash not used as part of the death benefit. At this point, any reserve previously received in the form of a loan, plus any residual unborrowed reserve value exceeding what you paid, will have to be taxed on the difference.

Reduced Paid-Up and Extended Term

There is something else you could do. You could put your policy on a "reduced paid-up" basis or on an "extended-term" basis. Let me explain these two "$4 insurance" terms. *Reduced paid-up* means that the existing reserve buys X dollars of life insurance on a fully paid-up basis. The amount purchased is considerably less than the face amount of the existing policy. *Extended term* means that the existing reserve will keep the existing policy in force at exactly the same face amount for X years, months, and days on a term insurance basis, until the reserve reaches zero. When it does, the insurance coverage is no longer in force.

Form 1099 is issued by an insurance company to the owner of a life insurance policy, with a copy to the Internal Revenue Service, when the policy is surrendered and there is a taxable gain. I have been informed that some insurance companies will not issue a 1099 form until the extended term expires or the reduced paid-up policy is surrendered.

Current IRS rules are not clear. At present, the reduced paid-up option seems to be the best choice for avoiding issuance of a form 1099. But before opting for this choice, check with your insurance company for its procedure.

Rescue Plans. Watch out for the so-called tax-qualified minimum-deposit rescue plan. This is nothing more than a replacement of your existing loan, which is carried forward to the new policy. Remember that a new policy must satisfy state laws and must meet the cash-value accumulation, guideline premium, corridor, and seven-annual-premium-payments tests, in order to meet the definition of life insurance and in order for loans not to be considered taxable events.

Some commentators say that an existing policy with a loan outstanding can be exchanged and a taxable event can be avoided provided that the existing loan is carried forward to the new policy. In 1986, the Internal Revenue Service issued private letter ruling 8604033, concerning the exchange of an existing policy with a loan for another like-kind policy with the same dollar amount of loan outstanding with the new insurance company. The private letter ruling stated that there was no taxable gain because the existing loan was not forgiven. The new policy was subject to the same dollar amount as the existing loan.

The existence of private letter ruling 8604033 has caused some companies to market a concept called a "tax-qualified minimum-deposit rescue plan." Here is some nuts-and-bolts information and advice that you should take into consideration before purchasing such a plan:

1. Interest is not tax-deductible on the loan carried forward to the new policy except under the existing rules.

2. A *private letter ruling* is just that: a private letter to the particular taxpayer applying for the ruling. It does not apply to other taxpayers and it certainly is not tax law.

3. Most important, even if a particular company will issue a new policy with an existing loan outstanding on it, and even if, in fact, the original policy had an inherent taxable gain, the original life insurance company is required, by current law, to issue you a 1099 form showing taxable income. And of course, a copy of your 1099 form also

goes to the Internal Revenue Service. It is then your responsibility, not the insurance company's, to use private letter ruling 8604033 as evidence that the same procedure should apply in your particular situation.

Deductibility of Interest on Individual Taxpayers' Personally Owned Life Insurance Policies

If you are a cash-basis taxpayer, and if you pay interest on a loan taken out on your life insurance policy, you may deduct 20 percent in 1989 and 10 percent in 1990; your deduction will be zero thereafter.

You must know what a cash-basis taxpayer is, in order to determine whether you qualify. In essence, a *cash-basis taxpayer* pays tax only on income actually received and can deduct only deductible expenses in the year actually paid. In any given calendar year, cash-basis taxpayers record as income only the income that has actually been paid to them. Conversely, they can deduct only those expenses deductible under current tax law that they actually paid out during the tax calendar year. Most individuals are cash-basis taxpayers.

Business-Owned Life Insurance Policies

Business entities in general must use the accrual method of accounting, although some (e.g., farmers and qualified personal service corporations) may continue to use the cash-basis method of accounting. These exceptions do not have to change over to the accrual method as do all other business entities, as mandated by the 1986 act.

Most business entities are not cash-basis taxpayers but accrual-basis taxpayers. An *accrual-basis taxpayer* can be defined as one who treats income as income when it is accrued, not when it is actually received.

Example

A customer purchases a TV set and pays by credit card. This type of transaction is income to the business, even though no cash changed hands.

Conversely, expenses of an accrual-basis taxpayer are treated as expenses when incurred and, if deductible, are deductible when incurred, not when paid.

Example

An accrual-basis taxpayer is notified by the life insurance company, on the premium notice, that X dollars of interest is due. When notified, the expense (interest) is incurred and (if deductible by the 4-out-of-7 test) is deductible whether paid or not, provided it meets the requirements of the 1986 Tax Reform Act. If the interest is not paid, however, the insurance company adds it to the loan. If the amount of the loan exceeds the reserve value, the policy will lapse.

For loans on business-owned life insurance policies purchased prior to June 21, 1986, all the interest is tax-deductible, if the policies are tax-qualified. For loans on policies purchased after June 20, 1986, if tax-qualified, interest is deductible to the extent that policy loans, in the aggregate, are not in excess of $50,000 per insured. Interest on loans in excess of $50,000 is not tax-deductible.

Business-Owned Life Insurance Comparison

The question that arises is: For business-owned life insurance, is tax-qualified minimum deposit still a viable way to pay for life insurance? In order to know the answer, you will have to compare yearly renewable term insurance with tax-qualified minimum deposit. A thorough comparison would be one using all three cost-disclosure methods (see Chapter 5): the traditional, interest-adjusted, and rate-of-return methods.

Example

Study Comparison of Yearly Renewable Term and Tax-Qualified Minimum Deposit (45-Year-Old Male, Nonsmoker)

Face amount: $100,000.

Traditional whole life, paying dividends as declared, used to purchase 1-year term insurance equal to the cash value, with the balance of the dividend used in reduction of the gross premium. The gross premium was paid in year 1. In years 3, 4, and 5, the gross premium was paid by first using the projected dividend in reduction of the premium and the balance due was paid by a loan against the reserve. In years 2, 6, and 7, the gross premium, minus the dividend plus interest, was paid. The complete reserve (the cash value), was borrowed at the beginning of year 8. A 34 percent corporate tax bracket was assumed for interest-deduction purposes. State income taxes, if any, were not considered.

Plan: Yearly renewable term insurance. Nonreissue and reentry rates.

Age: 45.

Sex: Male.

Nonsmoker: Yes.

Unisex rate: No.

Results:

1. The traditional method, strictly a cash-flow analysis, disregarding the time value of money, revealed a lower outlay of cash, i.e., premium payments for the first 5 years for yearly renewable term insurance. For the next 5

years, tax-qualified minimum deposit was lower, making the cumulative outlay for the first 10 years almost the same. From 10 years on, tax-qualified minimum deposit generated lower outlays, after taking into consideration the tax deduction.

2. Using the interest-adjusted index method and a 5 percent interest assumption on invested money (if not used to purchase life insurance), it was discovered that yearly renewable term insurance, taking into consideration the time value of money, produced a lower numerical figure for a net payment index than that yielded by tax-qualified minimum deposit.

3. Use of the rate-of-return method, expressed in terms of compound interest and with the time value of money taken into consideration, revealed that yearly renewable term insurance produced a greater rate of return upon death than did tax-qualified minimum deposit.

Comment:

1. In this study comparison, a fixed loan rate of 8 percent was used for the tax-qualified method of premium payment. (Refer to Chapter 13.)

2. At the time this book is being written, variable loan rates are in the range of 10.54 to 10.97 percent. (Refer to Chapter 13.)

3. A period of 20 years, age 45 to age 65, was chosen for this study comparison essentially because the insurance company's tax-qualified ledger statement only indicates an after-tax outlay up to age 65.

4. Perhaps the results would have been different if studied beyond age 65. In addition, the results may be different for ages other than 45.

Summary: Tax-Qualified Minimum Deposit

1. Perhaps, as an individual, you felt you had several reasons for adopting a tax-qualified minimum deposit method, such as a high marginal federal ordinary tax bracket, the ability to deduct the interest, or the possibility that it might be a less expensive way to provide a death benefit than yearly renewable term insurance. You should rethink this issue because of the Tax Reform Act of 1986.

2. If, as an individual, you are thinking of terminating your tax-qualified minimum-deposit life insurance policy, consider all the tax implications and all the possibilities for restructuring your present policy before you make any moves toward termination.

3. Watch out for so-called tax-qualified minimum-deposit rescue plans. They are nothing more than a replacement of your existing loan, which will be carried forward to the new policy.

4. When considering tax-qualified minimum deposit as an alternative to yearly renewable term for new business-owned life insurance, you

will be well advised to compare the two on all three methods of cost disclosure, i.e., traditional, interest-adjusted index, and rate of return for the time period the insurance is needed.

5. Vanishing premium is a more suitable method of paying for life insurance than is tax-qualified minimum deposit.

6. Finally, always keep in mind, when you read anything dealing with taxes, that you must make sure that what you are reading is, in fact, current in our ever-changing tax environment.

Most Recent Fad: Single-Premium Life Insurance

Recently, single-premium life insurance has been the most talked-about plan of life insurance, thanks to the 1986 Tax Reform Act. This act, among other things, has resulted in:

1. *Reduction of individual marginal ordinary federal income tax brackets.*
2. *Change in depreciation rules for real estate when purchased for investment purposes.*
3. *Elimination of the Clifford Trust as an income tax-shifting device for purposes of accumulating money for education. Income tax shifting* is a device which allows interest or earnings to be taxed in a lower tax bracket.
4. *Reduction or elimination of current tax benefits for most nonqualified tax shelters.* If a tax shelter (e.g., oil and gas exploration, real estate rehabilitation, real estate development) is nonqualified, it cannot be submitted to the Internal Revenue Service for prior approval. Approval or disapproval of tax-deductible and nontaxable features will depend upon interpretation by the Internal Revenue Service, if and when questioned, for example in a tax audit. The 1986 act seriously affects nonqualified tax shelters in that most of the tax benefits are pushed ahead to future years. When considering a nonqualified tax shelter, make sure that you are able to answer the following questions:
   a. Is your current contribution allowed to be considered a deductible expense?
   b. When income is received, in the form of cash flows, is the income sheltered from taxes?

    c. Are there any other factors (e.g., depreciation) that can be used as an offset against cash flows, which are taxable?

    d. When the nonqualified tax shelter terminates, what are the tax ramifications?

    Based on items *a* to *d* above, what can you expect for a potential rate of return as expressed in terms of compound interest, for the use of your money, as an investment into the nonqualified tax shelter? If you are convinced that it is a sound economic investment, and if legitimate, highly regarded people are running the deal, then consider investing. If you are not convinced, however, that your rate of return before taxes can be at least 15 percent compound, do not invest.

5. *The eventual elimination of personal interest charges as a deductible expense.*

6. *Change in Individual Retirement Account (IRA) rules.* If you are covered by a company pension plan, or if your individual taxpayer's adjusted gross income is $35,000 or over, or if you and your spouse are a married couple filing a joint return with an adjusted gross income of $50,000 or over, the tax deductibility of an IRA contribution disappears. Even if covered by a pension plan, however, an individual whose income is less than $25,000 or a married couple whose joint income is less than $40,000 can still make deductible IRA contributions.

7. *A 15 percent excise tax on your retirement plan assets.* This applies when your yearly retirement distribution is in excess of a specific allowed amount. It also applies when you die and the accumulated value of your retirement plan assets is in excess of a specific amount.

The Last Great Tax Shelter?

Because the 1986 act still allows for the reserve of a life insurance policy to accumulate on a tax-deferred basis, some companies have decided to market single-premium life insurance as the last great remaining tax shelter.

Congress Takes a Serious Look at Single-Premium Life Insurance

Abuse of the fact that the reserve is still allowed to build up on a tax-exempt basis (as part of the tax-exempt death benefit) has already caused Congress to take a very serious look at single-premium life insurance—and Congress did not like what it saw. Consequently, it changed the rules for all nonterm life insurance policies issued on or after June 21, 1988. In order for a loan against the reserve, i.e., the cash-surrender value, not to be a taxable event, a policy must qualify for the seven-annual-premium-payments test. Clearly, a one-time payment (i.e., a single-premium policy) will not meet the test.

How Does It Work?

Single-premium life insurance requires the payment of one sum—a single, one-time premium. The minimum payment allowed by most companies is $5000.

Various tests (i.e., cash-value accumulation, guideline premium, and corridor) must be met in order for the policy to be considered life insurance. This is important for two reasons—reasons without which the appeal of single-premium life insurance is lost. These reasons are:

1. So that the death benefit, when payable to the beneficiary, will not be subject to federal income tax.
2. So that the reserve for whole life and universal life and the separate investment account for variable life, which is part of the tax-exempt death benefit, can accumulate tax-exempt.

Characteristics

The amount of the death benefit is determined by the dollar amount of the single premium (guideline premium test) and the insured's age. Single-premium life is not a cost-effective way to provide for much-needed life insurance, for it provides very little protection in relation to the premium spent. Remember the rate-of-return rule of thumb: the larger the present-value payment (which is the premium), the lower the rate of return upon death.

The *death benefit* can never be less than the amount guaranteed at the time of purchase. As the reserve (the cash value or the separate investment account) increases because of interest credited or increase in the investments, the original death benefit must increase. This is because of the cash-value accumulation and the corridor test whereby the face amount of life insurance must always exceed the reserve by a specific percentage at each specific age in order to qualify as life insurance.

Loans against the reserve are not taxable events for policies issued prior to June 21, 1988. For policies issued on or after June 21, 1988, they are taxable events, and for loans made prior to age 59½, there is an additional 10 percent penalty tax. In addition, a loan reduces the death benefit by the amount of the loan. This is because the reserve is part of the death benefit. When you make a loan, you have received that portion of the death benefit in advance.

The *cost to borrow against the reserve* (the interest charge) varies from company to company. Some companies impose a zero net cost on certain amounts borrowed. This means that they credit the same interest rate to borrowed and to unborrowed reserve amounts.

An X percent cost on amounts borrowed means that the borrowed amount is earning X percent less interest than the unborrowed amount. Make sure that you are provided with total disclosure about the cost of borrowing.

Loads.   With the majority of companies, 100 percent of your single-premium payment earns full tax-exempt interest. There are no front-end loads, which means that your single deposit is not reduced. Because of expenses (commissions, etc.), the insurance company is making its profit on the investment spread. This means that if it is earning X percent, it will credit to you less than X percent. The company makes its profit on the difference.

Most companies that are actively in the business of marketing single-premium life issue what is called, in the insurance business, a "rear-end-loaded contract." This means that if you decide to terminate your policy, there are penalties, and your money is reduced accordingly. For example, a company may impose the following surrender penalties:

Year	Percent
1	7
2	6
3	5
4	4
5	3
6	2
7	1

From the eighth year on, no rear-end surrender penalty charges exist, in this example. Make sure that you are given total disclosure about surrender charges.

Interest Credited.   The particular plan you are considering (e.g., whole life or variable life) will determine the investment strategy of the insurance company. Whole life will credit interest to the reserve. The current interest rate and the guaranteed interest rate will vary from company to company. Variable life will credit no interest to the reserve (the separate investment account). Its value will be solely dependent upon investment performance.

Terms Defined

Guaranteed Interest Rate.   The *guaranteed interest rate* is the interest rate by contract that the insurance company guarantees to credit on the reserve.

Current Rate.   The *current rate* is not guaranteed. It is the rate currently being paid. This rate is determined by the investment strategy (e.g., old money, new money; money market investments; capital market investments; pure portfolio rate; portfolio rate with a weighted average of old money and new money; or modified portfolio rate).

Separate Investment Account.   The *separate investment account* with most companies which issue a single-premium variable life product consists of a common stock account, a money market account, and a bond account. Some have specific bond accounts (e.g., zero coupon bonds), and some have a real estate investment account.

Tax Advantages

1. The reserve (the cash value or the separate investment account) is allowed, under current law, to build up on a tax-exempt basis. This means that a 7.75 percent interest factor in the marginal tax brackets listed below is worth:

Marginal tax bracket	Interest factor
15%	9.12%
28	10.76
33	11.57

2. The reserve can be borrowed. When borrowed, it is not a taxable event for policies issued prior to June 21, 1988.

3. The death benefit paid to your named beneficiary, provided it is considered life insurance proceeds, is not subject to federal income tax.

Tax Disadvantages

1. For policies issued on or after June 21, 1988, loans against the reserve (the cash-surrender value) are a taxable event. In addition, loans made prior to age 59½ are subject to a 10 percent penalty tax.

2. If you decide to terminate the policy, you may be subject to surrender penalties. Even with the surrender penalties, if the amount of

money you receive upon surrender is greater than what you paid, there is a marginal ordinary income tax due on the difference.

3. There is also a phantom income tax consideration. Any time you surrender a life insurance policy, to the extent that the reserve (the cash value or the separate investment account) exceeds what you paid for the policy, there is a marginal federal ordinary income tax due on the difference.

Example

$50,000 single payment; 7.75 percent interest assumption

Year	Reserve value policy	Amount subject to tax
5	$ 71,121	$ 21,121
10	105,474	55,474
15	153,190	103,190
20	222,493	172,493

Income tax due for the following tax brackets:

Taxable gain	15%	28%	33%
$ 21,121	$ 3,168	$ 5,913	$ 6,969
55,474	8,321	15,531	18,306
103,190	15,478	28,893	34,052
172,493	25,873	48,298	56,922

Where is the phantom income problem? Keep in mind that loans against the reserve, once the policy is surrendered, still result in a taxable event if the reserve value, borrowed or unborrowed, exceeds the one-time payment.

Summary: Single-Premium Life Insurance

1. For policies issued prior to June 21, 1988, the three tax advantages still hold true: (a) Reserve (i.e., cash value), because it is part of the tax-exempt death benefit, accumulates tax-exempt. (b) Loans against reserve are not taxable events. (c) If a policy qualifies as life insurance (i.e., if it meets various tests), the death-benefit proceeds are not subject to federal income tax.

2. For policies issued on or after June 21, 1988, the same tax advantages as listed in item 1 apply, except that loans against reserve are taxable events.

PART 3

Getting Down to Choices: Types of Life Insurance

10

Group Term Life Insurance Provided by Your Employer

($50,000 Tax-Free)

Always keep in mind that group term life provided by your employer usually does not provide you and your family with a postretirement death benefit. By this point in this book, you should have become convinced that your getting older does not automatically mean that your need for life insurance is being reduced or is nonexistent. Only a present-value calculation will provide the information you need—not an article in some publication telling you that as you get older your need for life insurance decreases.

Also be mindful that early retirement can cause loss of life insurance coverage. Many people have been persuaded by their employers to opt for early retirement—with the stipulation that insurance benefits, both life and major medical, will remain in force. The employer's goal of course is to save money. Unfortunately for the early-retiring employees, some such companies are now filing for bankruptcy. When this occurs, the retirees are left holding an empty bag: no benefits. The moral of this story is that you should pay for your life insurance in such a way that premium payments have vanished either before or by the time of retirement.

Group Term Life Insurance: What Your Employer May Provide

Up to $50,000 of group term life insurance per employee may be provided by an employer on a tax-exempt basis. This means that you, as the employee, do not have to report any of this term insurance as income on your federal income tax return.

Payments for group term life insurance may be made in one of two forms: noncontributory or contributory. *Noncontributory* means that you, as the employee, contribute nothing. Contributions are made entirely by your employer. All eligible employees must be included in this category of payments, if the employer provides noncontributory payments.

Contributory means that you, as the employee, contribute something toward the cost. An employee who does not wish to participate does not have to do so.

Generally speaking, group term life insurance is issued without medical examination and without proof of insurability. This means that present and past medical history is not taken into consideration.

To take advantage of group term life (even though you don't have to participate), you must sign up for it when you become eligible. There is a reason for this. If a person wanted to participate later, the insurance company would suspect that the person was electing to participate because of poor health and just wanted to take advantage of the opportunity to receive life insurance without medical examination and without regard to medical history.

Cost in Excess of $50,000 Is Taxable Income

For amounts of insurance in excess of $50,000 provided to an employee by the employer, the employee must report as taxable income an amount of money for the excess coverage as determined by the "I (note that this is a capital letter, not a Roman numeral) table" (Table 10-1). The "I table," published by the Internal Revenue Service, lists rates used to calculate the value of group term life insurance in excess of $50,000. Shown below is an example of use of the "I table."

Table 10-1. The "I Table"

Age	Cost per month per $1000 of coverage	Annualized cost
29 & under	$ .08	$ .96
30–34	.09	1.08
35–39	.11	1.32
40–44	.17	2.04
45–49	.29	3.48
50–54	.48	5.76
55–59	.75	9.00
60 & over	1.17	4.00

Example

Noncontributory plan: Employer pays entire premium.

Excess amount: $100,000.

Annualized charge: $3.48 per $1000 of coverage.

Amount of money that must be reported as taxable income on W2 statement: $348 ($100,000 × $3.48).

Effective real costs: $52.20, $97.44, and $114.84—assuming 15, 28, and 33 percent marginal federal tax brackets, respectively. Additional income of $348 taxed at 15, 28, and 33 percent means that an additional $52.20, $97.44, and $114.84 must be paid in taxes.

Contributory plan: Employee pays part of premium.

Excess amount: $100,000.

Annualized charge: $3.48 per $1000 of coverage.

Employee's contribution to group term life insurance plan: $2 per $1000 of coverage annually. In this example, for $150,000 of coverage, the employee pays $300. Because the employee contributes $300, only $48 is reportable as additional taxable income—the difference between $348 and the $300 the employee paid.

The cost to you for amounts in excess of $50,000 for group term life provided by your employer can be substantial—and rates on the "I table" increase every 5 years. If the insurance increases because of increased wages or salary, the tax on the "I table" rate is significant, especially in later years.

Postretirement Death Benefit

Most group term life insurance plans allow you to convert to a nonterm life insurance plan, without medical examination and without proof of insurability, usually within 30 days of retiring or terminating employment. You are not allowed to convert to term insurance. Be advised that the cost of converting at retirement is expensive. For $150,000 of traditional whole life paying dividends as declared at age 65, the cost is approximately $7856.50 annually, not taking projected dividends into consideration. In addition, there is a conversion charge to the employer when employees convert their group term coverage.

Employer Considerations

Group term life insurance programs created for employees involves an ongoing nonrecoverable cost for employers. The time value of the money being spent should also be considered. The cost for the employer is the after-tax cost for the premium paid. The term "after-tax" is used because the premium paid is tax-deductible. The after-tax cost for each dollar in premium paid, assuming a maximum federal corporate tax bracket of 34 percent, is 66 cents. That's before state taxes are considered.

If only 7 to 12 percent of an employee group dies prior to age 65 (normal retirement age), 93 to 88 percent of the money spent by the employer is lost. The loss is further increased as a result of the time value of money, which means the money spent for group term life could have been invested, saved, or used for business expansion. There is a loss because no benefits are generated if life insurance is not in force when someone dies. If the insurance is not in force, because of retirement or termination of employment, the rate of return is always minus 100 percent compound for dollars previously spent for the coverage.

Employers who wish to provide selected employees (employers may pick and choose) with both a preretirement and a postretirement death benefit, and who wish to recover their cost either with or without a time-value-of-money factor, should consider split-dollar life insurance. Employers who wish to provide both a preretirement and a postretirement death benefit for selected employees, and who want to be able to deduct the premium currently as compensation to the employee, should consider whole-dollar life insurance.

Payroll Deduction Purchase

Regardless of the plan of life insurance being offered by your employer, payroll deduction purchase is warranted only if it fits with your objectives and comfort zone and is equal in cost and benefits to what you could purchase as an individual based upon your own specific medical history.

There are some things you should know if you plan to buy voluntary term insurance with your own money via payroll deduction through your employer.

First of all, this type of purchase is not the same as a contributory group term plan. This purchase is completely separate from the formal group term plan of your employer. Your employer (through payroll deductions) and the insurance company (by allowing additional insurance within certain limits to be issued without medical examination) are merely making it convenient for you to buy additional life insurance if you need it.

Is Payroll Deduction Purchase a Good Deal?

Whether or not this additional insurance is a good deal depends on what it costs. Perhaps you could buy yearly renewable term insurance from your own agent at a better price, although admittedly less conveniently than buying it through your employer. In addition, if you need and want to provide a postretirement death benefit and wish to vanish all premiums by the time you retire, term insurance will not fit the bill—because there is no cash buildup in a term policy. The moral to this story is that you should pay for your life insurance in such a way that premium payments have vanished either before or by the time of retirement.

Are There Alternatives?

There are alternatives to term life. Traditional whole life and graded premium life, universal life, interest-sensitive whole life, variable life, and universal variable life paid for on a vanishing-premium basis are alternatives you should consider. As a matter of fact, many employers are now offering universal and whole life on a payroll deduction basis. When you purchase life insurance on a payroll deduction basis, you are using mass purchasing power. This means, among other things, that the insurance company uses a particular type of medical underwriting to make it easy to enroll large numbers of people. Make sure that you find out the type of medical underwriting used. The major types are as follows:

1. Ratebook rate
2. Nonmedical underwriting
3. Medical underwriting
4. Simplified-issue underwriting
5. Guaranteed-issue underwriting

Why Is the Type of Underwriting Important?

The type of underwriting used will determine whether you are receiving the proper charge based on your current or past medical history. For example, if you are a nonsmoker with no adverse health history and the type of underwriting being used is guaranteed issue, you are paying for those who have an adverse medical history.

Types of Underwriting

Ratebook Rate Underwriting

In essence, the *regular ratebook rate* is the best possible rate per $1000 of life insurance, as listed in the regular ratebook of the insurance company. The rate is not loaded for any form of medical impairment or for an occupational category. Nonsmokers get a lower regular rate than smokers.

Nonmedical Underwriting

Answers to a detailed nonmedical form are required in *nonmedical underwriting*. The nonmedical form can be used by agents or brokers of a specific life insurance company that has given them a nonmedical privilege. The nonmedical form can be used only when the amount of life insurance, based on the proposed insured's age, is within the nonmedical limits of the insurance company. If there is no adverse current or past medical history which would cause the insurance company to increase the rate, the insurance is issued at the proper ratebook rate. ("Proper," in this context, means that nonsmokers get the nonsmokers' rate and smokers get the smokers' rate.) The rate listed in the ratebook can only be increased because of current or past medical history or a specific occupational category.

Medical Underwriting

If the amount of life insurance applied for and the proposed insured's age are such that the nonmedical form cannot be used, medical underwriting is the answer. *Medical underwriting*, again depending upon the amount of life insurance applied for and the proposed insured's age, requires the underwriting form (medical questionnaire) to be filled out by either (1) a paramedic or (2) a physician.

Besides the filling out of the form, certain medical tests must be performed, usually including:

1. Blood pressure test

2. Urine specimen

In addition, depending upon the amount of insurance and the age of the applicant, the following may be required:

3. Resting EKG

4. Stress test (EKG during exercise)

5. Chest x-ray

6. Blood test for acquired immune deficiency syndrome (AIDS)

When the medical form has been completed and all required tests have been done, then, based on the medical evidence, the insurance is issued at the appropriate rate. The rate charged to the individual can be increased over the regular ratebook rate only because of current or past medical history or a specific occupational category.

Simplified-Issue Underwriting

Simplified-issue underwriting is similar to nonmedical underwriting, but the form used is much shorter, only requiring the answers to about four specific questions. This form of underwriting is used mainly in large enrollments, such as payroll deductions or professional associations. As in nonmedical underwriting, if there is no adverse current or past medical history which would cause the insurance company to increase the rate, the insurance is issued at the proper ratebook rate for either a smoker or a nonsmoker. The regular rate can be increased only because of current or past medical history or occupational category. The amount of life insurance that can be purchased is usually limited.

Guaranteed-Issue Underwriting

Guaranteed-issue underwriting is dramatically different from ratebook rate, nonmedical underwriting, medical underwriting, and simplified-issue underwriting. With most life insurance companies, guaranteed issue means that if the proposed insured is actively at work, the insurance is issued automatically without regard to current or past medical history. Because the insurance company knows that it will be insuring some adverse risks, it requires that *either all or a certain percentage of all eligible participants enroll.* This guarantees the insurance company an adequate spread of ratebook-insured (nonimpaired) versus impaired insureds. In addition:

1. The insurance company will increase the ratebook rate to take into consideration the insuring of some impaired risks.
2. If dividends are paid as declared, the company may not increase the ratebook rate premium but will pay lower dividends.

In essence, for insureds who have no adverse current or past medical history which would cause them to have to pay a higher rate, guaranteed-issue underwriting is not a very good buy; they are paying for the impaired risks.

Other Factors to Consider

Make sure that you are being provided total disclosure about:

1. *The premium charged.*   Is it lower than what you could pay for like-kind coverage on your own because of the theory that the selling effort is less?
2. *The cost disclosure method being used.*

Summary

1. Group term life insurance generally does not provide for a postretirement death benefit.
2. Life insurance premiums should vanish either before or at retirement.
3. Up to $50,000 of group term life can be provided by an employer without cost to the employee.
4. For amounts in excess of $50,000, there is reportable income which will increase the taxes to be paid by the covered employee.
5. To convert group term life is expensive both for the covered employee and for the employer.
6. Split dollar and whole dollar (see Chapter 19) is more suitable for those employers who wish to provide both pre- and postretirement death benefits.
7. Payroll deduction purchases, to be worthwhile, must be equal in costs and benefits to what you could purchase as an individual, based upon your own specific medical history.

11

Term Insurance

(Initially the Biggest Bang for the Buck)

Certainly, term insurance is the most inexpensive form of life insurance—when it is initially purchased. It may continue to be the most inexpensive, depending upon how long the insurance remains in force.

The bottom line in life insurance buying decisions is that it is essential that you have the exact amount of life insurance you need. If you can afford that exact amount only on a term insurance basis, then term insurance most definitely should be your choice.

Yearly Renewable and Convertible Term

Yearly renewable term life insurance is one of the most popular choices when term insurance is purchased on an individual basis. As the name implies, this is insurance issued for 1 year at a time. At the end of the year the insurance may be renewed for another year. At each renewal the premium goes up. The face amount of the insurance remains the same. The premium charged in each year represents the actual cost of dying.

The insurance company dictates how long the insurance can be renewed as term insurance. Prior to an age determined by the insurance company, term insurance can be converted to a nonterm plan without medical examination and without regard to medical history.

Reissue and Reentry

Reissue and *reentry*, as used in discussion of yearly renewable term life insurance, are interchangeable terms that apply to existing term policy-holders who are given the opportunity to reenter by the insurance company. What this means is that the policyholders can reenter, or the company will reissue policies to them, at various time intervals (determined by the insurance company) as though they were new applicants for life insurance. If, as "new applicants," they successfully pass the underwriting requirements, they will be charged lower premiums.

Insured people who pass the underwriting requirement are assumed at that point to be better risks. Insured people who do not pass are not charged a higher premium; they continue to pay the nonreentry (re-issue) premium as stated in their insurance contract.

The reissue and reentry rates, as shown on the original ledger statement when being presented as a specific recommendation, *are not* guaranteed. The actual rates will be the rates the insurance company is charging at the time of reissue and reentering if an insured qualifies. This fact should be stated on the ledger statement. (See the sample ledger statements in the Appendix.)

Some companies issue yearly renewable term insurance on an *indeterminate premium basis*. This means that there is a current premium charge and a maximum premium charge. The current rate is not guaranteed, but the maximum rate is guaranteed to be the highest charge that can be imposed. The current rate will be increased if the insurance company experiences additional costs (e.g., more deaths than anticipated, expenses higher than expected, or interest earnings assumptions not realized).

5-Year Renewable and Convertible Term

With 5-year renewable and convertible term, as with yearly renewable term, the face amount of the insurance remains the same. The premium, however, unlike the premium of yearly renewable term, does not increase yearly, but rather increases at the end of each 5-year period.

The insurance company dictates how long the insurance can be renewed as term insurance. *Convertible* means that the insurance can be converted to a nonterm plan without medical examination and without regard to medical history, at or prior to a specified age, as determined by the insurance company.

As in the case of yearly renewable term, some companies issue 5-year term on an indeterminate premium basis.

Advocates of Term Insurance

Most advocates of term insurance, particularly those with an economics background, feel that flexibility and cost have high priority in developing a life insurance program. The reasons for this belief are: ever-changing tax laws; concerns about the federal budget; interest rates that are at times extremely volatile; and the likelihood of high inflation, which produces serious negative purchasing power. In the judgment of its advocates, term insurance, with its simplicity and initial low cost, fits the bill.

I am not an economist. I will, however, in the balance of this chapter, offer a reasonably informed layperson's reaction to the opinion of these advocates of term insurance.

Tax Laws

I agree with those who feel that life insurance decisions should not be made solely with taxes in mind. My having said this, however, does not mean that I recommend term insurance when it is not warranted. As a rule of thumb, if life insurance is needed for more than 10 years, using term insurance as a solution is generally not cost-effective. (Please refer to the Appendix, and compare the rates of return upon death, in sequential years beyond 10, for the following ledger statements: yearly renewable term, traditional whole and graded premium life, interest-sensitive whole life, universal life, and variable life.)

Chapter 9, "Life Insurance Fads Past and Most Recent," covers how life insurance is affected by changes in tax laws, i.e., the 1986 Tax Reform Act (which affects tax-qualified minimum deposit) and the 1988 Technical Corrections Act (which affects single-premium whole life).

The Federal Budget and Volatile Interest Rates

Considerable space is spent in this book on the investment strategy of the life insurance company (which is very important for all nonterm life insurance plans)—old money, new money; modified and pure portfolio rate; money market investments; capital market investments; and the inverse relationship that exists between bond prices and interest rates. There is no question that the federal budget, interest rates, and just about anything else having to do with finance, such as use of so-called junk bonds to finance corporate take-over situations, have a definite bearing on the ability of life insurance companies to meet their projections, their assumptions, and, equally as important, their guarantees.

You should demand to know how your life insurance company is investing its (your) money. To what extent, if any, is it investing in junk bonds? With which investment banking firms does it do business? What, if any, effect has arbitrage had on its investments?

Terms Defined

Old Money

Old money is money invested by an insurance company in a previous time period (e.g., 1 year ago, 2 years ago, 5 years ago), not currently.

New Money

New money is money being invested currently (today) by an insurance company.

Portfolio Rate—Pure

The *portfolio rate—pure* is a blend of old money and new money, resulting in an average yield on the entire asset structure of the life insurance company. This term is in contrast with the *weighted-average portfolio rate*, which consists of old and new money on a weighted-average basis, and the *modified portfolio rate*, which rolls over a specific percentage of previously invested money into new money each year.

The type of portfolio rate—pure which is not on a weighted-average basis, and a percentage of which is rolled over to new money each year, is usually allocated to all policies issued by those companies that use this approach. In essence, this approach treats all policyholders the same. This type of investment strategy is for traditional whole and graded premium life. Some companies also use it for their universal life product.

The weighted-average portfolio-rate approach is usually used for specific blocks of policies, not necessarily for the entire "book of existing policies" in force. This type of investment strategy also is used for traditional whole and graded premium life, and some companies also use it for their universal life product.

Modified Portfolio Rate

Modified portfolio rate is my own term for the investment strategy of life insurance companies that use a weighted-average percentage rollover concept. This type of investment strategy is used primarily for universal life and interest-sensitive whole life.

Weighted Average

Weighted average means that X weight is given to old money and X weight to new money. The combined result is the weighted average (e.g., X percent), which then is used in the following manner:

1. X percent is the dividend interest-rate assumption used to warrant the dividend projections for a traditional whole and graded premium life policy paying dividends as declared.
2. X percent is the current interest rate to be credited on the reserve (cash value) of a universal life or interest-sensitive whole life policy.

Percentage Rollover

Percentage rollover means that X percent of previously invested money plus interest earned on the reserve (the cash value) is rolled over each and every year into a new money rate. An example is given below.

Example

Year 1: Premium paid, $2001; guaranteed interest rate throughout the life of the policy, 4.5 percent; current interest rate being paid, 8.75 percent.

Year 2: Current interest rate, 8.5 percent; new $2001 premium gets 8.5 percent; 20 percent of the first year's $2001 plus interest is rolled over to 8.5 percent money; remaining money gets 8.75 percent.

Year 3: Current interest rate, 9 percent; new $2001 premium gets 9 percent; 20 percent of the remaining first year's money plus interest is rolled over to 9 percent money; remaining first year's money gets 8.75 percent; 20 percent of second year's money plus interest is rolled over to 9 percent; remaining money gets 8.5 percent.

Year 4: Current interest rate, 10 percent; new $2001 premium gets 10 percent. Of the remaining first year's money, 20 percent plus interest is rolled over to 10 percent money; remaining first year's money gets 8.75 percent. Of the remaining second year's money, 20 percent plus interest is rolled over to 10 percent money; remaining second year's money gets 8.5 percent. Of the third year's money, 20 percent plus interest is rolled over to 10 percent money; remaining third year's money gets 9 percent.

Year 5:   Current interest rate, 12 percent; new $2001 premium gets 12 percent. Of the remaining first year's money, 20 percent plus interest is rolled over to 12 percent money; remaining first year's money gets 8.75 percent. Of the remaining second year's money, 20 percent plus interest is rolled over to 12 percent money; remaining second year's money gets 8.5 percent. Of the remaining third year's money, 20 percent plus interest is rolled over to 12 percent money; remaining third year's money gets 9 percent. Of the fourth year's money, 20 percent plus interest is rolled over to 12 percent money; remaining fourth year's money gets 10 percent.

This procedure continues year after year. The guaranteed rate is always 4.5 percent. As you can see by the example, eventually each year's premium gets rolled over 100 percent to new money.

The effective rate credited to the reserve, when a variety of different interest rates are causing different amounts of values, is done on a weighted-average basis. The rates used in the above example are for illustrative purposes only. The figure $2001, as new money each year in the form of a newly paid annual premium, is also used for illustrative purposes. It is unlikely that each $2001 paid, in the form of an annual premium, will go 100 percent into the reserve. Only that portion of the $2001 which was not reduced for commissions, expenses, or policy fees will go into the cash value.

Inverse Relationship between Bond Prices and Interest Rates

When interest rates go up, bond prices go down; when interest rates go down, bond prices go up. There is an inverse relationship between bond prices and interest rates. Because of this fact, the specific plan of life insurance you choose must have an appropriate investment strategy.

Management of money to produce an acceptable rate of return is serious business. Make sure that you understand what an insurance company has to do to back its promises, and find out what the company's guarantees are for each specific plan of life insurance. Other types of nonterm insurance (e.g., traditional whole and graded premium life, universal life, interest-sensitive whole life, and variable and universal variable life), even though they are more complicated than term insurance, should be purchased when warranted. Your choice is your individual decision; it should be predicated upon your specific objectives and your comfort zone in financial matters.

Inflation

Life insurance benefits (the death benefit to the beneficiary and the reserve within the policy in the form of cash-surrender value) are always paid in the form of *constant dollars*, except for variable life, which can be considered a *real dollar* form of life insurance.

When a benefit is paid in the form of a constant dollar within an inflationary environment, its purchasing power is reduced. For example, assuming a 3.71 percent inflation rate, $1 to be paid 10 years from now will be worth 69 cents in today's dollars. In order for $1 paid 10 years from now to be worth $1 *in today's dollars*, $1.44 would have to be paid. And that $1.44, to be paid 10 years from now with an inflation rate of 3.71 percent, is worth, on a present-value basis, $1.

In addition to benefits from life insurance being paid in the form of constant dollars, the premium paid for life insurance is always in the form of a constant dollar, which means it is not indexed to increase based on the inflation rate. This means that a $100,000 death benefit payable 10 years from now will not be worth $100,000 in today's dollars. Assuming 3.71 percent compound inflation, $100,000 in today's dollars will be worth $69,469 in 10 years. This pertains to all constant dollar financial services products.

It also means that the premium will not increase each year. The premium, as in the case of the benefit, remains constant.

One of my students once asked, when the subject of inflation was being discussed in class,[1] "Is there a way to calculate which plan of life insurance or method of premium payment provides the highest ratio of insurance after taking inflation into consideration?"

I replied, "Yes, provided you have the proper tool—a hand calculator capable of doing financial decisions or software for your personal computer." I use a Hewlett-Packard 41-C series hand calculator with a financial decisions module. The calculator steps are as follows:

Step 1. Calculate the present value of a future sum, i.e., the face amount to be paid by the insurance company to your beneficiary. The

---

[1] In a CLU course which I taught at Northeastern University, Insurance and Financial Services Institute, Boston.

time period (the number of years you select) is up to you. The discount rate (or interest rate) is the inflation rate you assume. I enter the face amount as a future value, the time period chosen, and the interest rate (e.g., 3.71 percent). Then I ask the calculator to solve for present value.

Step 2. Calculate the present value of the stream of premium payments to be paid by you for the plan of life insurance or method of premium payment you are considering. The time period (the number of years) you select must be the same as the time period selected in step 1. The discount rate (interest rate) you select must be the same interest rate as used in step 1. Enter the stream of premium payments for the time period chosen (e.g., 10 years of premiums) and the interest rate (3.71 percent), which is the discount rate, and ask the calculator to solve for net present value.

Step 3. Divide the present value of the future sum to be paid (death benefit to the beneficiary) by the present value of the premium payments. The result is the ratio of insurance to premium payments. The higher the ratio, the greater the amount of insurance, taking inflation into consideration.

The erosion of the purchasing power of money, caused by inflation, is nothing to take lightly. The best way to make sure it does not affect the death benefit to be paid to your beneficiary is to determine the amount of life insurance you need on a real dollar basis, not on a constant dollar basis. If such a policy is not affordable, attempt to increase the future value of the death benefit through the dividends by purchasing additional paid-up life insurance (for whole and graded premium life, refer to Chapter 13), through the selection of option II (for universal life, refer to Chapter 15), and through the separate investment account performance (for variable life, refer to Chapter 16).

Conclusion

Ever-changing tax laws, concern for the federal budget, volatile interest rates, and inflation should be recognized as serious problems. They should not, however, automatically mandate the selection of term insurance as the only plan of life insurance to be purchased. The bottom line, as always, is how long you need the life insurance for. If you need it for longer than 10 years, term insurance is most likely not the right choice.

Summary

1. Term insurance is simple to understand.

2. With term insurance, however, it is extremely expensive to provide a postretirement death benefit.

3. Make sure, if you purchase term insurance, that you can convert to a nonterm plan without medical examination and without regard to your medical history.

4. Having a waiver of premium (a provision that the premium is waived if you become totally disabled; refer to Chapter 17) on a term policy is most important. Most companies allow the term insurance to be converted to a nonterm plan without payment of the premium. In addition, some companies give a fully paid-up policy at age 65, provided total disability occurs no later than age 60 and remains continuous to age 65.

5. You should always retain in your files the original official ledger statement given to you with your life insurance policy. This will enable you to find out whether or not the insurance company is meeting its projections; all you have to do is compare the original ledger statement with the yearly statements that you receive pertaining to your policy.

12

Buy Term, Invest the Difference

(Facts versus Rhetoric)

How many times have you read, heard on a talk show, or been told by a friend or fellow employee that you should purchase only term insurance and invest the difference? Although this has happened to me many times, no advocate of this principle has ever told or showed me what I would have to earn in compound interest on the invested difference in order to have the same amount of cash in my self-determined investment vehicle as I would have had in a nonterm policy, as well as exactly the same death benefit. The topic of this chapter is one of the great controversies of life insurance.

When you are considering buying term insurance and investing the difference (that is, the difference between what would be spent for the nonterm policy and what would be spent for term insurance), the sole consideration is: What would you have to earn in compound interest to provide exactly the same amount of money in a self-determined investment vehicle and exactly the same tax-exempt death benefit as would be provided by a nonterm policy?

Term versus Nonterm Life Insurance Plans

This chapter is devoted to a comparison of term and nonterm life insurance plans. Traditional whole life purchasing additional paid-up life-insurance by the declared and paid dividend is used as the nonterm plan. I have chosen it as an example because it is the life insurance plan that I designed and purchased for myself, and because I consider it a good one: Dividends are used to purchase paid-up life insurance; gross premiums are paid from age of issue to age 65; from age 66 on, gross premiums are paid by the dividends, which means that—in effect—the premiums vanish at age 65. For purposes of this chapter, I have designated $100,000 as the initial face amount of life insurance for a 45-year-old male who is a nonsmoker.

The two capital-formation scenarios discussed in this chapter are as follows:

- *Scenario A.* Capital is created by death only. The insurance is presumed to stay in force (that is, to provide a death benefit) throughout the insured's life expectancy, which is 29 years for a 45-year-old male.

- *Scenario B.* Capital is created by death, and a living benefit is also created. At age 65, the total cash benefit of the whole life policy (i.e., $89,420) is used to purchase $149,500 of paid-up life insurance. This means that no matter when death occurs, $149,500 is paid and no further premiums are required. In addition, once the policy is on a paid-up basis, dividends are paid directly to the owner of the policy as a living benefit. The life expectancy of a 65-year-old male is 15 years. Therefore, in this scenario it is assumed that a stream of income payments in the form of paid-up dividends will be paid for 15 years.

The calculation that must be performed to determine the amount of compound interest required in the buy-term, invest-the-difference scenario is referred to in the life insurance business as a "Linton yield calculation." The Linton yield calculations for scenarios A and B were performed by Lori Comeau, ASA, of Boston, an actuary for one of the nation's leading life insurance companies.

Please be advised that any nonterm plan can be evaluated in a buy-term, invest-the-difference scenario (e.g., grade premium whole life, interest-sensitive whole life, universal life, variable life, or universal variable life), provided that the Linton yield calculation can be performed.

Rules

For purposes of a meaningful comparison of scenarios A and B, certain rules have been formulated, as follows:

Rule 1. Exactly the same amount of money that is spent for whole life (i.e., $2001 each and every year from age 45 to age 65, for a total of 20 years) is to be spent for term insurance and the invested difference.

Rule 2. Each and every year, an amount of term insurance is to be purchased which, when combined with the separate self-determined investment vehicle, must equal exactly the same amount of money (i.e., cash-surrender value) and exactly the same tax-exempt death benefit being provided by the whole life policy *or* exactly the same amount of paid-up life insurance with its increasing reserve and the yearly paid-up dividends paid to the owner of the whole life policy as a living capital-formation benefit.

Scenario A

It takes until year 9 to produce a positive rate of return in the cash-surrender value of the whole life policy. Therefore, buying term and investing the difference is not a consideration if insurance is not needed beyond 10 years; under these circumstances, term insurance should always be the choice. The values shown here will be in sequential years from year 15 to life expectancy (i.e., 29 years or age 74).

Year	Total cash-surrender value	Total tax-exempt death benefit
15	$ 43,890	$135,297
20	$ 79,762	$180,071
29	$174,946	$283,645

Shown below is compound interest required to be earned if you buy term and invest the difference:

Year	Percent
15	8.19
20	9.44
29	10.46

To achieve the above required net after-tax compound interest rates for marginal federal ordinary income tax brackets, the before-tax compound interest required for buying term and investing the difference is as follows:

Tax bracket	Year 15	Year 20	Year 29
15%	9.64%	11.11%	12.31%
28	11.38	13.11	14.53
33	12.22	14.09	15.61

Scenario B

Scenario B is the same as scenario A for the first 20 years. In year 20 (age 65), the scenario changes to capital formation both as a living benefit in the form of yearly paid-up dividends and as a constant death benefit in the amount of $149,500, which is purchased by the total cash ($89,420) within the policy at age 65. The yearly paid-up dividends are tax-exempt until the cumulative sum of all dividends received exceeds the cost of the policy, which is the gross premium of $2001 paid each year for 20 years (i.e., $40,020). See Table 12-1.

If you buy term and invest the difference, compound interest required for years 21 to 35 is shown below.

Table 12-1

Year	Reserve (cash-surrender value)	Death benefit	Yearly paid-up dividend	Dividend taxable?
21	$ 91,492	$149,500	$ 7,651	No
22	93,549	149,500	7,872	No
23	95,581	149,500	8,099	No
24	97,580	149,500	8,331	No
25	99,540	149,500	8,564	$497*
26	101,461	149,500	8,795	Yes
27	103,346	149,500	9,019	Yes
28	105,204	149,500	9,231	Yes
29	107,040	149,500	9,434	Yes
30	108,861	149,500	9,630	Yes
31	110,667	149,500	9,828	Yes
32	112,447	149,500	10,043	Yes
33	114,197	149,500	10,258	Yes
34	115,898	149,500	10,476	Yes
35	117,541†	149,500	10,686‡	Yes

*The actual tax depends on the amount subject to tax and your actual marginal federal ordinary income tax bracket (i.e., 15%, 28%, or 33%). †The reserve increases each year until it reaches $1000 per $1000 of paid-up insurance at age 100. If alive at age 100, the insured is given $149,500 as a living benefit. ‡Paid-up dividends increase each year and are payable as long as the insured is alive.

Year	Compound interest required
21	15.98%
22	15.83
23	15.69
24	15.56
25	15.44
26	17.97
27	17.81
28	17.65
29	17.50
30	17.36
31	21.72
32	21.52
33	21.33
34	21.13
35	20.93

The goal is for the buy-term, invest-the-difference strategy to achieve the required net after-tax compound interest rate for the years listed above. That is, the same amount of reserve value should be maintained in the separate investment vehicle, there should be $149,500 of tax-exempt death benefit (consisting of term insurance plus the investment fund), and the yearly cash withdrawals from the separate investment vehicle should be the same dollar amount as the paid-up dividends. In order to achieve this goal, the before-tax compound interest required for 15, 28, and 33 percent marginal ordinary taxpayers is as follows:

Year	15%	28%	33%
21	18.80	22.19	23.85
22	18.62	21.99	23.63
23	18.46	21.79	23.42
24	18.31	21.61	23.22
25	18.16	21.44	23.04
26	21.14	24.96	26.82
27	20.95	24.74	26.58
28	20.76	24.51	26.34
29	20.59	24.31	26.12
30	20.42	24.11	25.91
31	25.55	30.17	32.42
32	25.32	29.89	32.12
33	25.09	29.63	31.84
34	24.86	29.35	31.54
35	24.62	29.07	31.24

Variables

Three variables involved in comparison of the two scenarios in this chapter are discussed below.

The Cost of Term Insurance

The first variable, the cost of term insurance, is one that must be taken into consideration. The term rates used in the example shown are competitive, but I am positive that both lower and higher rates exist. Lower rates than those used in this example would mean that you would have to earn less on the invested difference. Higher rates would mean that you would have to earn more on the invested difference. The term insurance rates used in this chapter for the Linton yield calculation are for a 45-year-old male who is a nonsmoker, on a 5-year renewable and convertible term basis, with a policy fee of $40. These rates are on a current premium basis, and thus are not the maximum rates that could theoretically be charged.

Marginal Ordinary Federal Income Tax Bracket

The second variable, your actual marginal ordinary federal income tax bracket, must also be taken into account. The lower your marginal bracket, the less difficult it is to earn the necessary before-tax compound rate of return.

In assessing this situation, do not listen to rhetoric; demand facts. Ask for a Linton yield calculation that provides the factual answer. Then divide the answer by your marginal tax bracket subtracted from 100 to determine the before-tax compound return required on an investment.

You may very well conclude that, all things being equal, you should be able to buy term and invest the difference, and end up with a better result. In the real world, however, all things are rarely equal. The evidence is quite conclusive: most people do not invest the difference. Instead, year in and year out, they spend the difference.

Besides, in the real world, there is no waiver-of-premium benefit for the separate investment fund if you become totally disabled. You must ask yourself where, if you become totally disabled, you will get the money you need to invest. And most likely, the answer will be that you will not be able to get that money.

On the other hand, for the $100,000 traditional whole life policy used in this example, if you are a 45-year-old male nonsmoker, in the event of total disability (as defined by the waiver-of-premium rider) you can get a waiver-of-premium benefit for an additional $86 per year.

Always keep in mind that, if you do get such a waiver-of-premium benefit with traditional whole life, graded premium whole life, interest-sensitive whole life, and variable life, and if you do become disabled, the premium will be waived and new money will be added to the reserve each and every year. The reserve will be manifested to you, the policyholder, in the form of cash value or a separate investment account. Approximately 25 percent of all universal life products now also offer a waiver-of-premium feature, not just on mortality charges but also on the "planned premium." In the past, universal life plans waived only the mortality charges, and no new money was added to the reserve (the cash value).

The Temperament of a Successful Investor

The third variable that must be considered is your temperament: Do you have the temperament to be a successful investor? Can you follow the maxims of successful investors? I learned the maxims of successful investing that I believe in from John Marks Templeton. They are:

- Keep a long-range view, not a short-range one. This means you should not constantly be in and out of the market.
- Remember that your main objective is maximum total real return after taxes and inflation.

  Gross rate of return − taxes to be paid = net rate of return after taxes − inflation rate = real rate of return

- Maintain enough self-discipline to avoid the fad of the moment. When something is already popular, it is too late to buy.
- Have patience. The best time to buy may very well be when everyone else is selling.
- Be just as concerned about down market performance as you are about up market performance.
- Be consistent. Invest on a dollar-average basis, month by month.
- Avoid market timing. I do not trust market timing as an investment strategy. Theoretically, it is a great marketing tool—but if it actually worked, every one of us would be a millionaire.
- Remember that managing money is serious business. Seek the help of a professional who has a long-standing track record in both up and, just as important, down markets. Do not consider investing money a hobby.
- Do not be overly concerned about how much money other people are making off you, as long as your money is being managed with your best interest in mind. The essential consideration is: How much money are they making for you?
- Always be a rate-of-return advocate. Know what you are getting for your money, as measured in terms of compound interest.

Conclusion

When you are considering buying term insurance and investing the difference, find out exactly what, at your age, you would have to earn in compound interest to produce exactly the same financial scenario as the nonterm policy.

13

Traditional Whole Life and Graded Premium Life

(This Old Soldier Will Not Fade Away)

Whole life is the traditional level premium plan of life insurance. The word "traditional" is used to distinguish this plan from interest-sensitive whole life. *Level premium* means that the premium will not increase. A level premium makes sense because it enables many people to afford life insurance, if needed, at advanced ages. Remember that we are all living longer and that incurring heavy medical expenses without adequate insurance reimbursement could place a serious financial burden on those important to us.

Self-Insurance

The longer the person covered by traditional whole life or graded premium life insurance lives, the greater the portion of the death benefit that is made up of the reserve (the cash value). Some suggest that, as a result, the insured is becoming self-insured. This is true. Even though the reserve of level premium life insurance is part of the death benefit, the entire death benefit is not subject to federal income tax when received by the named beneficiary.

Becoming self-insured in this way is a positive act, because of the creation of reserve. When life insurance is needed for a long period of time, buying term insurance does not make sense. Term insurance does not provide self-insurance, because of the increased premium payments (which become extremely substantial) and because not one penny of the premium paid creates a reserve in the form of a cash value.

You should be aware that a true self-insured death benefit plan—i.e., a sinking fund created instead of purchasing any form of life insurance—does not provide a tax-exempt death benefit to your beneficiary. Such a fund would not be considered life insurance proceeds. Only a death benefit in the form of life insurance proceeds payable to your beneficiary is exempt from federal income tax.

There are two types of traditional whole life. The first, paying dividends as declared and paid, is issued by both mutual and stock life insurance companies. In the second type, no dividends are paid.

Mutual life insurance companies, in theory, are owned by their policyholders. *Stock companies* are owned by their stockholders. There is a ripple of a trend among some mutual companies to demutualize themselves into stock companies for the sole purpose of being able to raise capital, when necessary. It is virtually impossible for a mutual company to raise capital. Corporations raise capital by issuing stocks or bonds, or both.

When dividends are declared and paid, the policy is referred to as a "participating policy," or in insurance jargon, a "par." When a policy does not pay dividends, it is referred to as a "nonparticipating policy," or a "nonpar."

Today, most stock companies no longer offer a traditional whole life policy with or without dividends. They now offer interest-sensitive whole life.

Graded premium whole life paying dividends as declared is exactly the same as traditional whole life in its investment strategy and dividend interest-rate assumption, except that the gross premium is not level. The gross premium starts out lower than the premium for whole life. It increases each year and then ultimately levels off after a specific number of years. The ultimate level premium, once reached, is higher than the gross premium for whole life issued at the same age.

Traditional whole life insurance policies have been kicked around more than some politicians. Are they outmoded? Some say yes. I suggest that you compare them with other plans of life insurance, based upon the cost-disclosure method of your choice and using ledger statements. Then study the investment strategy of the insurance company for each plan that you are considering. Armed with this information, then and only then will you know whether traditional whole life and graded premium life are out of date. For the type of detailed information that can be furnished to you for a traditional whole life policy, refer to the worksheet (Figure 7.1) in Chapter 7. This can be used with the official ledger statement.

Dividends

Dividends earned on a whole life policy may be used in one of the five ways listed below.

1. Dividends may be paid to you in cash.
2. They may be used to reduce gross premium.
3. They may be used to purchase additional paid-up life insurance.
4. Dividends may accumulate at interest with the insurance company. When the interest paid on the dividends is $10 or more, the interest must be reported as taxable income on your federal tax return.
5. An amount of 1-year term insurance equal to the cash value may be purchased with dividends.

Life Insurance Dividends Are Not Stocks or Bonds

Dividends paid on a life insurance policy should not be confused with dividends paid on stocks or interest paid on bonds. When declared and paid, the dollar amount is dependent upon the insurance company's expenses, mortality costs, and rate of return on its investments. Dividends are not guaranteed. They are estimates or projections into the future.

Dividend projections should not be given the same consideration as they have had historically—certainly not beyond the first 10 years. Capital market investments (i.e., bonds) backing the investment strategy do not usually have maturity dates beyond 10 years. Therefore, it is not possible to know whether dividend projections beyond 10 years will be the same as, lower than, or higher than the original dividend projections on the ledger statement at the time of purchase. In addition, even before 10 years, dividend projections in today's economic environment could very well be different from the original projections because of the dividend interest-rate assumption being changed because of the influence of new money.

Remember to ask what the interest-rate assumption is, to see if it warrants the dividend projections. Also find out whether it is based on old money, new money, or a blend of both, which is a portfolio rate. Starting in 1987, some companies lowered their dividend interest-rate assumption. This was done to maintain integrity in their dealings with the companies' existing policyholders and the buying public, because new money currently cannot be invested at the previous year's higher yields. This change, in most instances, will result in a reduction in dividends as compared with ledger statements from previous years—especially dividends projected to be payable many years in the future.

Taxes

Generally, dividends paid on a traditional whole life policy are not taxable to you. They are considered a return of unearned premium. If, however, the total of all dividends paid to you in cash should exceed what you paid for the policy, then the yearly dividend received at that point would be taxable to you.

Always keep in mind that when you personally receive more from a life insurance policy than you paid, you will have a taxable gain on your hands. The gain is taxed at ordinary marginal income tax rates. Also keep in mind that a loan against the cash value, like any other loan, generally should not be considered a taxable event, provided that, for a policy issued on or after June 21, 1988, the seven-annual-premium-payments test is met.

Most commentators feel certain that the 1986 act does not make a loan against the reserve a potentially taxable event. This is the only way money can be withdrawn, unless the death benefit is reduced (e.g., from $100,000 to $75,000), thus freeing up some of the reserve, or unless the policy is put on a paid-up basis, which then produces a stream of yearly paid-up dividends.

The 1986 act does mandate, however, that when benefits are reduced, a withdrawal within 15 years of the date of issue may create a taxable event, regardless of whether the seven-annual-premium-payments test is met for all policies issued or ending after December 31, 1984.

Direct Recognition

In the practice of *direct recognition*, a life insurance company rewards (or "directly recognizes") policyholders who do not borrow on their life insurance by distinguishing them from policyholders who do borrow.

Dividends are substantially higher for those who do not borrow. The following points should be mentioned:

1. Most companies use direct recognition; some may not.

2. You must study the official ledger statement of the life insurance company in order to know whether or not direct recognition is used in the life insurance plan being recommended for your consideration. Look for a declaration on the official ledger statement that says something like this: "Illustrated dividends assume no loans on the policy. Policy loans will reduce the dividends." Such a declaration tells you that direct recognition is being used. (See the sample ledger statements in the Appendix.)

3. Even when you borrow, if the insurance company gives you the option of paying a variable rather than a fixed interest charge, your dividends will not be reduced, provided the variable loan rate is at least as high as the interest rate assumed by the insurance company to warrant the dividend projections. If the variable loan rate is in excess of the interest rate assumed by the insurance company to warrant the dividend projections, the dividends will increase.

Example

Loan outstanding: $10,000
Fixed interest rate: 8 percent
Dividend interest-rate assumption: 11 percent
Variable loan rate: Changes monthly
New yearly dividend to be paid: $1000

If the fixed interest rate of 8 percent is paid, the $1000 dividend will be reduced by $300; an 11 percent rate on $10,000 yields $1100, but the owner of the policy receives only $800. This happens because the insurance company assumes an 11 percent dividend interest rate (this is what the company must earn on premium payments) to warrant its dividend projections. When the money is borrowed out, the company earns only 8 percent (the interest charged to the owner of the policy), which is 3 percent less than required. Three percent of $10,000 is $300, and therefore the dividend is reduced by $300.

In order for the dividend not to be reduced, a variable loan rate of at least 11 percent must be paid. In order for the dividend to be increased, a variable loan rate in excess of 11 percent must be paid.

The bottom line regarding direct recognition is that a fixed-interest-rate loan of X percent, if it is lower than the X percent dividend interest-rate assumption used by the life insurance company, results (when factoring in the reduction of the dividend) in an effective fixed interest rate greater than the guaranteed fixed loan rate. (See the Appendix for discussion of this point in relation to traditional whole and graded premium life ledger statements.)

The concept of *disintermediation*—movement of money from one financial services product to another—was of great concern to insurance companies a few years ago when new-money market interest rates were extremely high. Now it is of little concern because of the concept of direct recognition. Insurance companies are no longer concerned about loans against cash value, because now they can protect themselves through direct recognition and through shorter maturities within their investment strategy, i.e., bonds with maturities not in excess of 10 years.

The phenomenon of disintermediation is more likely to occur during periods of high new-money interest rates such as those experienced in the early 1980s. When the economy is influenced by high interest rates, savers move their money from its current places if the interest rates are not as high as other rates within the economy. Under such circumstances, life insurance companies experience heavy loans against their policies unless policyholders are assured that the reserve within their policies is being credited with an interest rate reflective of what is going on currently within the economy. The concept of disintermediation essentially caused creation of interest-sensitive life insurance products—e.g., current traditional and graded premium life with double-digit dividend interest-rate assumption, interest-sensitive whole life, universal life, variable life, and universal variable life.

Dividends Providing Supplemental Retirement Income

When a traditional whole and graded premium life policy is *fully paid up*, for each $1000 of paid-up insurance, no more premiums are due; the insurance company pays a paid-up dividend per $1000 of insurance. In addition, there is the yearly increase of the reserve, representing the interest paid on your money (the cash value), which has been used to pay up the insurance.

With a traditional whole life and graded premium policy, when you reach your desired retirement age you may choose one of two options, depending upon your capital-formation needs (death benefits, living benefits, or both):

1. You may continue your existing policy. Ideally, at this point either your premiums will have vanished or the yearly dividend used in the

reduction of the gross premium will result in a very low premium outlay.

2. If some death benefit is still needed but you also wish to receive supplemental retirement income for yourself, you may use the total reserve and the value of the dividends (if any) to fully pay up the policy.

For example (and do be aware that this is an example only; these are not standard figures that would apply throughout the industry), in policies issued by one life insurance company, it takes $598.11 to fully pay up $1000 of insurance at age 65.

The anatomy of a paid-up dividend, from a financial viewpoint, is as follows:

1. In an instance of the self-insured concept, the ratio of insurance being provided (found by dividing $1000 by $598.11, the amount required to pay up the policy) is 1.67. Dividing $598.11 by $1000 produces a percentage result of 60 percent, which means that 60 percent of the $1000 death benefit is your own money in the form of the reserve.

2. For policies in force at least 20 years, the dividend amount per $1000 of insurance (paid up at age 65 at the end of the year, which is the same as if it were paid up at the beginning of the person's sixty-sixth year) is $51.18. This, related to the cash sum of $598.11, is 8 percent ($51.18 divided by $598.11 is 8 percent). In addition, 1 year later the reserve has increased from $598.11 to $611.99, which is a 2.32 percent increase. (Note that this item too is an example; it does not represent figures standard for the life insurance industry.) Please keep in mind that paid-up dividends, like all dividends, are not guaranteed; as always, they are estimates—projections into the future.

3. The reserve and the paid-up dividend per $1000 of life insurance increase yearly. Examples of paid-up dividends[1] and reserves[2] for 15 years are shown based on the current life expectancy of a 65-year-old male.

---

[1] Tax-exempt until the cumulative sum of all paid-up dividends received exceeds the cost of the policy (i.e., basis), which is the sum of premiums paid, exclusive of premiums paid for riders such as waiver of premium.

[2] Reserve increases tax-exempt because it is part of the constant tax-exempt paid-up death benefit.

Age	Paid-up dividend	Reserve
66	$51.18	$611.99
67	52.66	625.75
68	54.18	639.34
69	55.73	652.71
70	57.29	665.82
71	58.83	678.67
72	60.33	691.28
73	63.75	703.71
74	63.11	715.99
75	64.42	728.17
76	65.74	740.25
77	67.18	752.16
78	68.62	763.86
79	70.08	775.74
80	71.48	786.23
81	72.76	796.21
82	73.92	806.96
83	74.93	816.72
84	75.85	826.12
85	76.85	835.23

4. In addition to paid-up dividends to provide supplemental retirement income, a postretirement death benefit is always provided. This is in the form of X dollars of paid-up insurance, i.e., $1000.

Whole Life and Graded Premium Rate-of-Return Comparison

Because of differences in premium payments and the effect of the time value of money, the numerical interest-adjusted index figures shown on ledger statements for whole life and graded premium life issued for the same gender, age, and face amount, and with the same insurance company, will not be the same.

Table 13-1 shows, for sequential years, the rate-of-return-upon-death scenario for a $100,000 policy issued to a male aged 45. The owner pays the gross premium on each policy listed for 20 years; the dividends are applied to purchase of additional paid-up life insurance, and the premium is vanished starting in year 21 by using the dividends. Table 13-2 shows the rate of return before taxes upon surrender.

It is interesting to note that the rate of return upon death becomes greater for whole life at life expectancy even though the premiums paid during the first 20 years were higher than for graded premium life. This occurs for two reasons: (1) the increased death benefit (i.e., future

Table 13-1. Death Benefit: Rate of Return upon Death

	Whole life		Graded premium Life		Difference
	Death benefit	Rate of return	Death benefit	Rate of return	
Year 1	$100,000	4,897.50%	$100,000	15,977.17%	11,079.67%
5	101,460	90.50	100,672	143.78	53.28
10	110,848	30.00	105,791	44.12	14.12
20	180,071	12.87	147,283	14.92	2.05
29	283,645	9.77	186,451	9.42	0.35

Table 13-2. Surrender Benefit: Rate of Return before Taxes*

	Whole life		Graded premium life		Difference
	Reserve (cash value)	Rate of return	Reserve (cash value)	Rate of return	
Year 1	$ 0	−100%	$ 0	−100%	None
5	7,696	−8.62	2,069	−25.81	17.19
10	23,069	2.57	10,070	−3.02	5.59
20	89,420	7.16	56,368	5.41	1.75
29	174,946	7.40	102,504	6.10	1.30

*When the rate of return upon surrender is positive, taxes are due. The difference between the cash-surrender value and premiums paid is subject to marginal ordinary federal income tax. The above positive rates of return have not taken taxes into consideration.

value) over graded premium life generated by the dividends and (2) the ultimately increased level premium of graded premium life (i.e., present-value payments).

The guaranteed interest rate paid on the reserve is indirectly increased by the declared and paid dividends. The guaranteed interest rate is usually 4.5 or 6 percent, depending upon the mortality table being used. If the dividends are used to reduce the gross premium, then the present-value payment (premium) for life insurance is less. If the dividends are used to purchase additional paid-up life insurance, then the future value to both the beneficiary and the insured is increased: For the beneficiary, the death benefit is increased by the paid-up additional life insurance, and for the insured, the paid-up additional life insurance has a reserve.

Conclusions

1. Actual dividend performance is extremely important to the insurance company. This fact should provide a degree of certainty to you. You should be able to rightfully assume that management is responsible and would not illustrate projected dividends that it did not believe could be paid.

2. When and if inflation starts perking again, in addition to a possible rise in new-money interest rates, traditional whole life and graded premium life will appear to be an unwise choice. This will be true because the nonadvocates of traditional whole or graded premium life will play upon prevailing high current new-money interest rates which may occur if inflation increases. The new-money rates will be openly manifested with specific interest-sensitive life insurance products (e.g., interest-sensitive whole life or universal life). It is unlikely that these advocates will point out that in the long run a higher rate of return should be achieved in the capital market than in the money market.

3. Traditional whole life provides some flexibility, particularly when the paid-up dividend additions rider is used, but not as much flexibility as universal life. The paid-up dividend additions rider, in addition to accumulating deposits (separate money, other than the actual premium due on the policy) at interest, also provides a death benefit. The rider accommodates large sums of money. It can also be used to shorten the premium-paying period by allowing for additional money to be deposited, besides the regular premium. A further advantage is that it can be used by women who wish to pay the same as men in order to increase the reserve of their policies. Use of this rider is affected by the seven-annual-premium-payments test for policies issued on or after June 21, 1988.

4. Waiver of premium in the event of total disability, as in the case of interest-sensitive whole life and variable life, waives the entire premium. Cash value and dividends accrue just as though the premium were paid. Approximately 25 percent of all universal life products now offer a waiver-of-premium feature not just on mortality charges but also on the "planned premium." In the past, universal life plans waived only the mortality charges, and no new money was added to the reserve.

5. You should file the original ledger statement with your policy. Ideally, the investment strategy employed and the dividend interest-rate assumption will be indicated on this original ledger statement. Keep in mind that you are always dealing with a "moving target" when it

comes to dividends; actual dividends may be the same as, less than, or greater than the original projections. Finally, ideally the insurance company will state on the ledger statement that in its opinion the ledger statement meets the definition of life insurance tests and the seven-annual-premium-payments test.

6. Remember that all traditional whole and graded premium life policies issued or exchanged after December 31, 1984, must meet the definition of life insurance tests, and are also subject to the rules of taxation of withdrawals or a reduction in benefits. A policy issued on or after June 21, 1988, must meet the seven-annual-premium-payments test in order for a loan not to be considered a taxable event.

14

Interest-Sensitive Whole Life

(Sensitive to What?)

Here are some examples of the influence of volatile interest rates and ever-changing economic factors on our lives.

Example 1

Currently you have X dollars remaining to be paid on your home mortgage. Your bank is charging you X percent interest, but on new home mortgages the bank is currently charging a higher rate than X percent. You go to your banker and ask whether or not the bank wishes to get rid of your percentage money. If the answer is yes, you should be provided with a discount to pay off your balance (putting aside the fact that the amount of the discount is subject to federal income tax).

Example 2

A few years ago, you purchased a bond paying X percent interest. If your X percent interest rate is higher than that available today on new bond purchases, and if you decide to sell your bond today prior to maturity, you will have to receive an amount of money in excess of the value at maturity. This concept is called "selling a bond at a premium."

Example 3

Conversely, many years ago you bought another bond paying X percent. If you decide to sell your bond today, and if the current interest rate available on new bond purchases exceeds your X percent, you will have to sell your bond for a value less than the maturity value. This concept is referred to as "selling a bond at a discount."

What Is the Life Insurance Company's Message?

Life insurance companies that are offering interest-sensitive whole life are conveying to you, the buyer, that at all times your policy will be current. You will be paid on your reserve cash value an interest rate that reflects what is going on currently in the economy.

Consider the following statements which have been taken verbatim from a sales brochure put out by a life insurance company. (The only change is the substitution of "Interest-Sensitive Life" for the proprietary name of the company's product.)

> Interest-Sensitive Life policyholders are currently accumulating funds at X percent. The projected rate is X percent. Their accumulation rates are reviewed regularly and are guaranteed never to fall below minimum rates quoted in each policy. High accumulation rates create lower premiums. Interest-Sensitive Life is the only whole life policy that provides current risk rates, accumulation based on current interest, and no direct policy expenses—the policy that's current the rest of your life.

Design

The death benefit, unlike a traditional whole life policy using dividends to purchase additional paid-up life insurance, does not increase unless the reserve (the cash value), which is dependent upon the actual interest credited and actual mortality charges, forces an increase in the death benefit because of the cash-value accumulation and the corridor test. The death benefit must exceed the reserve (the cash value) by a specific percentage. The larger the reserve, the greater the death benefit.

Mortality charges are the costs imposed by the insurance company for the amount of insurance for which it is at risk. For term insurance, it is risking the entire face amount. For nonterm plans, it is risking the difference between the face amount and the reserve (the cash value or the separate investment account). Mortality charges increase with age.

Current mortality charges are the charges reflected in the ledger statement, which influence the reserve value. This is shown as an example in Tables 14-1 and 14-2 under the heading "Current mortality." Current charges are less than the maximum charges that can be imposed. Some ledger statements have either no current charges or very low mortality charges. Maximum mortality charges are the maximum charges that can be imposed as stated in the policy contract. You should know the ratio between current and maximum charges.

Here are some things you should keep in mind in dealing with mortality charges such as those shown in Tables 14-1 and 14-2:

Table 14-1

	Company A		
Age	Current mortality	Guaranteed maximum mortality	Ratio of current charges to maximum mortality
25	1.32	1.44	92%
35	1.56	1.68	93
45	3.00	3.24	93
55	7.20	7.80	92
65	19.56	21.12	93
75	48.14	58.80	82

Table 14-2

	Company B		
Age	Current mortality	Guaranteed maximum mortality	Ratio of current charges to maximum mortality
25	1.21	1.52	80%
35	1.50	1.69	89
45	2.90	3.32	97
55	6.41	7.83	78
65	15.42	21.17	73
75	35.08	59.09	59

1. The mortality charge is what the insurance company is risking per $1000 of life insurance.

2. The mortality table used by both company A and company B is the 1980 Commissioner's Standard Table (1980 CSO table).

3. The mortality charges are for a male nonsmoker.

4. Be advised that some companies have lower mortality charges for different amounts of life insurance. This is known as the "band approach."

5. Mortality charges are on an annual basis; the monthly charge has been multiplied by 12.

Conclusions

1. The higher ratio of current charges to maximum charges means that current mortality charges will not increase by much, if anything, in the future.

2. The ratio of current charges to maximum charges should be indicated by the insurance company on the ledger statement. Most likely, however, it will not be, and you will have to ask for it.

Riders

There is some flexibility in interest-sensitive whole life when a rider is used (to accommodate additional money being deposited above the basic premium), provided the rider does not violate the definition of life insurance tests and the seven-annual-premium-payments test. However, like traditional whole and graded premium life, interest-sensitive whole life does not have as much flexibility as universal life.

Interest-sensitive whole life is also similar to traditional whole and graded premium life and variable life in that waiver of premium in the event of total disability waives the entire premium. Cash value accrues just as though the premium were paid. Approximately 25 percent of all universal life products now also offer a waiver-of-premium feature not just on mortality charges but also on the "planned premium." In the past, universal life plans only waived the mortality charges, and no new money was added to the reserve.

Profit

There are only two ways an insurance company can make money. The first is on the investment spread. If, with the investment strategy employed, it earns X percent and credits less than what it earns on the cash value, it makes its money on the difference. Conversely, if it credits the entire X percent it earns on the cash value, it must make its profit through higher than necessary mortality charges. For these reasons, gross rates of return mean nothing. One company may be crediting X percent higher than another company, but that does not mean its policy is a better buy.

Lower current mortality charges generally should mean that the insurance company has priced its product to make a profit through the investment spread. Higher current mortality charges generally should mean that the insurance company has priced its product to make a profit not through the investment spread but rather based on the mortality charge.

Rear-End Load

Unlike a traditional whole life policy, which is a front-end-loaded product, interest-sensitive whole life is a rear-end-loaded product. This means that there are two sets of values in the event the policy is surrendered: the accumulation account and the cash-value account. The accumulation account is higher than the cash-value account. The cash-value account is what you get if you surrender the policy, and is the value which must appear, when required, on the balance sheet. At a specific time, the accumulation account and the cash-value account are the same. This indicates that the rear-end load has ended. The two sets of values are shown on the ledger statement under *both* the "Guaranteed interest" column (the actual amount of interest by contract that must be paid on the reserve, i.e., cash-surrender value) and the "Current interest" column (current interest, not guaranteed, that is being paid as of the date of the ledger statement). In the policy itself (a legal contract), *only* the guaranteed interest rate is used in producing the two separate tables of values.

Loans

Most commentators feel certain that the 1986 Tax Reform Act does not make a loan against the reserve (the cash value) a potentially taxable event, provided that, for a policy issued on or after June 21, 1988, the seven-annual-premium-payments test is met. This is the only way money can be withdrawn, unless the death benefit is reduced (e.g., from $100,000 to $75,000), thus freeing up some of the reserve. The 1986 act does mandate, however, when benefits are reduced, that a withdrawal within 15 years of the date of issue may create a taxable event even if the seven-annual-premium-payments test is met, for all policies issued or exchanged after December 31, 1984.

Disintermediation—The Movement of Money

The concept of *disintermediation*, which was of great concern to insurance companies several years ago when new money market interest rates were extremely high, now is of little concern if the current rate is not paid on borrowed money. Insurance companies no longer care about loans against the cash value provided they can protect themselves. And they can indeed protect themselves, by not paying the current rate on borrowed money and by having appropriate investments for their investment strategy, e.g., maturity dates on bonds that can protect the insurance company in the event of changes in interest rates.

Unless a variable loan rate is available, the current interest rate will not be paid on borrowed money. This differs from the practice with traditional whole life in that, if a variable loan rate is paid equal to the dividend interest-rate assumption, the dividends will not be reduced if a loan is made against the cash value.

When the investment strategy employed by the insurance company is a new-money approach, the popularity of such an approach will be very high when new-money rates are high. Emphasis on new money is more apparent in a modified portfolio rate.

Enthusiasm for a new-money rate approach, however, should be tempered with extreme discipline. The evidence is quite conclusive that in the long run a higher rate of return is achieved in the capital market than in the money market.

Major Concerns

The major concerns about interest-sensitive whole life insurance are the same as those for all life insurance plans: Will the investment strategy employed by the life insurance companies be realized? The ability of the life insurance company to meet its dividend projections or current interest-rate assumptions is a major issue and should not be taken lightly. In addition, you must understand the concept of current mortality charges versus the maximum charges as provided in the contract—and how the insurance company has priced its product to make a profit, i.e., investment spread, mortality charges, or a combination of the two.

Conclusions

1. As with traditional whole and graded premium life, the premium in interest-sensitive whole life is level.

2. As with traditional whole and graded premium life, the reserve in interest-sensitive whole life is guaranteed, and there is a guaranteed interest rate, usually 4.5 or 6 percent, depending upon the mortality table used.

3. In interest-sensitive whole life, unlike traditional whole and graded premium life, the increase from 4.5 or 6 percent is not influenced

by dividends but rather by a current interest rate which is paid in excess of the guaranteed rate.

4. Interest-sensitive whole life providers do not have the responsibility for making sure that dividend projections become dividends actually declared and paid. Interest-sensitive whole life lacks a degree of certainty that the current interest rate can be maintained.

5. As with dividends for traditional whole and graded premium life policies, a current interest-rate assumption for an interest-sensitive whole life policy should be viewed with caution. The specific investment strategy employed will dictate the length of time the current rate should be used in a ledger statement. This is particularly important if the investment strategy is a modified weighted-average portfolio rate. If it is a pure portfolio rate, use of the current rate may be prudent for the first 10 years.

6. Some life insurance commentators feel that interest-sensitive whole life is the only whole life product that should be purchased. They believe that it will provide a greater rate of return to you than traditional whole and graded premium life paying dividends as declared.

7. You should keep the original ledger statement on file with your policy. Ideally, the investment strategy employed and the ratio of current mortality charges used in the ledger statement to indicate the maximum charges that can be imposed by contract will be shown. In addition, the insurance company may reveal how it priced its product to make a profit (it may, however, be unrealistic for us to expect this revelation in today's competitive world). Keep in mind that you are always dealing with a moving target.

8. In addition to the current interest rate being subject to change, current mortality charges (if used) are also subject to change. If they are increased, the values indicated on the original ledger statement will not be realized, even if the current interest-rate assumption is always paid.

9. Finally, it is to be hoped that the insurance company will state on the ledger statement that in its opinion the ledger statement meets the definition of life insurance tests and the seven-annual-premium-payments test.

10. Remember that all interest-sensitive life policies issued or exchanged after December 31, 1984, must meet the definition of life insurance tests and are subject to the rules of taxation of withdrawals or reduction in benefits. A policy issued on or after June 21, 1988, must meet the seven-annual-premium-payments test in order for a loan not to be considered a taxable event.

15
Universal Life
(Flexibility and Custom Design Are the Appeal)

There is no question but that universal life remains one of the most talked-about plans of life insurance in the marketplace. "Universal life" is a generic name. The technical name for universal life is *adjustable premium whole life*. It is a version of the level premium system of life insurance (e.g., traditional whole and graded premium life or interest-sensitive whole life). The main attraction of universal life is its flexibility.

Why Is Universal Life Flexible?

Universal life is the only life insurance plan that can be truly custom-designed. You, the consumer, can design it to your own specifications. Here are some items on which flexibility is built into the plan:

1. *Length of time you wish to pay premiums.* This is not arbitrarily decided by the insurance company as it is with traditional whole life or interest-sensitive whole life. You decide.

2. *How long you want the death benefit to be in force.* For example, you can have the plan in force until age 65, 75, 85, or 95, at your discretion.

3. *What interest-rate assumption you want credited to the reserve (the cash value).* When the investment strategy employed by the life insurance company is a modified portfolio rate approach, the current rate should be used for only 1 year. From the second year on, the

rate should be at least 1 to 3 percent less than the current rate. When the investment strategy employed by the life insurance company is based on the pure portfolio rate, it may be appropriate to use the current interest rate for the first 10 years.

Once you have decided how you want to handle items 1, 2, and 3, the official ledger statement, which is produced by the computer service of the life insurance company, tells you how much you have to pay (the premium).

When the objective is to accumulate a specific predetermined amount of reserve for a particular purpose (e.g., X dollars at retirement, X dollars for educational purposes, and X dollars to keep life insurance in force for a specific period of time), the only plan of life insurance that can theoretically achieve such a goal is universal life. The word "theoretically" is used here because the actual results are dependent upon (1) realization of interest-rate assumptions and (2) no increase in the mortality charges cited in the ledger statement.

How Is Flexibility Achieved?

Flexibility is achieved through the use of the computer, which allows the universal life product to be split. Each part becomes self-evident and independent of each other part—unbundled, if you will. You know specifically:

1. What percentage of each premium paid is allocated for an expense charge
2. How much of each premium paid goes into the reserve
3. The mortality charges imposed by the insurance company and taken from your cash-value account month by month, year by year
4. Administrative fees, if any

The independence built into universal life allows for flexibility which cannot be achieved in the same manner and degree with other products (e.g., traditional whole and graded premium life, interest-sensitive whole life, and variable life).

Is Universal Life Money in the Bank?

There is a very serious misconception regarding universal life. Some consumers believe that when one purchases a universal life policy and the insurance company is currently crediting X percent toward the cash value, that this is the same as if you were putting your money in the bank at X percent. This is simply not true. No matter when you surrender the policy, you personally will never receive, either before or after taxes, interest equal to the actual interest rate credited. If you did, life insurance would have no cost to it.

If you want to know what you are getting for your money and what your beneficiary is getting, as expressed in terms of compound interest, you must request a rate-of-return calculation.

Investment Strategy

The investment strategy for most universal life plans is based on a weighted-average modified rollover portfolio rate versus a pure or weighted-average portfolio rate. Life insurance management (home office executives) believe that you, the public, perceive universal life as an ongoing interest-sensitive product. "Ongoing" means that if interest rates go up you will expect to receive a higher rate. If you do not receive the higher rate, you will move your money to another company that is paying a higher rate. In contrast to most of the modified rollover portfolio rates in the market today, a pure portfolio rate changes slowly. That is because it is based on the insurance company's complete investment portfolio. The advantage of the pure portfolio rate is that the money you have in it tends to grow at a good, steady interest rate that may move up even while short-term rates go down. The disadvantage is that a pure portfolio rate may lag behind when other new-money rates, within the modified rollover portfolio rate approach, are moving up.

Design

You can individually design the death benefit in one of two ways:

1. *Option I.*   You can have a level death benefit, for the face amount of the policy.
2. *Option II.*   You can have an increased death benefit, for the face amount of the policy plus the reserve.

As with interest-sensitive whole life, the death benefit in both option I (face amount only) and option II (face amount plus reserve, i.e., cash-surrender value) can increase because of the cash-value accumulation and the corridor test. The greater the cash value (or reserve), the larger the death benefit. The death benefit must exceed the reserve by a specified percentage at each age.

Universal Life Maxims

1. Provided there is enough cash value at any point in time, scheduled premium payments can be skipped because the mortality charges can be paid from the cash value. Unlike traditional whole and graded premium life and interest-sensitive whole life, the skipping of premium payments does not result in creation of a loan.

2. Money can be withdrawn (on a nontaxable basis) either on a nonloan or on a loan basis, provided that, for policies issued on or after June 21, 1988, the seven-annual-premium-payments test is met. If money is withdrawn on a nonloan basis within 15 years from the date of issue and the benefits have been reduced (e.g., changed from option II to option I), reduction in face amount of an option I (e.g., reduction from $100,000 to $75,000), which frees up some of the reserve, may create a taxable event. This is true, regardless of whether the seven-annual-premium-payments test has been met, for all policies issued or exchanged after December 31, 1984.

3. The concept of disintermediation is of little concern if the current rate is not paid on borrowed money. This was of great concern to insurance companies several years ago when new money market interest rates were extremely high. However, insurance companies no longer object to loans against the cash value, provided they can protect themselves—and they can indeed protect themselves by not paying the current rate on borrowed money. They also protect themselves through the rear-end load and their appropriate investment strategy.

4. Most universal life plans currently in the marketplace are rear-end-loaded. This means that there are two tables of values in the event that the policy is surrendered or borrowed against: the accumulation account and the cash-value account. The accumulation account is higher than the cash-value account. The cash-value account is what you get if you surrender the policy, and it is also the amount of money you can borrow against; this is the value which must appear on a balance sheet when required. At a specific point in time, the accumulation account and the cash-value account are the same. This means that the rear-end load has ended.

5. There are only two ways an insurance company can make money. The first is on the investment spread. If, with the investment strategy

employed, the company earns X percent and credits less than what it earns on the cash value, it makes its money on the difference. Conversely, if it credits the entire X percent it earns on the cash value, it must make its profit through higher mortality charges. For these reasons, gross rates of return mean nothing. Just because one company is crediting X percent as compared to a lesser percentage for another company does not mean that the first company is offering a better buy.

Major Considerations

There are three major considerations with respect to universal life, as follows:

1. *The actual interest rate that will be credited on the cash value.* As with traditional whole life and interest-sensitive whole life, the cash value is guaranteed a specific interest rate (e.g., 4.5 or 6 percent), depending on the mortality table being used. As with interest-sensitive whole life, the 4.5 or 6 percent is increased by the current interest rate being paid. If the interest-rate assumption shown on the ledger statement is not realized, the values will not be as illustrated. Also, if designed in a particular manner (e.g., if all premiums are to vanish at age 65, or if the death benefit is to remain in force to age 85) and the interest assumption is not realized, the insurance will not stay in force to age 85, and the premium cannot vanish at age 65.
2. *The mortality charges.* Throughout the life of the policy, there are mortality charges for each age. Current mortality charges are reflected in the values illustrated in the ledger statement. Guaranteed maximum mortality charges, as stated in the policy, are not reflected on the ledger statement in the current interest-rate assumption column. The guaranteed maximum mortality charges represent the highest charges that a company could end up charging. What is seen in the universal life marketplace today is that many universal life ledger statements are based on very low or, in some cases, no mortality charges. At the same time, the policies feature, by contract, very high guaranteed maximum mortality charges.
3. *How the insurance company prices its universal life policy.* Pricing involves not only the investment strategy of the insurance company but the ratio of current mortality charges to the maximum charges that can be imposed by contract. The result is that the current interest rate is paid on the cash value. The questions listed below are also of concern.

    a. How does the insurance company make a profit—through the investment spread or through higher than necessary mortality charges?

    b. You should understand the effect of the rear-end load. There are two separate values—a value for accumulation purposes and a cash-surrender value which is the actual money that you get if the policy is surrendered. When necessary, this second value is the one which appears on the balance sheet. When the two values are the same, the rear-end load has ended.

Conclusion

An understanding of the following factors is essential: (1) what is meant by the guaranteed interest rate versus the current rate, and by current versus maximum mortality charges, (2) what the company's investment strategy is, and (3) how the insurance company has priced its product to make a profit (i.e., investment spread or mortality charges).

Summary

1. Approximately 25 percent of all universal life products now offer a waiver-of-premium feature not just on mortality charges, but also on the "planned premium." In the past, universal life plans only waived the mortality charges and no new money was added to the reserve (the cash value). Waiver of premium in the event of total disability, as with whole life, interest-sensitive whole life, and variable life, waives the entire premium; cash value and dividends accrue just as though the premium were paid.

2. The premium for universal life is initially higher than for yearly renewable term, but is lower than for traditional and interest-sensitive whole life.

3. A provider of universal life, like a provider of interest-sensitive whole life, does not have the responsibility for making sure dividend projections become actually declared and paid dividends. There is no certainty that the current interest rate can be maintained.

4. You can have all the flexibility in the world—skip premiums altogether, adjust premiums up and down, withdraw money when you want, etc.—but remember, if you don't have enough money in the policy to keep the insurance in force, the death benefit will not be paid.

5. Unless a variable loan rate is available, the current interest rate is not paid on borrowed money.

6. Remember that all universal life policies issued or exchanged after December 31, 1984, must meet the definition of life insurance tests and are subject to the rules of taxation of withdrawals or a reduction in benefits. A policy issued on or after June 21, 1988, must meet the seven-annual-premium-payments test in order for a loan on it not to be considered a taxable event.

7. Keep the original ledger statement on file with your policy. Ideally, both the investment strategy employed and the ratio of current mortality charges used in the ledger statement to the maximum charges that can be imposed by contract will be shown. In addition, the insurance company may reveal how it priced its product to make a profit (this, however, may well be an unrealistic expectation in today's competitive world). Keep in mind that you are always dealing with a moving target. The current interest rate is subject to change; if current mortality charges are being used, they also are subject to change. If current mortality charges are increased, the values indicated on the original ledger statement will not be realized, even if the original current interest-rate assumption is always paid. Finally, it is to be hoped that the insurance company will state on the ledger statement that in its opinion the ledger statement meets the definition of life insurance tests and the seven-annual-premium-payments test.

16
Variable Life
(Buy Term, Invest the Difference with Us)

Variable life is a version of traditional whole and graded premium life, interest-sensitive whole life, and universal life, in that the premium is level and in that it accumulates a reserve (cash value), called the "separate investment account." It differs dramatically, however, from traditional whole and graded premium life, interest-sensitive whole life, and universal life, in that there is no guaranteed interest rate to be credited to the reserve. Traditional whole and graded premium life, interest-sensitive whole life, and universal life have a guaranteed interest rate that usually ranges from 4.5 to 6 percent, depending upon the mortality table being used.

In a variable life policy, the death benefit for the first policy month will be equal to the guaranteed face amount (e.g., $100,000). For policy months after the first, the death benefit can increase or decrease, depending upon the performance of the separate investment account, but it will never be less than the initial face amount.

In order for the death benefit to increase, the performance of the separate investment account must exceed a specific interest rate which is set individually by each insurance company.

Whereas traditional whole and graded premium life, interest-sensitive whole life, and universal life are insurance products, variable life is classified as a security. As such, it can be offered only through a current prospectus. Further, it can be sold only by people who have passed a specific securities examination. Because it is a security, variable life must be registered with the Securities and Exchange Commission.

Variable life has a separate investment account, usually consisting of the following:

1. A common stock account

2. A money market account

3. A bond account

Some variable life policies have specific bond accounts (e.g., zero coupon bonds) and other specialized accounts (e.g., gold, foreign securities, real estate).

When you take out a variable life policy, *you* decide where the premium you pay, minus specific charges, is going to be invested. You can choose to invest solely within the common stock account, the bond account, the money market account, or the specialized accounts, or you can invest proportionately within two or more of these accounts. You also have the right to switch from one account to another, although the number of times you can switch within a calendar year may be limited.

Ledger statements for variable life are required by the SEC to illustrate assumed rates of return of 0, 4, and 8 percent. The SEC also allows rates of return of 6 and 12 percent to be illustrated. The actual separate investment account performance can be greater than 12 percent and less than 0 percent.

Interest-Adjusted Index

Because there are no guarantees about cash flows (i.e., reserve) and dividend projections for variable life, the interest-adjusted index is not used as a cost-disclosure method in comparing like-kind variable life policies. However, the premium compounded at 5 percent interest is shown on the variable life ledger statement. The point is that if you did not use your money (the premium) to buy a variable life policy, your money would be worth X dollars at various time intervals, compounded at 5 percent interest.

Why Variable Life?

Advocates of variable life stress the potential reserve accumulation and death benefit increase that can be provided to you and your beneficiary from the investment performance of the separate investment account. Daniel H. Teas II, CLU, ChFC, MSFS, of Colorado Springs, Colorado, believes that variable life offers the ideal solution for consumers who would otherwise desire to buy term insurance and invest the difference.

Before you invest in variable life, you should find out who will be responsible for managing the separate investment account of the policy you are interested in. Find out about the track record of the money manager or managers at the company that issues the policy. Have they managed other investment accounts? If so, for how long? Find out what their investment performance has been in both up and down markets.

Particular attention should be paid to the common stock account. Generally speaking, common stock investing is not the expertise of life insurance companies. Some common stock accounts of variable life products are managed by an outside investment advisor, completely separate from the life insurance company.

Variable life is a security in which you take all the risks about how much reserve will accumulate within the separate investment account. You also decide when and where the money will be invested. The responsibility for moving the money in anticipation of changes in the market, in order to achieve a significant rate of return, is yours also. And you may or may not be well rewarded for assuming all these risks and responsibilities.

You will be well advised to consider whether or not you have the temperament to be a successful investor. Can you follow the maxims of successful investing? (See Chapter 12.) The requirements for successful investing are the same for the variable life investor as for the buy-term, invest-the-difference investor.

The Bottom Line on Variable Life

Finding out the answers to the following questions will give you the bottom line on variable life.

1. Will the performance of the separate investment account produce a greater death benefit than traditional whole and graded premium life, interest-sensitive whole life, or universal life?

2. Will the performance of the separate investment account produce a greater amount of money in the form of a reserve, when and if the policy is surrendered, than traditional whole and graded premium life, interest-sensitive whole life, and universal life?

3. Will the separate investment account prove to be a real dollar financial services product rather than a constant dollar product? A $100,000 life insurance policy purchased today has a purchasing-power value of $100,000; $100,000 payable at death 10 years from now, assuming a 3.71 percent compound inflation rate, is worth

$69,469 in today's dollars. In order for the $100,000 death benefit, payable at the beginning of year 10, to be worth $100,000 in today's dollars, $143,948 would have to be the value. If $100,000 of variable life is purchased today and if, 10 years from now, the separate investment account increases the death benefit to $143,948, then variable life will have proved to be a real dollar financial services product.

4. Keeping item 3 in mind, the critical question becomes: What gross rate of return must be realized to increase the death benefit to $143,948? After taking into consideration the "internal hits" (the company's commissions, mortality charges, management fees, etc.), look at the 12 percent interest-rate assumption on a variable life ledger statement, which is the highest interest-rate assumption allowed to be illustrated. If a $100,000 death benefit does not increase to $143,948 in 10 years, this tells you that a 12 percent gross rate of return does not produce a net rate-of-return increase of 3.71 percent compounded on the initial face amount of life insurance, after taking into consideration the internal hits.

Mortality Charges

Variable life, like interest-sensitive whole life and universal life, has current and maximum mortality charges. You should find out the ratio of current charges to maximum charges for companies that employ this concept.

Some companies employ a guaranteed fixed maximum mortality charge. Mortality charges that are guaranteed by contract are fixed; they cannot increase. Make sure that you get total disclosure about mortality charges.

Gains

Gains for variable life investors are the same as for traditional whole and graded premium life, interest-sensitive whole life, and universal life buyers. On the reserve value (separate investment account), if gains are in excess of what you have paid, an ordinary income marginal tax is due on the difference, when and if the policy is surrendered.

Most commentators feel certain that the 1986 act does not make a loan against the separate investment account a potentially taxable event, provided that, for policies issued on or after June 21, 1988, the seven-annual-premium-payments test is met. This is the only way money can be withdrawn, unless the death benefit is reduced (e.g., from $100,000 to $75,000), freeing up some of the reserve. The 1986 act does mandate, however, that when benefits are reduced, a withdrawal within 15 years of the date of issue may create a taxable event, regardless of whether the seven-annual-premium-payments test is met, for all policies issued on or after December 31, 1984.

Qualification for Definition of Life Insurance

The Internal Revenue Service has recently released a private letter ruling which holds that a variable life insurance contract issued by a life insurance company meets the definition of "life insurance" in section 7702 and the death benefit proceeds payable upon the death of the insured will be excludable from the income of beneficiaries under section 101(A)(1). PLR (private letter ruling) 8835059 (June 10, 1988).

Without significant analysis, the ruling holds that the variable life policy is a life insurance contract under section 7702 of the code and the death benefit proceeds payable are excludable from the gross income of the beneficiary under section 101(A)(1)of the code. Also the policy owner is not in constructive receipt of the cash value of the policy prior to actual surrender of the policy. The ruling does note that temporary regulations do not address when the owner of a policy has such control that he may be treated as owner of the assets in a policy account. Therefore this ruling could be revoked when regulations under section 817(d) are released.[1]

Retirement Exchange

Find out whether, at your desired retirement age, the insurance company will allow a section 1035 exchange—in other words, whether you can exchange your variable life policy for the company's traditional whole life policy. If this exchange is allowed, the whole life policy will be fully paid up from the value of the separate investment account. Once paid up, the traditional whole life policy will produce dividends. The dividends will be tax-exempt until they exceed the amount paid in the form of premiums for the variable life policy.

---

[1]*Washington Report*, Bulletin 88-134, Oct. 26, 1988. Published for members of the Association for Advanced Life Underwriting (AALU).

The insurance company should have no objection to your making such an exchange, provided that:

1. The face amount of the paid-up policy is not greater than the death benefit of the variable life policy at the time of exchange.

2. The exchange does not, in a bookkeeping context, produce a negative impact for the insurance company.

3. The specific expense factors allocated to the product line by the insurance company are not violated by the exchange.

The exchange, if allowed, results in a constant dollar financial services life insurance product for your retirement years. Most important, a stream of supplemental retirement income is provided by the paid-up dividends. It is impossible to provide supplemental living benefits from variable life unless a loan is created against the separate investment account or the death benefit is reduced (e.g., from $100,000 to $75,000), freeing up some of the reserve. When a loan is made against the separate investment account, the death benefit is reduced by the loan and interest is charged. As examples of typical interest charges, consider these figures: One company charges 6 percent, and pays 5 percent on the borrowed money, resulting in a net cost of 1 percent. Another company charges 8 percent, and pays 7.15 percent on the borrowed money, resulting in a net cost of 0.85 percent. (These figures are examples only and should not be considered universally applicable to variable life products.)

Only you can decide whether or not you wish to be paying interest charges that are nondeductible (from federal income taxes) during your retirement years. Also keep in mind that the separate investment account is a constantly moving target. Its value is strictly dependent upon market fluctuations. A downward reversal combined with loans could very well put you in a serious negative position.

Variable Life Maxims

1. For the active investor, variable life provides the opportunity for a variety of investment moves.

2. It is very unfortunate that the SEC does not allow a variable life ledger statement to assume an interest rate higher than 12 percent. When the appeal is one of investment performance, it is very important to be able to know what the net rate of return would be at higher interest results. After the internal hits have been taken into consid-

eration, however, variable life advocates skilled in rate of return will be able to make this type of calculation for you.

Example

One company offers a $100,000 variable life policy for a nonsmoking male, aged 45, with an annual premium of $2394. Based on the maximum allowed illustrated interest-rate assumption of 12 percent, the results are as shown below, for the sequential years listed.

	Cash value	Rate of return	Load—the difference between 12% and rate of return
Year 1	$ 1,205	−49.67%	−61.67
5	12,572	1.64	−10.36
10	35,485	7.05	4.95
15	72,874	8.43	3.57
20	132,756	8.95	3.05

The cumulative load of 3.05 percent shown for year 20 means that a gross investment return of 12 percent nets out to 8.95 percent before taxes, after the necessary reductions and expenses.

Knowing this, you can determine what your separate investment account would be worth in year 20 if the gross investment return averaged 15 percent versus 12 percent. The answer is that it would be $191,991 at 15 percent versus $132,756 at 12 percent. This was determined by using a hand calculator with a financial decisions module and entering $2394 as payment, 20 years as time, and 11.95 as interest (15 percent minus the cumulative load of 3.05 percent). The calculator was asked to solve for future value, which is $191,991, the result of compounding $2394 each year for 20 years at 11.95 percent interest.

3. Because the financial services professional must pass a security exam to sell variable life, and because many life insurance agents are therefore not in a legal position to sell the product, its use at this time is somewhat limited.

4. The concept of disintermediation is of little concern to either you or the life insurance company, when it comes to variable life. The insurance company is protected because a loan against the separate investment account does not earn the interest that the separate account is earning. You are protected by your ability to move assets from one investment vehicle to another within the separate investment account.

Summary

1. If, over a long period of time (e.g., 5, 10, 15, 20, or even 25 years) you can average 15 percent compound on your money, regardless of where you invest it, you should consider yourself extremely fortunate. With this in mind, it is my personal opinion that 15 percent compound is the maximum interest you should assume that the separate investment account could provide.

2. In dealing with variable life, remember that you are running a marathon, not a race. Do not get carried away with bull market results, and do not panic about bear market results. Develop a long-range view, and know your own investment temperament.

3. The premiums for variable life, like those for traditional whole and graded premium life and interest-sensitive whole life, are level; they never increase.

4. For variable life, as for traditional whole and graded premium life and interest-sensitive whole life, waiver of premium in the event of total disability waives the entire premium. New money, in the amount of the premium, is added to the separate investment account just as though the premium were paid. Approximately 25 percent of all universal life products now also offer a waiver-of-premium feature not just on mortality charges, but also on the "planned premium." In the past, universal life plans only waived the mortality charges and no new money was added to the reserve (the cash value).

5. Remember that all variable life policies issued or exchanged after December 31, 1984, must meet the definition of life insurance tests and are subject to the rules of taxation of withdrawals or a reduction in benefits. A policy issued on or after June 21, 1988, must meet the seven-annual-premium-payments test in order for a loan not to be considered a taxable event.

6. Keep the original ledger statement on file with your policy. It is to be hoped that the insurance company will state on the ledger statement that in its opinion the ledger statement meets the definition of life insurance tests and the seven-annual-premium-payments test.

17

Additional Benefits Provided by Riders

(Before Buying the Accessories, Check Your Oil)

Life insurance and automobiles have something in common. They both offer accessories. Automobile accessories commonly offered include cruise control, power windows, sun roof, automatic shift, and power antenna. Life insurance offers its own accessories, called "riders," which include such items as:

- Waiver-of-premium rider
- Yearly renewable term insurance rider
- One-year term insurance rider
- Cost-of-living (COLA) rider
- Accidental death benefit (ADB) rider
- Purchase option rider
- Paid-up dividend additions rider

Before you choose your automobile accessories, you test-drive the car—but no one should test-drive a new car without first checking to make sure that there is oil in the engine. An analogous check is needed for life insurance. Before you start deciding which, if any, accessories you want, make sure that your life insurance engine has oil. This oil takes the form of two benefits, which, unlike riders, do not cost you money. These benefits are:

1. *Automatic premium loan (APL).*   An APL can become part of your policy contract if you simply request it in the application. This provision protects your policy against inadvertent lapse. If you forget to pay your premium, the premium amount is automatically paid from the dividends or, if there are no dividends available, from the cash value via a loan.

2. *Spendthrift provision.*   Some policies have a spendthrift provision as part of the policy contract. If not, request it. This provision insulates your policy from being attached by creditors, unless it can be proved that you had an intention to defraud the creditors.

These two provisions take care of the oil for your life insurance engine. Now it's time to discuss the accessories.

Waiver-of-Premium Rider

A waiver of premium works in a situation something like this. You, as the insured, must first be totally disabled for 6 continuous months. During the first X months (usually 36 or 24 depending upon the company) of a disability, you are considered totally disabled if you cannot work in your regular occupation because of the disability. After X months, you are considered totally disabled if you cannot work in any occupation for which you are or may become reasonably fitted by education, training, or experience. If you meet this requirement, premiums are waived. Premiums are not waived beyond your sixty-fifth year. If at age 65 you have been totally disabled on a continuous basis for the full 5-year period prior to your sixty-fifth year, and if your policy is nonterm, it becomes fully paid up for its face amount with some companies. Check with each company you are considering about the plan of life insurance it allows to be used for paid-up purposes, provided that it offers this feature. Once the policy is paid up, you personally are entitled to the paid-up dividends, provided that your policy is dividend-paying.

Your cost basis for tax purposes is the total premiums paid either by you or through the waiver-of-premium provision. From the date of original issue to your sixty-fifth year, your paid-up dividends are tax-free until the sum of all dividends received exceeds your basis cost.

Term policies of some companies also become fully paid up on a nonterm basis (check with the company about the plan of life insurance they allow for paid-up purposes) for the face amount of your term policy, in a waiver-of-premium situation. Once the policy is paid up, you personally are entitled to paid-up dividends, provided that yours is a dividend-paying policy. For the nonterm plan used for paid-up purposes, your basis cost for tax purposes is the sum of all premiums waived from the date of total disability to your sixty-fifth year.

Example

Say you become disabled at age 45. The nonterm plan of life insurance used for paid-up purposes is traditional whole life. Your term policy has a face amount of $100,000. The premium for traditional whole life at age 45 is $2001. Your basis is $2001 times 20 years, which is $40,020. Your paid-up dividends will be tax-free until the sum of all dividends received exceeds $40,020.

Conclusions

Waiver of premium, in my opinion, is essential. Some life insurance commentators do not recommend a waiver-of-premium provision for term insurance. I do not agree, on the basis of personal experience. I became disabled at age 54. My very substantial premiums were waived. In addition, my term insurance was converted to traditional whole life without the necessity of paying the whole life premium.

Life insurance premiums waived (paid to the insurance company *not* by the owner of the policy but through the waiver-of-premium rider) are not deemed taxable income to the owner of the policy. The waived premiums are exempt from federal income tax because they are considered a payment for either a personal injury or a sickness.[1]

Although premiums paid for riders are not generally considered part of the basis cost for life insurance purposes,[2] it is my own independent opinion that life insurance premiums paid through the waiver-of-premium rider do become part of the basis cost.

A contrary opinion is offered by the *only* court case on this subject, which was heard way back in 1952.[3] The court concluded that the waived premiums dealt with the computation of gain (premiums paid, i.e., basis cost versus cash-surrender value). This case, however, dealt with a matured endowment contract, not a life insurance policy. An endowment contract differs from a life insurance policy in that it endows for a specific amount of money as a living benefit at a specific age, e.g., 65.

[1]Internal Revenue Code, section 104(A)(3). *Tax Facts I*, National Underwriter Company, Cincinnati, 1988, p. 103.

[2]Revenue Ruling 55-349, 1955. *Tax Facts I*, National Underwriter Company, Cincinnati, 1988, p. 11.

[3]*Estate of Wong Wing Non. Tax Facts I*, National Underwriter Company, Cincinnati, 1988, p. 11.

Because the only court case dealing with waiver of premium was heard in 1952, and because the only revenue ruling on this subject is a 1955 ruling, and that ruling did not deal with a life insurance policy, it would seem to me, in order to make this issue crystal-clear, that the life insurance industry or a specific life insurance company should ask for either a private letter ruling or, better yet, a formal IRS ruling dealing with waiver of premium on a life insurance policy in relation to the question of basis cost for waived premiums.

Yearly Renewable Term Insurance Rider

A yearly renewable term rider can be added to most nonterm plans. The rider provides level term insurance for a period of 1 year and is renewed at the end of each year without medical examination. The premium increases each year. The length of time the rider can remain in force, as a rider, depends on the specific company. The rider can be exchanged (converted to a nonterm plan) without evidence of insurability. The rider should cost less than the company's individual yearly renewable term policy because it is issued as a rider on a base policy—an underlying policy providing a specific amount of insurance. This rider should be used when you cannot afford the amount of life insurance you need on a nonterm basis. Eventually you can either terminate or convert the rider, depending upon your financial situation and your present-value money needs.

One-Year Term Insurance Rider

A 1-year term insurance rider is paid by the dividends, provided that it is a dividend-paying policy. This rider is used when you wish your death benefit to increase by the amount of the reserve (the cash value). On each dividend date (usually the anniversary date of the policy), 1-year term insurance equal to that year's reserve (cash value) is purchased. If your dividend is insufficient, because of the amount or because of your age, to purchase 1-year term insurance equal to the cash value, a lesser amount will be purchased. If the dividend is more than sufficient, you may have the balance of the dividend paid to you in cash, or you may use it to reduce the gross premium or purchase additional paid-up life insurance, or you may allow it to accumulate at interest. At any time prior to your sixty-fifth year, you may convert the rider to a nonterm plan (check with each company for its definition of "nonterm") without evidence of insurability.

This rider should be used when it is impossible for you to purchase all the insurance you need, as calculated on a real dollar basis. It should also be used if you expect to borrow against the reserve. Remember that the seven-annual-premium-payments test for policies issued on or after June 21, 1988, must be met in order for a loan not to be a taxable event. If you do borrow against the reserve, the rider will keep your death benefit level at the original face amount.

A word of caution: The rider is paid from the dividends. Therefore if you decide to use the vanishing premium method, your payments will not vanish, as illustrated in the ledger statement. If possible, ask for a ledger statement reflecting the purchase of 1-year term and check on when the premium will vanish.

Cost-of-Living Rider

The cost-of-living rider uses the dividends, provided that the policy is dividend-paying, to provide 1-year term insurance coverage which, each year, will be adjusted in accordance with changes in the cost of living, as measured by the Consumer Price Index (CPI). The mix of insurance purchased can be all 1-year term, all paid-up additional life insurance, or a combination of the two. The mix depends on the amount of insurance to be purchased, the amount of the yearly dividend, and your age.

The additional coverage to be purchased may have a limitation (check with the company). The amount of coverage provided in the form of 1-year term insurance may be converted to a nonterm plan without evidence of insurability. This rider differs from the 1-year term rider equal to the cash value because the amount of insurance is unknown. It should be used when you have calculated your insurance on a real dollar basis and cannot afford to purchase the required amount. Again, as in the case of the 1-year term rider, the ability to vanish the premium will be affected by this rider.

Accidental Death Benefit Rider

The accidental death benefit is generically referred to as "double indemnity." You should consult with each company for its complete definition. Briefly, such a definition should state that the benefit is payable if you die within 120 days from the date of an accidental bodily injury, and if your death is a result of the injury. If both of these conditions are met, the death benefit payable to your beneficiary will double. Most riders of this type provide that if the accidental bodily injury occurs while you are a fare-paying passenger on a public conveyance being operated for passenger service by a common carrier (e.g., an airplane), the benefit payable to your beneficiary will triple.

Purchase Option Rider

The purchase option rider grants the option to purchase additional life insurance, without proof of insurability and usually at specific times. For example, one company provides seven options, at ages 22, 25, 28, 31, 34, 37, and 40. The option dates can be advanced in the event of marriage or the birth of children. The maximum amount that can be purchased is $50,000 times 7, or $350,000, provided that the rider is issued on an initial policy having a face amount of at least $50,000. The cost of the rider varies with age. The average cost is about $1.50 to $2 per $1000. For $50,000, that would come to $75 or $100 a year. Check with each company for its own rules. When this book was being prepared, one company that I asked about its rider features had not factored in an additional cost or changed its rules because of AIDS—e.g., it had not added the requirement of a blood test in order to utilize the option.

Paid-Up Dividend
Additions Rider

The paid-up dividend additions rider is used to purchase additional paid-up life insurance. The paid-up amount of insurance has its own reserve (cash value). The rider is used to provide flexibility for a traditional whole life or graded premium life policy.

Most companies impose a sales charge for this rider. Check with each company. When used properly, this rider can be of benefit to you. Use of this rider may well be affected by the seven-annual-premium-payments test for policies issued on or after June 21, 1988.

Summary

1. Waiver of premium is an essential rider.
2. Premiums paid for riders are not considered part of your basis cost for life insurance purposes.

PART IV

Who Should Write the Check to Pay the Premium?

18

The Perfect
Payment Scenario

Five Criteria: How Do Various Payment Methods Stack Up?

The word "perfect" suggests being entirely without fault or defect—flawless. Is there a perfect way to pay for life insurance?

The Five Criteria for the Perfect Payment Scenario

The answer to the question whether there is a perfect way to pay for life insurance depends on how "perfect" is defined. I believe that there are five criteria for measuring perfection in paying for life insurance, as listed below and described in Table 18-1. These criteria will be considered throughout this chapter in discussion of the various methods of payment:

1. Does someone else pay the premium, leaving the insured with nothing to report as additional income on his or her tax return?
2. After the premium is paid, is it tax-deductible?
3. When the entire death benefit is received by the insured's beneficiary, is it exempt from federal income tax?
4. When the entire death benefit is received by the insured's beneficiary, is it reduced in value because of the federal estate tax? (State

154

Table 18-1. Various Scenarios for Paying for Life Insurance

The Writing of the Check

	Personal basis	Qualified retirement plans	Group term life	Whole dollar	Split dollar	Death benefit only	Deferred compensation	Key person	Stock redemption buy-sell	Professional corporation	Partnership buy-sell
1. Does someone else pay the premium, leaving the insured with nothing to report as additional income on his or her tax return?	No	No	Yes & no	No	No	Yes	Yes	Yes	Yes	Yes	Yes
2. After the premium is paid, is it tax-deductible?	No	Yes, except for PS-58 charge	Yes	Yes	No	No	No	No	No	No	No
3. When the entire death benefit is received by the insured's beneficiary, is it exempt from federal income tax?	Yes	No	Yes	Yes	Yes	No	No	Not applicable	Yes	Depends	Yes
4. When the entire death benefit is received by the insured's beneficiary, is it reduced in value because of the federal estate tax?	Depends	Depends	Depends	Depends	Depends	Depends	Depends	Not applicable	Depends	Depends	Depends
5. If the reserve (cash-surrender value or separate investment account) is greater than what has been paid, is the difference exempt from tax when the policy is surrendered?	No	No	Not applicable—no living capital-formation benefit	No	No	No	No	No	No	No	No

inheritance taxes are not considered here because each state has different inheritance laws.)

5. If the reserve (cash-surrender value or separate investment account) is greater than what has been paid, is the difference exempt from tax when the policy is surrendered?

In this chapter, every conceivable way of paying for life insurance will be examined, and each will be measured against the above criteria for the perfect payment scenario. At the outset, the reader should be advised that in life insurance, as in most of life, perfection is elusive. No one method of paying for life insurance can meet all five criteria—but some come close. Here, we'll look at just how close to perfect various life insurance payment methods come.[1]

Table 18-1 features a matrix of various payment methods measured against the perfect payment scenario. As you are reading this chapter, it may be helpful to refer to this table for a side-by-side comparison of the various payment methods. The remainder of this chapter will show you how the various methods of payment stack up against the perfect payment scenario.

You Personally Write the Check: How It Stacks up against the Perfect Payment Scenario

The Five Criteria

1. Someone else *does not* pay the premium.
2. You pay the premium and it is *not* tax-deductible.
3. The death benefit, when received by your beneficiary, is not subject to federal income tax, provided that it is considered life insurance proceeds.
4. The death benefit, when received by your beneficiary, is not reduced in value because of federal estate tax provided that one of the following conditions holds true:
   a. From inception (date of issue of the policy), someone else (other than you) is the owner.
   b. From inception, you were the owner, but you lived at least 3 years after irrevocably assigning away all incidents of ownership to a new owner.

[1]The business or corporate interests of the various methods discussed in this chapter (e.g., group term life, whole dollar, split dollar, death benefit only, deferred compensation, key person, stock redemption buy-sell, and professional corporation) are assumed to be business entities *other than* S corporations. (See the definition of "S corporation" later in this chapter.) The tax treatment for S corporations is different. If your business is an S corporation, consult with both your life insurance agent and your tax adviser for specifics.

c. From inception, you were the owner and did not irrevocably assign away all incidents of ownership to a new owner, but either the value of the death benefit qualified for the marital deduction or, if not, you did not leave an estate in excess of $600,000.

5. If the cashing-in value (the reserve upon surrender) is greater than the premiums paid, there *is* a marginal ordinary federal income tax due on the difference. This must be paid by the owner of the policy.

Summary

1. No

2. No

3. Yes

4. Depends

5. No

Commentary.   Although this method is the *least* exciting (someone else is not paying the premium) and although it carries *no* tax advantage (the premium is not tax-deductible), it is the most straightforward. All factors (e.g., ownership, beneficiary terminology, access to reserve, reduced paid-up determination, and the receiving of paid-up dividends) rest with you or your chosen owner. For supplemental retirement purposes, i.e., the receiving of living capital-formation benefits (paid-up dividends), this method provides the highest cost basis, which results in *X* years of paid-up dividends not subject to federal income tax. This is true because the premium is not subsidized (paid by someone else or allowed to be tax-deductible).

Your Retirement Plan Writes the Check (Tax-Qualified Retirement Plans): How It Stacks up against the Perfect Payment Scenario

Pension, Profit Sharing, Keogh, 401k

The Five Criteria

1. Someone else (your employer) pays the premium (via the pension or profit-sharing plan). The dollar amount of the life insurance premium depends upon the type of plan, i.e., *defined contribution* (pension or profit-sharing) or *defined benefit* (pension). If you are

self-employed, you may make your own retirement plan contribution via a nonincorporated retirement plan called the "Keogh plan."

Defined contribution pension or profit-sharing plan. The life insurance premium cannot exceed 49 percent of the aggregate contribution to the pension or profit-sharing plan when traditional whole life, interest-sensitive whole life, or variable life is purchased. When term insurance is purchased, the premium each year is limited to 25 percent of the aggregate contribution. There are at present no Internal Revenue Service formal rulings or regulations about whether universal life is 49 or 25 percent of aggregate contributions. Opinion statements by the Internal Revenue Service and private letter 8725088, however, lean toward the 25 percent limit rather than the 49 percent.

Defined benefit pension plan. The amount of life insurance cannot exceed 100 times the monthly pension benefit at retirement.

Traditional whole life and graded premium paying dividends as declared. Dividends must be used to reduce the gross premium each and every year. This procedure assures that the initial death benefit will always remain the same. It is assumed that the initial death benefit does not exceed 100 times the monthly retirement benefit (e.g., for a monthly retirement benefit of $1000, the maximum amount of life insurance is $100,000).

Interest-sensitive whole life. Make sure, based on the current interest rate, if always paid, that the initial face amount of the policy does not increase because of the cash-value corridor test. If the initial face amount increases, it will be in excess of 100 times the monthly retirement benefit. Check the ledger statement.

Universal life. Option I should always be the choice. Make sure, based on the current interest rate, if always paid, that the initial face amount does not increase because of the cash-value corridor. If the initial face amount increases, it will be in excess of 100 times the monthly retirement benefit. Check the ledger statement.

Variable life. Variable life could present a problem if the rate of return of the separate investment account exceeds a specific rate-of-return amount. This is determined by each insurance company. The initial face amount will increase, thus causing the death benefit to be greater than 100 times the monthly retirement benefit. This problem may cause you to want to avoid variable or universal-variable life for purchase within a defined benefit pension plan. One way of avoiding this potential problem, which is associated with interest-sensitive whole life, universal life, and variable life, is to purchase an initial amount of life insurance less than 100 times the monthly retirement benefit.

You must report, as taxable income, the economic benefit of the "pure insurance coverage," which is defined as the difference between the face amount and the cash value. The economic benefit charge is calculated from either the government's PS-58 table or the insurance company's in-force term rates if they are lower than the PS-58 rates. For Keogh plans, the economic benefit charge is a nondeductible item.

Example

Face amount: $100,000
Cash value or separate investment account value: $10,000
Pure insurance at risk: $90,000
PS-58 charge for age 45: $6.30
Reportable charge: $90,000 × 6.30 = $ 567
Additional income tax due from taxpayers in the following marginal tax brackets:

15%	$ 85.05
28	158.76
33	187.11

The accounting for the PS-58 charge for Keogh plans is different. Although the tax result is the same, it is not reportable as income. Rather, it is a nondeductible expense.

2. The retirement plan contribution by your employer is tax-deductible. Your own retirement plan contribution to the Keogh plan is also tax-deductible. In both cases PS-58 charges must be taken into consideration because of the purchase of life insurance.

3. The pure insurance-at-risk death benefit (difference between the face amount and the reserve) is not subject to federal income tax when received by your beneficiary. The reserve portion (i.e., cash value or separate investment account) of the death benefit is subject to federal income tax, because the premium attributable to the creation of the reserve is tax-deductible. The pure insurance-at-risk is not tax-deductible (i.e., either because of the reporting of PS-58 charges as income or because of the inability to deduct); therefore it is not subject to federal income tax.

4. The total death benefit is includable in your estate for federal estate tax purposes. You cannot irrevocably assign all incidents of ownership to a new owner. The owner of the policy is the trustee of the retirement plan. The death benefit, however, will not be reduced by the federal estate tax if it qualifies for the marital deduction or if you did not leave an estate in excess of $600,000.

5. The surrender value (the reserve) vests to you as the covered employee in accordance with the particular vesting schedule. All the money you received as a living retirement benefit is subject to marginal ordinary federal income tax, provided that all the contributions were made by your employer. There is no basis (cost) to you if your employer made all the contributions or if you deducted all your own contributions (as with the Keogh plan).

Summary

1. No

2. Yes—except for PS-58 charge

3. No

4. Depends

5. No

Commentary.   The appeal of this method is the ability to purchase life insurance on a tax-deductible basis. How can life insurance within a retirement plan (not allowed for IRAs) be retained to provide a postretirement death benefit, if desired?

Life insurance on your life as part of a qualified retirement plan can be distributed to you personally at retirement under the following conditions in order to keep the insurance in force:

1. *The policy is distributed to you.*   The reserve portion of the policy (the cash value or separate investment account) will be subject to income tax when received by you. You then become the owner of the policy. The reserve of the life insurance policy is considered an asset of the retirement plan; therefore, when distributed, it constitutes a taxable distribution from the plan.

2. *The trustee of the retirement plan takes out a maximum loan against the reserve.*   It is then invested in an account of yours which is not life insurance. The policy is then distributed to you with a maximum loan, and you become the owner of the policy. The face amount of life insurance is reduced by the amount of the loan as a death benefit. You as owner are responsible for the payment of interest on the loan against the reserve. There is no taxable distribution to you because you received a policy with no value. In addition, your retirement plan account was not reduced in value because the loan value from the reserve is invested for you in your investment vehicle (which is not life insurance) within the plan.

Your Employer Writes the Check: How It Stacks up against the Perfect Payment Scenario

Group Term Life Insurance

The Five Criteria

1. Someone else (your employer) pays the premium if the plan is noncontributory. If your group term amount is in excess of $50,000, you must report the charge for the excess amount (the "I table" charge) as income, on your tax return.
2. Your employer is allowed to deduct the premium as an ordinary and necessary business expense.
3. The death benefit, when received by your beneficiary, is not subject to federal income tax, provided that it is considered life insurance proceeds.
4. The death benefit, when received by your beneficiary, is not reduced in value because of federal estate tax, provided that at least one of the following conditions is met:
   a. You live at least 3 years after irrevocably assigning away all incidents of ownership to a new owner other than yourself.
   b. You did not irrevocably assign away all incidents of ownership to a new owner, but the value of the death benefit either qualified for the marital deduction or, if not, you did not leave an estate in excess of $600,000.
5. There is no surrender value for group term life to either your employer or to you as the covered employee, if and when a group term life plan is terminated. Therefore no taxable event has occurred.

Summary

1. Yes and no
2. Yes
3. Yes
4. Depends
5. Not applicable

Commentary. The results of this method of payment are not as clear-cut as some others, when measured against the perfect payment scenario. If the amount of insurance is below $50,000, all criteria appear to be met. But if the amount goes above $50,000, this ceases to be the case.

Group term life provided by an employer on a noncontributory basis is a good deal for the employee, provided the amount of life insurance does not substantially exceed $50,000. It is also a good deal for the employer, because it is a fringe benefit provided to employees and because the premium is tax-deductible.

For large amounts of life insurance, substantially in excess of $50,000, however, group term life is not a good deal for either employee or employer. It is not good for the employee because of the "I table" charges which increase by age and must be reportable as taxable income. It is not good for the employer because it results in a greater cost; even after the deduction, group term life insurance costs 66 cents for every dollar spent (34 percent corporate tax bracket), without taking into consideration the time value of money. In addition, this cost is nonrecoverable.

Many commentators feel that if selected employees, chosen by the employer, receive large amounts of life insurance through a split-dollar method of premium payment instead of through group term life, both employer and employees are better off. The employer is better off because the sum of all premiums paid is recoverable either with or without a time-value-of-money factor. The employee is better off because both preretirement and postretirement death benefits are provided. If the employer wishes to trade off the ability to recover premiums paid for the ability to deduct the premium, the whole-dollar (section 162) plan should be considered instead of split-dollar.

The 1986 Tax Reform Act creates new discrimination rules for group term life insurance plans, as a result of section 89 of the Internal Revenue Code. Specifically affected are: eligibility to participate, rules for benefits, an optional test if the group life plan covers 80 percent of employees, and a special rule for determining discrimination in group term life plans. A thorough explanation of these rules is beyond the scope of this book. You should review them with a specialist in group term life insurance, in order to make sure that the group term life plan is not in violation of section 89 rules.

Whole Dollar—Section 162 Plan

The Five Criteria

1. The premium is paid by someone else—your employer, who pays it as long as you are on the payroll. Your employer has no incidents of ownership within the policy; you do (unless you choose an owner other than yourself). You must report as taxable income on your tax

return the entire premium paid by your employer. Dividends, if any, and cash value belong to the owner of the policy.

For example, say the premium paid and deducted by your employer as compensation to you is a $2001 premium. You must report $2001 as income. The cost to you in the form of additional federal income tax to be paid is as follows:

Tax bracket	Cost
15%	$300.15
28	560.28
33	660.33

2. Your employer deducts the premium as an ordinary and necessary business expense as compensation to you.
3. The death benefit, when received by your beneficiary, is not subject to federal income tax, provided that it is considered life insurance proceeds.
4. The death benefit, when received by your beneficiary, is not reduced in value because of federal estate tax, provided that at least one of the following conditions is met:
   a. From inception (date of issue of the policy), someone other than you is the owner of the policy.
   b. From inception, you were the owner, but you lived at least 3 years after irrevocably assigning all incidents of ownership to a new owner.
   c. From inception, you were the owner, and you did not irrevocably assign all incidents of ownership to a new owner. Either the value of the death benefit qualified for the marital deduction, or if not, you did not leave an estate in excess of $600,000.
5. If the cash value upon surrender (the reserve) is greater than the premium paid, a marginal ordinary federal income tax is due on the difference. This must be paid by the owner. "Premiums paid" means the premiums (e.g., $2001 for the number of years paid) the employee or owner reported as taxable income.

Summary
1. No
2. Yes
3. Yes
4. Depends
5. No

Commentary. The 1986 Tax Reform Act, which resulted in lower marginal ordinary federal income tax brackets, makes whole dollar extremely worthy of consideration. Some commentators refer to whole dollar as an "executive bonus compensation plan." This term has no legal meaning. It is simply a marketing expression.

Advantages to employer. The premium paid is tax-deductible as an ordinary and necessary business expense (under section 162 of the Internal Revenue Code) as compensation to the employee. The employer can choose which employees are to receive a whole-dollar plan.

Disadvantages to employer. All incidents of ownership, from inception, vest with the employee (or an owner chosen by the employee). With this plan, unlike the split-dollar method of premium payment, the employer will not be able to recover the amount of premiums paid. In addition, increased social security and retirement plan contributions may have to be paid because of the increased compensation to the employee.

Advantages to employee. The reserve (the cash value or separate investment account) in addition to dividends, if any, is vested to the owner of the policy, who is not the employer. The owner's true cost is the tax to be paid on the premium paid by the employer (e.g., $300.15 for 15 percent taxpayers, $560.28 for 28 percent taxpayers, and $660.33 for 33 percent taxpayers), not $2001, which is the premium. For tax basis purposes, however, if the owner surrenders the policy, the basis (cost) is the sum of premiums paid (e.g., $2001) times the number of years they were paid.

Disadvantages to employee. The actual amount of additional taxes to be paid will depend upon the premium amount and the marginal ordinary federal income tax bracket of the owner. In addition, state income taxes must be taken into consideration. Finally, because of increased compensation, additional social security payments *may* have to be withheld.

Split-Dollar Life Insurance

There are many variations of split-dollar life insurance. Common types are: employer pays all, single bonus, double bonus, roll-out, and even reverse split dollar. The focus here is on the most basic form (for matters of providing general tax information): employer pays all.

The Five Criteria

1. The employer pays the premium, and there is an agreement between employer and employee about splitting the premium, death
benefits, and reserve. As an example, your employer is the beneficiary of a part of the death benefit, equal to the sum of premiums paid either with or without factoring in the time value of
money. The employee is allowed to name a personal beneficiary
for the difference between the total death benefit and the employer's share. The employer has complete flexibility about which employees are selected for a split-dollar plan. The employee must report as taxable income (as calculated by the term rates of the
insurance company) a charge for the death benefit being provided
to the personal beneficiary. This fact of life is referred to as the
"doctrine of economic benefit."

Because the insured's death can occur at any time, an economic
benefit is being provided in the form of a life insurance death
benefit. Thus, a yearly charge in the form of reportable income is
mandated by current law. The charge is determined in the following way:

Example

Face amount: $100,000
Employer's share of death benefit: $10,000
Employee's share of death benefit: $90,000
Charge assessed against: $90,000

The dollar amount of the charge is determined by either the government's PS-58 table rates or the term rates of the insurance company.
The lower of the two may be used. The charge increases each year
because it is based on age.

Example

Age: 45
Employee's share of death benefit: $90,000
PS-58 rate: $6.30
Charge: $6.30 × $90,000 = $567.00

Therefore, $567.00 must be reported as taxable income. The actual
cost is the tax on the $567.00 ($85.05 for a marginal tax bracket of
15 percent, $158.78 for 28 percent, or $187.11 for 33 percent). State
income taxes have not been considered.

2. The premium paid by the employer is not tax-deductible. There is no version of split-dollar that allows the premium to be tax-deductible either by employer or employee.
3. The death benefit, when received by the employer, is not subject to federal income tax, provided that the alternative minimum corporate tax is not a consideration. The death benefit, when received by the personal beneficiary, is not subject to federal income tax. In both cases, the death benefit must be considered life insurance proceeds.

Many large companies in the past have paid little or no income tax. Because of this, the alternative minimum corporate tax was created, within the 1986 Tax Reform Act. The alternative minimum tax, if any, is calculated by taking into consideration regular taxable income plus tax preferences less certain deductions.

Of the preferences that must be added to taxable income, the particular tax preference which affects life insurance is the *business untaxed reported profits* (BURP). Why may a BURP affect life insurance? Because the profit from a life insurance policy must be included as book income for the years 1987 through 1989. Profit is the difference between the death benefit received and the cumulative sum of premiums paid. Also, from a living viewpoint, if the reserve is greater than the cumulative sum of premiums paid, the corporate alternative minimum tax must be considered. From 1990 on, profits and earnings will replace book income.

The bottom line seems quite clear. The corporate alternative minimum tax and its effect on life insurance, if any, is going to depend on what is on the specific financial statement prepared for the corporation.

Any life insurance having a corporate interest should be reviewed by the financial officer of the corporation or the tax adviser. This tax applies only to C corporations, not S corporations. An understanding of the types of corporations is necessary here; see the definitions below.

Corporation. A separate legal entity, often referred to as an "artificial person." A corporation is organized and created for a specific purpose. Examples include professional people (e.g., physicians, attorneys, dentists, or accountants) conducting their professions on a corporate basis, automotive businesses, insurance agencies, and health fitness businesses. After being organized and created, a corporation is chartered under the laws of a specific state. As a separate legal entity, the corporation has its own tax bracket, completely separate from the tax brackets of its shareholders and corporate officers. The essential characteristics of a corporation are: centralized management, limited liability, continuity of life, and transferability of shares.

C corporation. C corporations include all corporations that are not S corporations. The "C" stands for subchapter C of the Internal Revenue Code.

S corporation. This is a particular type of corporation which, prior to the Tax Reform Act of 1986, was referred to as a "subchapter S corporation" and which elects not to be taxed as a corporation. In order to qualify as an S corporation, certain requirements about the kind and number of shareholders, classes of stock, and sources of income must be met. Electing not to be taxed as a corporation means that all profits and losses are passed directly to the shareholders of the S corporation, as in a partnership. Profits and losses are then taxed on the basis of the individual shareholder's own tax bracket.

4. The death benefit, when received by the personal beneficiary, is not reduced in value because of the federal estate tax, provided that at least one of the following conditions is met:
   a. From inception, someone other than you is the owner for your personal beneficiary's share of the death benefit.
   b. From inception, you are the owner, and you live at least 3 years after irrevocably assigning all incidents of ownership to a new owner for your personal beneficiary's share of the death benefit.
   c. From inception, you are the owner, and you do not irrevocably assign to a new owner the incidents of ownership of your beneficiary's share of the death benefit. Either the value of the death benefit qualifies for the marital deduction, or if not, you do not leave an estate in excess of $600,000.
5. The surrender value (the reserve) is split between your employer and you. If your employer's share is equal to the sum of premiums paid, with no time-value-of-money factor, there is no gain and no tax due. If, however, there is a time-value-of-money factor, a marginal ordinary federal income tax is due on the difference between what is received and what your employer paid. For your share, there is a marginal ordinary federal income tax on the difference between what is received and the sum of all reportable charges over the years. Essentially, for all versions of split-dollar, the general tax information provided here applies.

Summary

1. No
2. No
3. Yes
4. Depends
5. No

Commentary .   For years, split dollar as a method of paying for life insurance has been used extensively by employers for its employees, by professional corporations, and by family members—and it still is being used. Split dollar is still a viable choice.

There are two split-dollar methods: endorsement and collateral. Under the endorsement method, your employer applies for the life insurance on your life and is the owner of the policy. Although your employer owns all rights within the policy, your rights and the rights of your personal beneficiary are protected by an endorsement on the policy. This modifies the employer's absolute rights as owner.

Under the collaterally assigned split-dollar payment method, you apply for the policy and you determine the owner and your personal beneficiary. Your employer is protected through the separate agreement by having you collaterally assign the policy. Your employer's interest in the policy is as an assignee, not as a beneficiary, and is limited to the exact amount of money spent as an employer.

Red Flag! It is not uncommon to use split-dollar plans in nonqualified deferred compensation arrangements between an employee and employer. When this is the case, the collaterally assigned split-dollar method should not be used, because deferred compensation payments must come from an employer. When the policy is to be used to fund the payments, the policy must be transferred to the employer (if collaterally assigned), who becomes the new owner. This is in violation of the transfer-for-value exceptions unless the insured is a shareholder or officer of the corporation. Such a violation causes some of the life insurance proceeds, at death, to be subject to federal income tax.

Death-Benefit-Only Plan

Under a death-benefit-only plan, the employer and employee enter into a contract whereby the employer promises a death benefit only, not a retirement benefit, to the employee's personally named beneficiary. This promise is contingent upon the employee's staying in the employ of the employer. The employer has complete flexibility about which employees are selected for a death-benefit-only plan.

The Five Criteria

1. Someone else (your employer) pays the premium. Your employer is both owner and beneficiary of the policy. You as an employee have no rights at all within the life insurance policy, and you have no reportable income to report on your tax return during active and retired working years.

2. The premium paid by your employer is not tax-deductible.
3. The death benefit, when received by your employer, is not subject to federal income tax, provided that it is considered life insurance proceeds and provided that the alternative minimum tax is not a consideration. The money paid to your personally named beneficiary by your employer is in the form of salary continuation payments. This is subject to marginal ordinary federal income tax because it is not life insurance proceeds. It is money from your employer. Your employer may take as a tax deduction the payments made to your beneficiary, provided your employer is a taxable entity.
4. The death benefit paid to your personally named beneficiary will not be reduced in value because of the federal estate tax if the following conditions are met:
   a. You do not have the right to receive nonqualified deferred compensation or any other benefits other than a qualified retirement plan from the same employer, even under a different plan.
   b. You do not die within 3 years of entering into the plan if you specifically told your employer the name of your beneficiary.
   c. You do not retain a controlling interest (i.e., having the benefit payable to your estate if all beneficiaries die before you do).
   d. You do not retain the right to change the beneficiary. If the death benefit is deemed to be includable in your estate, the value will not be reduced if it qualifies for the marital deduction or if you did not leave an estate in excess of $600,000.
5. The value upon surrender of the policy is paid to your employer. To the extent that the cash value exceeds the total of premiums paid, a marginal ordinary federal income tax, which must be paid by your employer, is due on the difference.

Summary

1. Yes
2. No
3. No
4. Depends
5. No

Commentary.   When taxable charges to you as an employee are of concern, the death-benefit-only plan provides an excellent solution. You should be aware that the life insurance policy, which is owned by your employer, is a part of the employer's assets. As such, it is subject to the creditors of your employer. The 1986 Tax Reform Act, which makes marginal ordinary federal income tax brackets lower, reduces the tax on money received by your beneficiary from your employer. Conversely, because the 1986 act also lowers corporate marginal tax rates, the tax deduction has a lower after-tax cost for your employer. The tax deduction is taken by your employer for payments made to your beneficiary, provided that your employer is a taxable entity.

Nonqualified Deferred Compensation

"Nonqualified" means that prior Internal Revenue Service approval is not required. Your employer decides to provide selected employees with a plan of deferred compensation. Your employer can choose which employees are to be offered the plan. If you are chosen, your employer and you as the designated employee enter into a contract. Your employer promises to pay, to you as a retired employee or to your personally named beneficiary, salary continuation payments contingent upon your staying with your employer during your working years.

The Five Criteria

1. Someone else (your employer) pays the premium. Your employer is both owner and beneficiary of the policy. All rights within the policy are controlled by your employer. You as an employee have no reportable taxable income.

2. The premium paid by your employer is not tax-deductible.

3. The death benefit is not subject to federal income tax when received by your employer, provided it is considered life insurance proceeds and the alternative minimum tax is not a consideration. The death benefit, in the form of salary continuation to your personally named beneficiary or to you as a retired employee, is subject to marginal ordinary federal income tax. Your employer may take as a tax deduction payments made to you as a retired employee or to your personally named beneficiary, provided that your employer is a taxable entity.

4. The death benefit will be reduced in value by the federal estate tax because the present value of future payments is includable in your estate at the time of your death, whether before or during retirement and if you left an estate in excess of $600,000. The death benefit will not be reduced in value because of the federal estate tax, provided that either the death benefit qualifies for the marital deduction or, if not, you do not leave an estate in excess of $600,000.

5. The value upon surrender of the policy is paid to your employer. To the extent that the cash-surrender value exceeds the total of premiums paid, a marginal ordinary federal income tax, which must be paid by your employer, is due on the difference.

Summary

1. Yes

2. No

3. No

4. Depends

5. No

Commentary. Because of lower marginal ordinary federal income tax rates (as mandated by the Tax Reform Act of 1986), deferred compensation has lost some of its appeal; you as an employee may not wish to defer income at tax brackets lower than the pre-1986 act.

It is not uncommon to design a split-dollar deferred compensation plan funded by life insurance. When this is the case, the split-dollar plan used should be the endorsement form, not the collateral assignment form. This is because of the existing transfer-for-value rules. However, the endorsement form, thanks to the 1986 act, presents another problem—the alternative minimum corporate tax.

Key Person Life Insurance

Key person life insurance is life insurance purchased to provide money to a business or a business owner for a financial loss in the event of death of an insured person. The insured is economically important to the business or the business owner.

The Five Criteria

1. Someone else (the business) pays the premium for life insurance purchased on a key person, where a bona fide insurable interest exists.

2. The premium is not tax-deductible by the business. The business is both owner and beneficiary of the policy. All rights within the policy are controlled by the business as owner. The insured key person has no reportable income. There must be, at the inception of a life insurance policy being issued, a bona fide

insurable interest existing between the insured and the beneficiary. Usually this means that the death of the insured causes
financial harm or loss to the beneficiary. If an insurable interest
does not exist, the insurance company will not issue the insurance. To do so would put life insurance into the category of wa-
gering or making a bet. As such, the death benefit would not be
exempt from federal income tax.

3. At the death of the key person, the business receives the death
   benefit. The value of the death benefit is not subject to federal income tax, provided that it is considered life insurance proceeds
   and provided that the alternative minimum corporate tax is not a
   consideration.

4. The value of the death benefit is not reduced by federal estate tax,
   because the insured key person possessed no incidents of ownership.

5. The value upon surrender belongs to the business as owner. To
   the extent that the cash-surrender value exceeds what has been
   paid, a marginal ordinary federal income tax, which must be paid
   by the business, is due on the difference.

Summary

1. Yes
2. No
3. Not applicable
4. Not applicable
5. No

Commentary. Some commentators refer to life insurance as "discounted dollars" when convincing a business to use life insurance as the
financial vehicle for providing dollars for the business in the event that
a key person dies.

The term "discounted dollars" means that 100 cents are never paid
for $1 of death benefit. Hence, $1 of death benefit is being provided at
a discount. The flaw of the discounted dollars concept is that it does not
take into consideration the time value of money. Life insurance is used
to underwrite time; X dollars is created once the insurance is in force.
Life insurance provides a substantial rate of return upon death, taking
into consideration the time value of money.

In order to determine whether or not the life insurance rate of return
can be duplicated in another financial services product (e.g., mutual

funds, certificates of deposit, or real estate) the following calculations must be made.

Step 1. First, establish the rate of return upon death for each and every year the insurance is required. Remember, the death benefit is not subject to federal income tax, putting aside the alternative minimum corporate tax consideration, which can best be handled by the financial officer of a business or the tax adviser to the business.

Step 2. Find out what before-tax rate of return must be achieved each and every year in the alternative financial services vehicle (e.g., money or capital market investments). In order to determine the before-tax rate of return, you must divide the rate of return provided by life insurance by the result of subtracting from 100 percent the marginal tax bracket of the business.

The marginal tax bracket of the business is 34 percent, which, subtracted from 100 percent, gives 66 percent. The rate of return provided by life insurance in a specific year is 18.95 percent; this, divided by 0.66, results in a before-tax rate of return of 28.71 percent. A return of 28.71 percent before taxes must be achieved by a 34 percent taxpayer in order to net 18.95 percent after taxes.

One final comment about life insurance owned by a business. In addition to the corporate alternative minimum tax consideration, there is a recent accounting change that may affect all life insurance policies having a reserve (cash-surrender value): Financial Accounting Standards Board (FASB) statement 96, called "FASB 96."

According to Thomas A. FitzGerald, JD, LLM, of White Plains, New York, FASB 96 requires that a deferral tax liability be recorded for any item of book income in the current year that will be taxable income in a future year. That could cause a change in the way cash-value life insurance is shown on financial statements for fiscal years beginning after December 15, 1988. FASB 96 will principally affect the financial statements of publicly traded businesses, since privately held companies often do not follow the FASB pronouncements as strictly as do publicly traded ones.

If you adhere to FASB statements, make sure FASB 96 is explained in detail. This statement pertains to all existing life insurance policies, not just new purchases.

Closely Held Corporate Stock Redemption

Generally, what distinguishes a closely held corporation from, say, a General Motors is that its shareholders are also its officers. Profits are usually distributed totally in the form of salaries. There is no large surplus account, and there is no ready-made negotiable market for the stock (e.g., no over-the-counter market and no New York Stock Exchange).

Unlike a partnership in which the death of a partner causes the existing partnership to terminate, the death of a shareholder does not legally cause a closely held corporation, or any corporation for that matter, to terminate its existence. In theory, a corporation has an everlasting life, at least in this world.

In many respects a closely held corporation is very similar to a partnership. There are two types of stock redemption agreements for a closely held corporation, as there are for a partnership: *entity* and *cross-purchase*. When the cross-purchase form is used, any remaining living stockholders are obligated to purchase the stock of the deceased stockholders at the predetermined price. When the entity form is used, the corporation, not the stockholders, is obligated to purchase the stock of the deceased stockholders at the predetermined price.

The Five Criteria

1. The premium is paid by the corporation for life insurance purchased under the entity form and by respective shareholders for that purchased on a cross-purchase basis. The corporation and the shareholders have no reportable income for tax purposes.

2. The premium in either form is not tax-deductible.

3. The death benefit, when received by the corporation, is not subject to federal income tax, provided that the alternative minimum tax is not a consideration. The death benefit received by respective shareholders under a cross-purchase form is not subject to federal income tax. The death benefit, when received by the deceased shareholder's beneficiary, is not subject to income tax because of its stepped-up-in-basis status. (Property inherited by reason of death receives a stepped-up-in-basis status, meaning that if you inherit property with a fair market value of $1, your basis is $1.)

4. The value of the death benefit is not reduced because of the federal estate tax. The deceased shareholder possessed no incidents of ownership regardless of which form is used. The federal estate

tax treatment for the deceased shareholder's beneficiary depends upon the specific estate planning employed.

5. If the policy is surrendered for the cash value, to the extent that the reserve value is greater than the sum of premiums paid, an ordinary income tax is due on the difference, payable in the tax bracket of the owner.

Summary

1. Yes

2. No

3. Yes

4. Depends

5. No

Commentary. Stockholders will be well advised to create a stock redemption agreement for the following reasons:

- It obligates the remaining living stockholders to purchase the predetermined value of the deceased shareholders' stock.
- The price at purchase is predetermined and agreed upon, as stated in the stock redemption agreement.
- The estate of the deceased stockholders is obligated to sell the predetermined interests to the remaining living stockholders. This will keep in-laws, outlaws, strangers, and everybody else out of the business.

Life insurance should be used to fund a stock redemption agreement for the same reason given elsewhere in this chapter for key person life insurance and for partnership buy-sell life insurance. The number of policies will depend on which form is used (entity versus cross-purchase), just as for a partnership buy-sell. A corporation has its own tax bracket. It is not uncommon, particularly in the case of a closely held corporation, for the corporation to have a lower tax bracket than the stockholder.

Before deciding upon which form to use, consider the following:

- *Tax brackets.* When closely held corporations (even under the 1986 Tax Reform Act) are in a lower tax bracket than the shareholder, the entity form will require lower before-tax dollars to pay a nondeductible premium. A 15 percent corporate tax bracket requires $1.18 before taxes to pay $1 in premium. For a 33 percent shareholder taxpayer, $1.49 before taxes is required to pay a $1 nondeductible premium. If the shareholder is in a lower tax bracket than the corporation itself, the cross-purchase form will require fewer before-tax dollars to pay a nondeductible premium.

- *Simplicity.* If the number of shareholders to be insured is minimal, then there is no real problem in administrating either an entity or a cross-purchase form of stock redemption. When the number of shareholders is not minimal, then the cross-purchase form results in a large number of policies to keep track of. A possible solution is the use of the cross-purchase trust.[2]

- *Basis.* When the entity form is used, the corporation purchases stock from the estate of the deceased shareholder or from the selling shareholder, if living. This type of purchase by the corporation does not involve any other shareholders. They will retain exactly the same number of shares with no increase in their cost basis. After the purchase is made by the corporation, however, they will own a larger proportion of the value of the corporation. Since their basis remains the same, when and if they sell while living, they will have a higher tax to pay on any gain.

- When the cross-purchase form is used, it is the shareholder who is making the purchase, not the corporation. Therefore, the basis will increase after any purchase of shares. The increase in basis means that, if and when they sell while living, they will have less tax to pay on any gain.

- *Entity form.* For example, assume that XYZ Corporation has a current value of $210,000. Three equal shareholders have a current value of $70,000 each. The original investment, the *basis*, for each shareholder was $10,000. Then the following events occur:

1. One of the three shareowners dies, and the corporation purchases the deceased shareowner's stock from the estate for $70,000.

2. The current value of the corporation is still $210,000. Each remaining shareowner's shares are now worth $105,000, but each still has a basis of $10,000.

3. One of the shareowners decides to retire and sells to the remaining shareowner. The shareowner selling has a gain of $95,000 ($105,000 minus the original basis of $10,000). Tax must be paid on the $95,000 gain. There is no distinction between long- and short-term gains. The tax on $95,000 will be according to the seller's actual marginal ordinary income tax bracket (15, 28, or 33 percent).

---

[2]An explanation of the cross-purchase trust is beyond the scope of this book. This is a legal matter and should be discussed with an attorney.

Cross-purchase form. Again, for purposes of comparison, assume that XYZ Corporation has a current value of $210,000, that three equal shareholders have a current value of $70,000 each, and that the original investment, the *basis*, for each shareholder was $10,000. This example goes as follows:

1. One of the three shareowners dies. The remaining two living shareowners collect $35,000 each and purchase the deceased shareowner's stock.

2. The current value of the corporation is still $210,000. Each remaining shareowner's shares are now worth $105,000 but have a basis of $45,000. The original $10,000 basis has been increased by the $35,000 purchase to $45,000.

3. One of the shareowners decides to retire and sell to the remaining shareowner. The shareowner selling has a gain of $60,000 ($105,000 minus the new basis of $45,000). Tax must be paid on $60,000. There is no distinction between long- and short-term gains. The tax on $60,000 will be according to the seller's actual marginal ordinary income tax bracket (15, 28, or 33 percent). If a shareholder is apt to want to sell shares during his or her lifetime, then the cross-purchase form will provide a higher basis than the entity form. If the shareholder is apt not to sell shares during his or her lifetime, then it does not matter to the heir which form is used.

Life Insurance Owned by and Payable to a Professional Corporation

Prior to passage of the Omnibus Budget Reconciliation Act (OBRA) of 1987, and assuming that the corporate alternative minimum tax was not a consideration, life insurance in certain specific situations was owned and payable to a professional corporation.

Pre-OBRA Environment. Prior to passage of OBRA, when life insurance was owned by and payable to a professional corporation, the professional corporation was both owner and beneficiary of the life insurance policy. All incidents of ownership were controlled by the professional corporation. The professional shareholder could choose to provide life insurance protection for his or her family through the corporation because the corporation was in a lower tax bracket than the professional, which meant that it was less expensive to buy life insurance with before-tax dollars.

The Five Criteria

1. Someone else (the professional corporation) paid the premium. For a professional corporation in a 15 percent federal income tax bracket to pay $1 of life insurance premium, the corporation had to earn, before taxes, $1.18 (state taxes are not considered here). For the professional in a 33 percent marginal ordinary federal income tax bracket, $1.49 had to be earned before taxes to pay $1.00 of life insurance premium (again, state taxes are not considered here). The professional shareholder had no reportable charges to report as income.

2. The premium was not tax-deductible by the professional corporation.

3. The death benefit, when received by the professional corporation, was not subject to federal income tax, provided that it was considered life insurance proceeds and provided that the alternative minimum corporate tax was not a consideration.

4. The value of the death benefit was reduced by the federal estate tax, provided that it did not qualify for the marital deduction. If the estate was not in excess of $600,000, there was no reduction in value by the federal estate tax, regardless of the marital deduction.

5. The value upon surrender belonged to the professional corporation. To the extent that the cash-surrender value exceeded what had been paid, a marginal ordinary federal income tax was due on the difference.

Summary

1. Yes
2. No
3. Depends
4. Depends
5. No

Commentary. The essential purpose of life insurance is to provide a death benefit. The single most important tax aspect is that the death benefit be exempt from federal income tax. How then does life insurance that is owned by and payable to a professional corporation get to the professional shareholder's beneficiary free of federal income tax? The following requirements must be met.

1. Upon the death of the professional shareholder, the professional corporation must be liquidated, not sold to another professional.

2. Upon liquidation of the corporation, the liquidated value becomes part of the professional's estate. The professional's beneficiary is entitled to the estate value.

3. The liquidated value, when received by the beneficiary, is subject to stepped-up-in-basis status. Stepped-up-in-basis status at death means that the value inherited, by reason of death, has a value—the fair market value at the time of death.

4. If the beneficiary receives X dollars as fair market value, X dollars is the beneficiary's basis. As long as the disposition of inherited assets by the beneficiary is no greater than X dollars, no marginal federal ordinary income tax is due.

In a one-shareholder professional corporation, corporate-owned life insurance through a professional corporation works best, from a tax viewpoint, to provide life insurance protection for the professional's family. Consider the following reasons for the validity of this statement:

1. More likely than not, a one-shareholder professional corporation will be liquidated upon the death of the professional shareholder.

2. Liquidation, as previously described under current law, will provide the professional's beneficiary with tax-exempt money because of the stepped-up-in-basis status.

3. Unless the professional corporation is liquidated upon the death of the professional shareholder, thus allowing for the use of stepped-up-in-basis status, tax-exempt money to the beneficiary is impossible.

4. It is essential to remember that liquidated assets of a professional corporation, or of the deceased professional's estate, are subject to creditors of both the professional corporation and the estate. Assets cannot be paid immediately to the beneficiary unless there are no creditors or liens or until all creditors or liens have been satisfied.

Post-OBRA Environment. The Omnibus Budget Reconciliation Act of 1987, among other things, did away with the graduated income tax brackets for professional corporations. Now the minimum federal tax bracket is 34 percent. This fact of life eliminates the pre-OBRA leverage of having the professional corporation in a lower tax bracket than the professional shareholder-employee.

Because of OBRA and the existence of the corporate alternative minimum tax, tax advisers should counsel professionals about the feasibility of having life insurance for the benefit of their families continue to be owned by and payable to their professional corporations. The alternative—distributing the policy to the professional (the cash-surrender value will be subject to federal income tax) and having subsequent premium payments if any (the premium may have vanished) payable by the professional—may be preferable.

Even though not as glamorous, the personal payment method, as previously described, will provide the highest basis (cost) if the policy is surrendered. The same is true if it is used to provide a fully paid-up postretirement death benefit and yearly supplemental retirement income to the professional in the form of paid-up dividends—thus providing greater tax benefits at the other end (retirement).

The Partnership or Partners Write the Check: How It Stacks up against the Perfect Payment Scenario

Partnership Buy-Sell

A *partnership* is a type of business in which each partner devotes his or her time to the financial success of the partnership, has full authority to act for the partnership, and is liable for the legal and financial obligations of the partnership. Law provides that upon the death of a partner, the partnership has ended. The remaining living partners have the financial responsibility to pay the deceased's fair share of the partnership to the estate of the deceased partner.

Buy-sell agreements are of two types: *entity* and *cross-purchase*. When the entity form is used, the partnership itself buys out the ownership interest of the deceased partners. When the cross-purchase form is used, each partner obligates his or her estate to sell his or her partnership interest not to the partnership but to the remaining living partners.

The Five Criteria

1. The premium is paid by the partnership for life insurance purchased under the entity form, and by the respective partners for life insurance purchased on a cross-purchase basis. The partnership and the partners have no reportable income for tax purposes.

2. The premium paid, in either form, is not tax-deductible.

3. The death benefit, when received by the partnership or the respective partners, is not subject to federal income tax. The death benefit, when received by the deceased partner's beneficiary, is not subject to income tax because of its stepped-up-in-basis status.

4. The value of the death benefit is not reduced in value because of the federal estate tax. The deceased partner possessed no inci-

dents of ownership regardless of which form was used, i.e., the entity or cross-purchase. The federal estate tax treatment for the deceased partner's beneficiary depends upon the specific estate planning employed.

5. If the policy is surrendered for the reserve, to the extent that the reserve value (i.e., the cash value) is greater than the sum of premiums paid, an ordinary income tax is due on the difference, payable in the tax bracket of the owner.

Summary

1. Yes

2. No

3. Yes

4. Depends

5. No

Commentary. Partners will be well advised to create a buy-sell agreement for the following reasons:

- Such an agreement obligates the remaining living partners to purchase the partnership interests of a deceased partner.
- The price at purchase is predetermined, as stated in the agreement.
- The estate of the deceased partners is obligated to sell the predetermined interests to the remaining living partners.

The number of life insurance policies needed in a partnership buy-sell arrangement depends upon the type of buy-sell agreement. When the entity type is used, there will be one policy for each partner insured, owned and payable to the partnership. When the cross-purchase type is used, each partner is insured and is required to obtain a policy on every other partner.

When the entity form is used, the cost basis (the investment in the partnership) of each living partner is increased by the proceeds *received* by the partnership. When the cross-purchase form is used, the cost basis of each living partner is increased by the amount *paid* for the deceased partner's interest.

PART V

The Economic Need for Present-Value Living Money

19

In God We Trust; All Others Pay Cash

**Disability and Retirement—
The Bills Must Be Paid**

Why We Need Present-Value Living Money

If you get sick or hurt, you will not be able to continue to live in the fashion to which you have become accustomed unless you have enough present-value money to provide the required yearly stream of income. If your current assets are not sufficient to provide the required yearly stream of income, you need disability insurance.

When you wish to slow down or retire, your present-value money needs can no longer be fulfilled from wages, salary, compensation, bonuses, etc. Remember that, at all times, whether you are working or retired, your *net income* (money that you have available for spending, after taxes) must support your *gross habits* (your own specific lifestyle). In order for you to continue to live in the fashion to which you have become accustomed, your present-value money needs will have to be met from another source or sources. All such sources are dependent in one way or another upon someone's "sending money ahead" while you are working—i.e., they are dependent upon your ability to save and upon your employer's good business sense and act of social responsibility in providing retirement plans for employees. Various sources for present-value money at retirement are Social Security; personal savings; living benefits from life insurance, i.e., paid-up dividends; pension, profit-sharing, and 401K plans; 403B tax-sheltered annuities for employees of 501(c)(3) organizations; Keogh plans; individual retirement accounts; supplemental retirement income plans, i.e., nonqualified deferred compensation, whole-dollar, and split-dollar life insurance.

Disability Insurance: How Much and What Kind?

How much and what kind of disability insurance should you have? You should have enough so that when it is combined with your other liquid assets it will provide you with the required yearly stream of income you need. The kind you need may depend in great part on your occupation and on how you are employed—i.e., on whether you are a self-employed person, the owner of a business, or an employee of a company or other employer. If you work for someone else, ideally you are being provided with long-term disability coverage by your employer, on either a group or an individual basis (where "long-term disability coverage" is defined as having a benefit period to age 65). The unfortunate aspect of working for someone else, in regard to disability coverage, is that most likely you have no say in the *design* of the disability plan provided by your employer.

What Kind of Disability Coverage?

The type of disability insurance you get should be noncancellable and guaranteed renewable, which means that the policy can never be canceled except for nonpayment of the premium, and that the premium can never be increased (level premium from date of issue). It is *unlikely* that group coverage will meet this requirement. Individually owned policies, however, *will* meet this requirement. (See Table 19-1.)

What Benefit Period?

The benefits should provide coverage to age 65 for both sickness and accident. Group coverage *should* be able to meet this requirement. Individually owned policies *will* meet this requirement.

Table 19-1. Disability Income Insurance Criteria

Criterion	Group policy	Individually owned policy
Noncancellable and guaranteed renewable	Unlikely	Yes
Benefit period to age 65 for both sickness and accidents	Should have	Yes
Coverage for both total and residual disability	Should have	Yes
Your own occupational definition of total disability	Should have	Yes
Dual-occupation determination in writing by insurance company	Should have	Should have
Total disability not required for residual disability benefits	Should have	Yes
Residual disability indexed for inflation	Should have	Yes
Waiting period determination	Should have	Individually determined
Lifetime rider for sickness and accident	Should have	Yes
COLA rider	Should have	Yes
Premium discounts	Group rate	Yes
Social security offset	Yes	No
Portability	Unlikely	Yes

SOURCE: Copyright © William D. Brownlie, CLU, ChFC, CIP, LIA, 1988. All rights reserved.

What Kind of Coverage?

Your disability policy should cover you for both total disability and residual disability. Group coverage *should* be able to meet this requirement. Individually owned policies *will* meet this requirement.

Definition of Total Disability

The definition of "total disability" contained in your policy should refer to your own specific occupation at the time of claim—the occupation you are engaged in at the time you become disabled, not your occupation when you purchase the policy. Group coverage *should* be able to meet this requirement. Individually owned policies *will* meet this requirement.

Dual Occupation

You may very well have a dual occupation or become disabled not through a sickness or accident but rather because of a state or federal law. Because of my experience in working with physicians, I can best illustrate this principle by giving you specific real-life dual-occupation situations in the medical profession.

Example

An *obstetrician-gynecologist* (a physician practicing in a dual speciality involving both delivering babies and dealing with the diseases and hygiene of women), suffers a heart attack, and is told by his or her personal physician to stop getting up at all hours of the night to deliver babies. He or she is still allowed to practice gynecology.

Example

An *otorhinolaryngologist* (whose specialty is concerned with the ear, nose and throat) is unable to perform surgery on the ear, nose, and throat because of an accident or sickness. His or her practice is now confined to office and hospital examinations and treatment of the ear, nose, and throat.

Example

An *ophthalmologist-ophthalmic surgeon* (who works with the structure, function, and diseases of the eye) becomes unable to perform surgery on the eye because of an accident or sickness. His or her practice becomes confined to office and hospital examinations and treatment of the eye.

Example

A *surgeon-teacher-researcher* (a physician based in a teaching hospital affiliated with a medical school) becomes unable to perform surgery within his or her medical specialty because of an accident or sickness. He or she can still do some research and teaching (but cannot instruct by giving demonstrations in the operating room).

Example

State or Federal Law

An *infectious disease specialist* who is hospital-based becomes antigen-positive (a carrier of tuberculosis but not infected). The particular state law is such that this physician's practice must be terminated. The physician thus becomes disabled, not through a sickness or an accident, but rather by a particular law.

Before you purchase the disability policy, find out in writing (signed by an officer of the insurance company) whether you will be considered totally disabled if you are unable to practice one aspect of your occupation but able to practice the other. Both group and individually owned policies *should* be able to meet this requirement.

Definition of Residual Disability

A "residual disability" is one that does not render you totally disabled but affects your earnings. With most insurance companies, if your monthly earnings are 20 percent less than before you became disabled, you will be paid even though you are not totally disabled. The amount of residual benefit will depend upon the particular company with which you are insured.

Try to make sure that your policy contains a provision which guarantees that you *never* have to be first totally disabled in order to qualify for residual disability. Group coverage *should* be able to meet this requirement. Individually owned policies *will* meet this requirement.

Residual Disability Indexed for Inflation

Make sure that your residual disability coverage is indexed for inflation. Each insurance company has different requirements and benefits. Most require that you have a 20 percent "loss of earnings" and be under the care of a licensed practitioner, and some also require a loss of time and duties. Say, for example, that when you first became disabled, your base earnings (as determined by the insurance company, usually based on your highest earnings in the 2 years prior to the disability), were $4166.67 per month, or $50,000 annually. They would subsequently increase to $4506.67 per month ($54,000 annually), according to the CPI, the measurement used by insurance companies. This increase assumes 4 percent compound inflation and a 3-year total disability. Your earnings would be $50,000 the first year, $52,000 the second year, and $54,080 the third year.

If, upon returning to work, you were able to earn only $2500 per month ($30,000 annually) because of your disability, you would qualify for one phase of residual disability because of the 40 percent loss; however, your residual benefit ($2500, a percentage of your actual monthly benefit) would be 45 percent, or $1125. Earnings of $30,000 in relation to $54,080 would mean a loss of 45 percent. Without indexing, your residual benefit would have been 40 percent of $2500, or $1000, a difference of $125. Group coverage *should* be able to meet this requirement. Individually owned policies *will* meet this requirement.

Waiting Period

A waiting period in a disability insurance policy is similar to a deductible on your automobile or homeowner's coverage, meaning the *longer* the waiting period and the *higher* the deductible, the *lower* the premium. Group coverage usually has only *one* predetermined waiting period. You decide the waiting period with an individually owned policy.

Keep in mind that benefits are always paid in arrears. A 30-day waiting period means that the first payment is mailed to you 60 days after the disability begins. A 60-day waiting period means that the first payment is mailed 90 days after the disability begins. A 90-day waiting period means that the first payment is mailed in 120 days.

Additional Benefits Provided by Rider

Additional benefits can be provided by a rider to the disability policy. There is a cost for these accessories to your policy. The following are necessary riders and you should purchase them.

Lifetime Sickness Rider.   With most insurance companies, the lifetime sickness rider provides that if you become totally disabled from a sickness prior to age 60, and if the sickness or disability remains continuously and totally in effect to age 65, then you qualify for lifetime sickness benefits. Group coverage *should* be able to meet this requirement. Individually owned policies *will* meet this requirement.

Lifetime Accident Rider.   A lifetime accident rider usually provides lifetime benefits, provided that, at the beginning of your sixty-fifth year, you are in fact totally disabled from an accident. Group coverage *should* be able to meet this requirement. Individually owned policies *will* meet this requirement.

Cost-of-Living Adjustment Rider.   The cost-of-living adjustment (COLA) rider is an optional choice. The purpose of the rider is to take inflation into consideration, after you become disabled, so that your monthly benefit will not be reduced in purchasing power. The COLA rider is completely separate from residual disability indexing. Group coverage *should* be able to provide a COLA. Individually owned policies *will* do so.

After You Become Disabled.   Say you purchase a monthly disability benefit of $2500. Five years from the date of purchase (at the end of the fifth year) you become disabled. The monthly benefit paid at the beginning of the sixth year, after the waiting period, is $2500. Assuming that your disability continues, the monthly benefit increases as follows (based upon 5 percent compound interest):

Beginning of year	Benefit
7	$2625
8	2756
9	2894
10	3038
11	3190

The monthly benefit continues to increase as you remain disabled. No medical examination is required, and your medical history is not a consideration. You should know:

- The actual interest rate used

- Whether the interest rate is compound or simple

- Whether the yearly option to increase is limited to an ultimate maximum amount

I believe that the COLA rider should be an optional choice because of the cost; it is not an inexpensive rider. If you do purchase this rider and if you become residually disabled, with most companies you should receive "double indexing."

Before You Become Disabled

According to Sharon Wanamaker, a disability insurance specialist, some insurance companies provide, at no additional cost, a yearly update feature, which usually can be purchased only prior to becoming disabled. This should not be confused with a COLA rider, which does have an additional cost.

If you purchase a monthly disability benefit policy for, say, $2500 per month, according to Wanamaker, one company (not her own) allows for a 7 percent compound yearly increase during a 5-year period. One year from the date of original purchase, you can purchase an additional $175 monthly benefit (7 percent of $2500; in 2 years you can purchase $187.25 (7 percent of $2675), in 3 years $200.36 (7 percent of $2862.25), in 4 years $214.38 (7 percent of $3,062.61), and in 5 years $229.39 (7 percent of $3276.99). The additional amounts can be purchased for an additional premium based on your age at that time, without medical examination and without regard to your medical history. At the end of the 5-year period, you can begin another 5-year period if you are able to meet medical and financial underwriting requirements.

Discounts

Companies issuing individually owned, noncancellable, guaranteed renewable disability policies provide some or all of the following premium discounts (these are examples only; actual percentages may differ):

1. A 10 percent discount if the premium is paid once a year (annually)

2. A 5 percent discount for nonsmokers

3. A 10 percent discount if three or more people are insured on a list bill (one bill for all insured)

4. A 20 to 25 percent discount for officially sponsored professional association plans, in which the insureds (e.g., physicians, dentists, or accountants) are members of a specific association

5. A 20 to 25 percent discount for corporate-sponsored programs, in which a definite employer-employee relationship exists

Benefits Reduced by Social Security Offset Rider

So far as I know, all group long-term disability programs provided by employers have a social security offset rider. This means that, when you become disabled, the insurance company requires you to apply for social security disability benefits. It is unlikely that you will qualify for social security disability. The Social Security office's definition of "total disability" is such that you would have to be almost dead to qualify. If you refuse to apply, however, the insurance company will reduce your monthly benefit by the amount that social security would have paid. The bureaucratic process then begins.

Step 1. You either call or go to a Social Security office and state that you wish to apply for social security disability. You should then be told to fill out form SSA-1650-441(1-P6) (4 pages), form SSA-3368-BK(7-85) (6 pages), form SSA-821-F4(7-85) (4 pages), a "Statement of Claimant" form (1 page), and a "Supplemental Interview" form (4 pages).

Step 2. You probably do not qualify, and so form SSA-L808.5-U2(5-82) will probably inform you of a "Social Security Notice of Disapproval of Claim." Upon receipt, you have 60 days to file for reconsideration, which the insurance company will insist that you do.

Step 3. After you file for reconsideration, form SPT-G-54 is sent to you, informing you of a second denial of claim. You have 60 days, after receipt, to apply for a formal hearing, i.e., a trial, which the insurance company will insist that you do. Form HA-501-45(9-85) is used for this purpose.

Step 4. Form HA-507-US(10-83), "Notice of Hearing," is sent to you, informing you of the date, time, and place for the hearing. If your application is refused again, you may ask the Social Security Appeals Council to review the hearing decision or dismissal—and the insurance company may insist that you do this.

If, when all the bureaucratic process is finished, Social Security still will not pay, the insurance company continues to pay your full monthly benefit. If Social Security decides to pay, the insurance company will reduce its monthly payment by the amount that Social Security pays. Incidentally, during the bureaucratic process, the insurance company pays your full monthly benefit, provided that you furnish it with copies of the paperwork that you must submit to Social Security.

On an individual policy, you can also add a social security offset rider to lower your premium. Be advised that if you add such a rider and then do become disabled, you will have to go through exactly the same bureaucratic process as described above.

Portability

An individually owned disability policy is inherently portable. Once issued, it can never be canceled by the insurance company except for nonpayment of the premium, and the premium can never be increased. This is *most likely not* the case with a group policy. If you terminate employment with your employer, your coverage is not allowed to go with you—meaning that it is unlike group term life insurance in that you cannot convert it to an individually owned policy. This lack of portability can be a serious problem if you have a preexisting medical condition, e.g., a heart condition. The preexisting medical condition *may* prevent you from being insured in a new employer's group plan.

Premiums and Taxes

A premium paid by your employer for either an individual or a group disability policy is tax-deductible by your employer and nonreportable to you as income, pursuant to section 106 of the Internal Revenue Code. A premium that you yourself pay is not tax-deductible.

Benefits Received and Taxes

When benefits are received from a disability policy fully paid for by your employer, the benefits are fully taxable. When benefits are received from a policy which you paid for, and the premium was not tax-deductible, the benefits are not subject to tax. If you are self-employed and incorporated, keep in mind that you are an employee of your own corporation.

Some commentators say that it is perfectly permissible for you to report as income the amount of the premium paid by your employer so that, if you become disabled, the benefits will be nontaxable to you. The truth is, however, that the Internal Revenue Code specifically states that a disability premium paid by an employer is *not* to be included as income on the individual's tax return. There is nothing in the Internal Revenue Code about how to include the premium paid by your employer as income so that your benefits will be nontaxable. If you wish to make your benefits nontaxable, the best bet seems to be to have your employer bonus the premium to you as income, and then you can pay the premium directly to the insurance company.

There are different rules for individual disability policies and for group policies. In order for the bonus plan above to work for a group policy, it would have to have been done over a 3-year period prior to a disability claim, because existing law says that the ratio of premium paid by the employer to premium paid by the employee over the 3-year period preceding the disability determines what portion of the benefits are taxable versus nontaxable [IRS regulation 1.105-1(c)(1)].

Section 89 (J)(10)(b) Red Flag!

Policies providing for "presumptive total disability" (e.g., total loss of speech, sight, hearing, use of both hands, both feet, or one hand and one foot, even though the insured is able to work), and/or a "nondisabling injury" feature (e.g., reimbursement for medical bills incurred due to injury, even though the insured is not disabled) are considered health benefits, not disability benefits says Allan Checkoway, RHU, Wellesley, Massachusetts. As such, if not handled properly (the premium attributable to the benefits provided) it could be a violation of the Section 89 nondiscrimination tests. See your insurance agent for the most suitable solution for your specific situation.

Retirement Reality

When it comes to retirement, the magic age of 65 no longer holds true. Retirement now occurs at a variety of ages, i.e., 45, 55, 65, and yes, 75. Life expectancy has increased to 65 for a female now 11 years old (that is, she can expect to reach age 76), and to 65 for a male now 6 years old (that is, he can expect to reach age 71). Experts in the statistical study of human populations estimate that these numbers can be expected to increase. The current life expectancies for the retirement ages mentioned above are shown in Table 19-2.

Each year that we live, our life expectancy changes, i.e., increases (see Table 19-3). This fact of life means that our present-value living money will have to extend over a longer period of time.

How Much Is Enough?

A hypothetical retirement illustration will help you to answer this question for yourself. (See Table 19-4.)

Example

Retirement income objective: $50,000 of yearly income in constant dollars.
Payments: $50,000 at the beginning of each year, starting in the year of retirement, i.e., from age 45, 55, 65, or 75 to current life expectancy.
Interest-rate assumption: 5.76 percent net after taxes (equivalent to 8 percent before taxes, taxed at marginal ordinary federal income tax rate of 28 percent).
Last payment: Received at the beginning of the last year (life expectancy).
   The principal (present-value living money needed as of retirement age) is exhausted—gone.

Method of Calculation

On a hand-held calculator (such as the Hewlett-Packard 41C series) with a financial decisions module, perform the calculations in the following manner:

1. Use a beginning-of-year (not end-of-year) calculation.

2. Enter $50,000 as payment.

3. Enter life expectancy in years as time.

4. Enter 5.76 percent as interest.

5. Instruct the calculator to solve for present value.

Annual Savings Required

The annual deposits, from age 35 to retirement, required to accumulate the necessary present-value living money for retirement at specified ages are shown in Table 19-5. (This table is based on the assumption

Table 19-2. Life Expectancy in Years

Age	Women	Men
45	33.8	29.6
55	25.5	21.7
65	18.2	15.0
75	12.1	9.6

Table 19-3. Ordinary Life Insurance Annuities—One Life—Expected Return Multiples

Table I — Ordinary Life Annuities — One Life — Expected Return Multiples

Male	Female	Multiples	Male	Female	Multiples
6	11	65.0	59	64	18.9
7	12	64.1	60	65	18.2
8	13	63.2	61	66	17.5
9	14	62.3	62	67	16.9
10	15	61.4	63	68	16.2
11	16	60.4	64	69	15.6
12	17	59.5	65	70	15.0
13	18	58.6	66	71	14.4
14	19	57.7	67	72	13.8
15	20	56.7	68	73	13.2
16	21	55.8	69	74	12.6
17	22	54.9	70	75	12.1
18	23	53.9	71	76	11.6
19	24	53.0	72	77	11.0
20	25	52.1	73	78	10.5
21	26	51.1	74	79	10.1
22	27	50.2	75	80	9.6
23	28	49.3	76	81	9.1
24	29	48.3	77	82	8.7
25	30	47.4	78	83	8.3
26	31	46.5	79	84	7.8
27	32	45.6	80	85	7.5
28	33	44.6	81	86	7.1
29	34	43.7	82	87	6.7
30	35	42.8	83	88	6.3
31	36	41.9	84	89	6.0
32	37	41.0	85	90	5.7
33	38	40.0	86	91	5.4
34	39	39.1	87	92	5.1
35	40	38.2	88	93	4.8
36	41	37.3	89	94	4.5
37	42	36.5	90	95	4.2
38	43	35.6	91	96	4.0
39	44	34.7	92	97	3.7
40	45	33.8	93	98	3.5
41	46	33.0	94	99	3.3
42	47	32.1	95	100	3.1
43	48	31.2	96	101	2.9
44	49	30.4	97	102	2.7
45	50	29.6	98	103	2.5
46	51	28.7	99	104	2.3
47	52	27.9	100	105	2.1
48	53	27.1	101	106	1.9
49	54	26.3	102	107	1.7
50	55	25.5	103	108	1.5
51	56	24.7	104	109	1.3
52	57	24.0	105	110	1.2
53	58	23.2	106	111	1.0
54	59	22.4	107	112	.8
55	60	21.7	108	113	.7
56	61	21.0	109	114	.6
57	62	20.3	110	115	.5
58	63	19.6	111	116	.0

SOURCE: *Tax Facts I 1988,* The National Underwriter Company, 1988, p. 641.

Table 19-4. Present-Value Living Money Required

Age	Women	Men
45	$779,761	$743,089
55	697,929	645,726
65	586,757	521,734
75	451,847	381,786

Table 19-5. Annual Savings Required

	Women		Men	
Age	Present-value money required	Annual savings	Present-value money required	Annual savings
45	$779,761	$33,395	$743,089	31,824
55	697,929	5,924	645,726	5,481
65	586,757	1,173	521,734	1,043
75	451,847	220	381,786	187

that the person is in a financial position to begin saving retirement money at age 35.)

Method of Calculation

On a hand-held calculator (as described on page 194), perform the calculations in the following manner:

1. Use a beginning-of-year (not end-of-year) calculation.

2. Enter the required present-value living money required (see Table 19-5) as the future value.

3. Enter the number of years from age 35 to retirement (for example, if you want to retire at age 45, enter 10; if you want to retire at age 75, enter 40) as time.

4. Enter 15 percent as interest.

5. Instruct the calculator to solve for payment. (See Table 19-5.)

Variables

The first and most obvious variable in the illustration used here is the choice of $50,000 as the desired income. Although an arbitrary amount, $50,000 is certainly *reasonable*, though not *lavish*. You, however, must decide your own specific amount, based upon your lifestyle.

Other variables, less well *understood*, are as follows:

1. $50,000 in *constant* versus *real* dollars fails to take into consideration the effect of inflation. Assuming a 3.71 percent inflation factor (the use of 3.71 percent has been explained in Chapter 4) means that a $50,000 future-value payment 20 years from now is worth $24,130 in today's dollars.

2. Calculating your individually selected retirement amount on a *real* dollar basis (as explained in Chapter 4) results in a *higher* present-value living amount as compared to a *constant* dollar calculation.

3. Interest-rate assumptions, i.e., 5.76 percent during *retirement* and 15 percent during the saving or accumulation period, are arbitrary. An assumption of 8 percent gross is indicative of a money market investment (e.g., annuities, money market funds, and U.S. Treasury obligations) in which principal—present-value money—is *not* subject to risk. An assumption of 15 percent for the accumulation period is very aggressive. It is based upon my own personal experience of using growth mutual funds, which have performed satisfactorily in both up and down markets, and which have been able to average 15 percent compound for each 5-year period that my money has been invested in them. Also factored into this assumption is my expected return, taking into consideration cash flows and liquidating value, on the real estate limited partnerships existing within my retirement plans, Keogh and IRA.[2] You must decide for yourself what interest rate you wish to assume both during the accumulation phase and during the retirement phase.

4. You may live *beyond* your life expectancy. This must be taken into consideration when you calculate your present-value living money needs either on a constant dollar or a real dollar basis. Failure to take this possibility into consideration may result in your running out of money during your lifetime.

Conclusions

Where is the present-value money for your retirement going to come from? Putting aside the unlikely possibilities—that you will unexpectedly inherit large amounts of money, win the lottery, or discover a remunerative cure for the ills of society—the money can only come from the sources mentioned at the beginning of this chapter. The best practical advice I can give you is to acquaint yourself with the financial decisions module of a hand-held calculator. The ability to perform financial decisions calculations has had a very positive influence on my business and personal life.

---

[2]Please do *not* write or call for the name of my mutual funds or my real estate limited partnerships. Under no circumstances will I be able to give out this information.

Appendix

How to Read a Ledger Statement

Sales Tool of the Life Insurance Industry

What Is a Ledger Statement?

When you buy a brand new automobile, you will find on the window of the automobile a sticker, which, by law, must be visible. That sticker completely describes the automobile you are going to buy. The sticker will tell you about the standard equipment, the accessories, the radio, the air conditioning, and so forth. In other words, the sticker describes the anatomy of the car you are going to buy. In exactly the same way, the official ledger statement produced by the computer service of the life insurance company describes the anatomy of the life insurance plan and/or method of premium payment under consideration for purchase; *or* the life insurance policy under consideration for replacement or exchange.[1]

Ledger statements are either produced by the mainframe computer in the home office of the life insurance company (where they are accessed for use via telephone lines) or on diskettes (software) provided by the life insurance company to its agents for use on their personal computers (PCs).

Some life insurance companies allow for a "range approach." This allows each agent to individually select for illustration purposes, as part of the ledger statement, the following: ⸚

---

[1]From William D. Brownlie, CLU, ChFC, CIP, LIA, *Life Insurance: Its Rate of Return,* The National Underwriter, Cincinnati,1983, p. 20.

- An interest-rate assumption, for interest-sensitive whole life and universal life

- A divided interest-rate assumption, for traditional whole and graded premium life

The range approach results in the agent's being able to choose interest rates and dividend interest-rate assumptions *above* and *below* those currently being employed by the life insurance company.

In my judgment, because of existing aggressive investment strategy assumptions, illustrations based on rates *above* current assumptions should not be allowed. The range approach should be limited to rates current and below current. ,

In this appendix, you will be walked through ledger statements for a variety of insurance products. The ledger statements are numbered and explained. (The italic numbers in the ledger statements refer to text explanations.) Also included is an explanation of what you should look for and ask for beyond what is on the ledger statement.

Sample Ledger Statements

Yearly Renewable Term

How to Navigate Your Way through a Ledger Statement for Yearly Renewable and Convertible Term—Non-Reissue and Reissue (Figure A-1)

1. The death benefit is "level," in this case, $100,000.

2. The plan of term insurance is yearly renewable to age 95.

3. Gender and issue age: male, age 45.

4. Insurability status (e.g., smoker or nonsmoker), or rated (extra charge because of having a higher risk for medical or occupational reasons). The "preferred" risk for this life insurance company refers to a nonsmoker, nonrated policyholder—the company's best insurability category.

5. The amount of life insurance payable to the named beneficiary. In this case, $100,000.

6. The beginning-of-the-year ledger statement versus the end-of-year statement.

7. The gross premium charged (not taking dividends into consideration) on a non-reissue basis.

8. The projected dividend payable at the end of the prior year, i.e., at the beginning of the following year. In this case, the first projected dividend is to be paid at the beginning of year 6.

+PLAN: Yearly Renewable Term to 95 __2__

Male: Issue Age __3__   __5__ Face Amount: $100,000

CLASS: Preferred Standard __4__

6	7	8	9	10	See 14	See 17	See 20
Beg. Pol. Year	Basic Ann. Prem &	Div. End of Prior Year*	Net Ann. Prem*	Reissue Premiums @ 1	Reissue Premiums @ 2	Reissue Premiums @ 3	Reissue Premiums @ 4
1	$ 238	$ 0	$ 238				
2	314	0	314				
3	395	0	395				
4	479	0	479				
5	568	0	568	$286 *11*			
6	842	171	671	388			
7	898	178	720	497			
8	984	183	801	614			
9	1,042	189	853	*13* $738 *12*	$378 *14*		
10	1,126	224	902		449		
11	1,244	245	999		592		
12	1,319	266	1,053		742		
13	1,421	317	1,104	*16*	$900 *15*	$498 *17*	
14	1,531	377	1,154			585	
15	1,689	417	1,272			773	*20*
16	1,781	460	1,321			964	
17	1,929	471	1,458	*19*		$1,164 *18*	$ 700
18	2,097	487	1,610				902
19	2,287	508	1,779				1,166
20	2,498	536	1,962				1,418
21	2,830	668	2,162				*21* $1,665
22	3,072	733	2,339				
23	3,372	860	2,512				
24	3,665	1,010	2,655				
25	3,920	1,125	2,795				
26	4,342	1,293	3,049				
27	4,674	1,309	3,365				
28	5,289	1,486	3,803				
29	5,692	1,625	4,067				
30	6,035	1,675	4,360				
31	6,480	1,725	4,755				
32	7,110	1,797	5,313				
33	7,867	1,992	5,873				
34	8,775	2,062	6,713				
35	10,280	2,130	8,150				
36	11,116	2,192	8,924				

See 23 — Reissue Premiums @ 5 (rows 21–24): *22* $1,034 / 1,405 / 1,758 / 2,083 ; *25* $2,380 *24*

See 26 — Reissue Premiums @ 6 (rows 25–28): *26* $1,580 / 2,231 / 2,720 / 3,159 ; $3,567 *27*   *28*

Dividends* used to reduce premiums.

Dividends are not guaranteed and will vary.

Figure A-1. Ledger statement for yearly renewable term.

(Continued)

LEVEL TERM LEDGER STATEMENT
Summary and Explanatory Notes

Summary:#29		Total Annual Premiums†	Total Annual Dividends*	Total Net Premiums*	Total Reissue Premiums@
5 years		$ 1,994	$ 171	$ 1,823	$ 1,712
10 years		6,886	1,190	5,696	4,038
15 years		14,090	3,027	11,063	7,228
20 years	30	24,682	31 5,697	32 18,985	33 12,378
Age 60		14,090	3,027	11,063	7,228
Age 65		24,682	5,697	18,985	12,378
Age 70		41,541	10,718	30,823	20,238

Interest-adjusted indexes* based on a 5.00% interest rate, for basic policy only: without reissue

	Life insurance net payment cost index	10 years: $5.45	20 years: $8.36	Age 65: $8.36
34	Life insurance surrender cost index	10 years: 5.45	20 years: 8.36	Age 65: 8.36
	Equivalent level annual dividend	10 years: 1.01	20 years: 2.21	Age 65: 2.21

35 &Plan renews automatically each year on payment of a renewal premium, but not beyond insured's age 95. Convertible to any life or endowment policy with a level face amount prior to the insured's age 90.

36 @If satisfactory evidence of insurability is submitted at the end of each 4-year period, but not beyond age 69, the lower premium rates may apply. Otherwise the original rates apply.

37 *Includes dividend values. The dividend levels in this illustration are based on the company's current experience with respect to mortality, persistency, taxes, expenses, and investments. They are not guaranteed. The dividends actually paid will be determined by the company's future experience in these factors and will likely differ from those illustrated, being either higher or lower.

38 Among these dividend factors, investment earnings are of major significance. The illustrated dividends assume continuation of the company's current investments experience. If all other dividend factors were to remain at current experience levels, future dividends would be higher or lower than those illustrated, depending upon future investment earnings. To demonstrate this, dividend levels resulting from future investments that are 2% higher and 2% lower than the illustrated scale are also available.

39 #Summary values are calculated as of the end of the year and, because of rounding, may differ slightly from values shown on the ledger page.

40 †Issuance of this plan for the values shown is subject to underwriting approval.

Figure A-1. (Continued)

9. Net annual premium (gross premium charged on a non-reissue basis taking projected dividends into consideration).

10. Reissue column.

11. At the beginning of year 5, the insured may apply for reissue rates. After satisfying the underwriting requirements of the insurance company (just as though applying for new insurance), the premium for year 5 will be $286, not $568. If underwriting requirements are not met, the net projected premiums in column 9 will apply.

12. At the beginning of year 9, those who qualified for reissue rates at the beginning of year 5 apply again. If their application is denied, their year 9 premium will be $738, then the non-reissue rates (column 9) apply. If they qualify for reissue rates, their premium in year 9 will be $378.

13. The net projected premium in year 10 is $902 for those who did not qualify for reissue.

14. The premium is $378 in year 9 for those who did qualify for reissue.

15. At the beginning of year 13, those who qualified for reissue rates at the beginning of year 9 apply again. If denied, their year 13 premium will be $900, then the non-reissue rates (column 9) apply. If they qualify for reissue rates, their premium in year 13 will be $498.

16. The net projected premium is $1154 in year 14 for those who did not qualify for reissue.

17. The premium is $498 in year 13 for those who did qualify for reissue.

18. At the beginning of year 17, those who qualified for reissue rates at the beginning of year 13 apply again. If denied, their year 17 premium will be $1164; then the non-reissue rates (column 9) apply. If they qualify for reissue rates, their premium in year 17 will be $700.

19. The net projected premium in year 18 for those who did not qualify for reissue is $1610.

20. The premium is $700 in year 17 for those who did qualify for reissue.

21. At the beginning of year 21, those who qualified for reissue rates at the beginning of year 17 apply again. If they are denied, their year 21 premium will be $1665, then the non-reissue rates (column 9) apply. If they qualify for reissue rates, their premium in year 21 will be $1034.

22. The net projected premium in year 22 for those who did not qualify for reissue is $2339.

23. The premium is $1034 in year 21 for those who did qualify for reissue.

24. At the beginning of year 25, those who qualified for reissue rates at the beginning of year 21 apply again. If they are denied, their year 25 premium will be $2,380, then the non-reissue rates (column 9) apply. If they qualify for reissue rates, their premium in year 25 will be $1,580.

25. The net projected premium in year 26 for those who did not qualify for reissue is $3049.

26. The premium is $1580 in year 25 for those who did qualify for reissue.

27. The premium in year 29 for those who did qualify for reissue rates at the beginning of year 25. In year 29, the insured is beyond age 69; therefore, reissue rates no longer are available.

28. The net projected premium in year 29 (based on the life expectancy for a 45-year-old male) for those who did not qualify for reissue is $4067. For those still alive after age 74 who want to have their insurance continue in force, the net projected premiums in column 9 will apply.

29. Reflects that this is a summary page.

30. Cumulative sum of gross non-reissue premiums (dividends not taken into consideration) for the years shown. Although mathematically correct, the numerical figures do not take into consideration the time value of money.

31. Cumulative sum of projected dividends that are assumed will be paid for the years shown. Although mathematically correct, the numerical figures do not take into consideration the time value of money.

32. Cumulative sum of net projected premiums on a non-reissue basis (gross premium minus projected dividends) for the years shown. Although mathematically correct, the numerical figures do not take into consideration the time value of money.

33. Cumulative sum of premiums on a reissue basis. Although mathematically correct, the numerical figures do not take into consideration the time value of money.

34. Interest adjusted indexes for the years shown on a non-reissue basis.

35. Statement about the renewability as term insurance and convertibility to a nonterm plan.

36. Statement about reissue rules.

37. Dividend statement.

38. Investment statement relating to dividends.

39. Statement about summary values which are based on the end of the year, not the beginning of the year.

40. Underwriting statement (medical, social, and economic).

Ledger Statements Do Not Tell All.   You should be told verbally or in writing the following additional information:

- Plain talk about what *reissue* means. It is satisfactory new evidence of insurability as determined by the insurance company. You may apply for reissue at the end of every 4 years, but not beyond your sixty-ninth year. If you are able to reenter, your premium will be lower. The actual premium will be what the insurance company deems proper at the time, which may be higher or lower than the reissue premiums shown on the current ledger statement.

- The rate of return expressed in terms of compound interest should be given either on the ledger statement or by the life insurance agent. Ideally, it should be provided for each year. If the agent does not have the proper financial decisions software, it will be economically impossible to provide yearly rates of return. A financial decisions calculator (I use the Hewlett-Packard 41C series with the financial decisions module) can be used on an economical basis to provide rates of return for various years, e.g., first year, fifth year, tenth year, twentieth year, and to your life expectancy.

- The rate of return upon death on a non-reissue basis is as follows:

Year	Rate of return
1	41,916.81%
5	200.04
10	58.83
20	17.45
29 (life expectancy)	6.85

- The rate of return upon death on a reissue basis is as follows:

Year	Rate of return
1	41,916.81%
5	200.62
10	61.26
20	20.53
29 (life expectancy)	9.78

- Once the rate of return upon death is known, then it can be determined what you would have to earn before taxes in another financial services product (e.g., mutual funds, certificates of deposit, real estate, or commodities) to duplicate the tax-exempt rate of return provided by life insurance. You determine the before-tax rate of return required by dividing the life insurance rate of return by your marginal tax bracket subtracted from 100 percent (e.g., for 15 percent, the factor is 0.85; for 28 percent, 0.72; for 33 percent, 0.67; and for 34 percent, 0.66).

■ The before-tax rate of return required in another financial services product to duplicate the rate of return upon death on a non-reissue basis should be on the ledger statement:

Year	*15% taxpayer*	*28% taxpayer*	*33% taxpayer*	*34% taxpayer*
1	49,313.89%	58,217.79%	62,562.40%	63,510.32%
5	235.34	277.83	298.57	303.09
10	69.21	81.71	87.81	89.14
20	20.53	24.24	26.04	26.44
29 (life expectancy)	8.06	9.51	10.22	10.38

■ The before-tax rate of return required in another financial services product to duplicate the rate of return upon death on a reissue basis should be shown on the ledger statement:

Year	*15% taxpayer*	*28% taxpayer*	*33% taxpayer*	*34% taxpayer*
1	49,313.89%	58,217.79%	62,562.40%	63,510.32%
5	236.02	278.64	299.43	303.97
10	72.07	85.08	91.43	92.82
20	24.15	28.51	30.64	31.11
29 (life expectancy)	11.51	13.58	14.60	14.82

■ The rate of return upon surrender is always −100 percent compound. This should be shown on the ledger statement.

■ You should be reassured that the ledger statement is the official ledger statement of the insurance company.

Traditional Whole Life Paying Dividends as Declared

How to Navigate Your Way through a Ledger Statement for Traditional Whole Life Paying Dividends as Declared (Figure A-2)

1. Length of time in years that the gross premium (e.g., $2001) is to be paid.

2. Plan of life insurance. Here it is traditional whole life paying dividends as declared. Ordinary life and whole life are interchangeable terms having the same meaning or significance.

<u>1</u>   20 PAY LIFE ILLUSTRATION

†PLAN: Ordinary Life___<u>2</u>   <u>5</u>___BASIC ANNUAL PREMIUM: $2,001.00
CLASS: Preferred Standard___<u>3</u>
Male Age 45___<u>4</u>   <u>6</u>___FACE AMOUNT: $100,000

<u>7</u> Beg. Pol. Year	<u>8</u> Pre- mium Payable*	<u>9</u> Cash Pre- mium Payment*	<u>10</u> Guar. Cash Value	<u>11</u> Total Cash Value*	<u>12</u> Ann. Incr. in Total Cash Value*	<u>13</u> Total Cash Value Incr.(−) Cash Prem.*	<u>14</u> Div. Adds Death Benefit*	<u>15</u> Total Death Benefit*
1	$2,001	$2,001	$ 0	0	0	−$2,001	0	$100,000
2	2,001	2,001	1,026	1,058	1,058	−943	113	100,113
3	2,001	2,001	2,938	3,043	1,985	−16	354	100,354
4	2,001	2,001	4,890	5,130	2,087	86	780	100,780
5	2,001	2,001	6,881	7,347	2,217	216	1,460	101,460
6	2,001	2,001	8,909	9,724	2,377	376	2,456	102,456
7	2,001	2,001	10,971	12,289	2,565	564	3,830	103,830
8	2,001	2,001	13,069	15,085	2,796	795	5,646	105,646
9	2,001	2,001	15,202	18,150	3,065	1,064	7,965	107,965
10	2,001	2,001	17,366	21,526	3,376	1,375	10,848	110,848
11	2,001	2,001	19,432	25,135	3,609	1,608	14,362	114,362
12	2,001	2,001	21,520	29,152	4,017	2,016	18,573	118,573
13	2,001	2,001	23,626	33,632	4,480	2,479	23,544	123,544
14	2,001	2,001	25,746	38,531	4,899	2,898	29,109	129,109
15	2,001	2,001	27,878	43,890	5,359	3,358	35,297	135,297
16	2,001	2,001	30,016	49,735	5,845	3,844	42,119	142,467
17	2,001	2,001	32,160	56,220	6,485	4,484	49,829	150,519
18	2,001	2,001	34,304	63,404	7,184	5,183	58,476	159,553
19	2,001	2,001	36,445	71,235	7,831	5,830	67,884	169,393
20	2,001	2,001	38,580	79,762	8,527	6,526	78,085	180,071

<u>16</u>   *Dividends are used to purchase paid-up insurance in years 1 through 20.
Thereafter, dividends are used to reduce premiums, and if necessary, a portion
of the paid-up insurance is surrendered to pay the balance of the premium.
"Div. Adds Death Benefit" reaches its lowest point in year 20.

Figure A-2. Ledger statement for traditional whole life paying dividends as declared.

(*Continued*)

3. Insurability status—e.g., nonsmoker, smoker (would be standard)
   or rated (extra charge because of being a higher risk for medical or
   occupational reasons). Preferred risk for this company means nonsmoker, nonrated. It is the company's best insurability classification.

4. Gender and issue age—male, age 45.

5. Gross premium (premium charged not taking dividends into consideration) not including any additional benefits provided by rider
   (e.g., waiver of premium).

<u>20</u>   PAY LIFE ILLUSTRATION

Beg. Pol. Year	Premium Payable*	Cash Premium Payment*	Guar. Cash Value	Total Cash Value*	Ann. Incr. in Total Cash Value*	Total Cash Value Incr.(−) Cash Prem.*	Div. Adds Death Benefit*	Total Death Benefit*
21	$ −3,984	0	$40,702	$ 87,033	$ 7,271	$ 7,271	$ 85,431	$187,939
22	−4,544	0	42,805	94,954	7,921	7,921	93,586	196,232
23	−5,178	0	44,882	103,597	8,643	8,643	102,638	205,420
24	−5,878	0	46,925	113,028	9,431	9,431	112,655	215,572
25	−6,655	0	48,929	123,322	10,294	10,294	123,723	226,773
26	−7,510	0	50,892	134,563	11,241	11,241	135,923	239,103
27	−8,445	0	52,820	146,848	12,285	12,285	149,336	252,644
28	−9,458	0	54,718	160,272	13,424	13,424	164,033	267,466
29 _17_	−10,551	0	56,596	174,946	14,674	14,674	180,088	283,645
30	−11,723	0	58,458	190,978	16,032	16,032	197,564	301,243
31	−12,993	0	60,303	208,489	17,511	17,511	216,551	320,351
32	−14,389	0	62,124	227,616	19,127	19,127	237,172	341,092
33	−15,963	0	63,912	248,530	20,914	20,914	259,620	363,658
34	−17,699	0	65,651	271,379	22,849	22,849	284,057	388,211
35	−19,613	0	67,331	296,317	24,938	24,938	310,667	414,934
36	−21,690	0	68,947	323,488	27,171	27,171	339,605	443,982
37	−23,913	0	70,499	353,028	29,540	29,540	371,007	475,489
38	−26,277	0	71,989	385,077	32,049	32,049	404,998	509,580
39	−28,780	0	73,426	419,802	34,725	34,725	441,699	546,378
40	−31,441	0	74,818	457,379	37,577	37,577	481,251	586,024

Summary# Page __18__

	19 Guar. Cash Value	20 Total Cash Value*	21 Cash Premium Payments	22 Total Cash Value Less Prem. Pymts.*	23 Guar. Paid-up Insurance	24 Total Paid-up Insurance*
5 Years	$ 6,881	$ 7,696	$10,005	$ 2,309−	$17,453	$ 19,519
10 Years	17,366	23,069	20,010	3,059	37,811	50,228
15 Years	27,878	47,945	30,015	17,930	52,791	90,792
20 Years	38,580	89,420	40,020	49,400	64,503	149,504
Age 65	38,580	89,420	40,020	49,400	64,503	149,504

<u>25</u>   Terminal dividend*   15th year: $348.00   20th year: $2508.00

Interest-adjusted indexes* based on a 5.00% interest rate, for basic policy only:

<u>26</u>   Life insurance 10 years: $16.24   20 years: $ 9.89   Age 65: $ 9.31
net payment cost index

Life insurance 10 years: 3.09   20 years: 1.95−   Age 65:   2.25−
surrender cost index

Equivalent 10 years: 3.77   20 years: 10.12   Age 65:   10.70
level annual dividend

<u>27</u>   Premium information: Annual   Semiannual   Quarterly   Pac.
Ordinary Life $2,001.00 $1,025.70 $520.56 $173.20

Figure A-2. (*Continued*)

---

20   PAY LIFE ILLUSTRATION
            Explanatory Notes

*Includes dividend values. Dividends are not guaranteed.___28
Illustrated dividends are based on the company's current mortality, expense, and investment experience. Actual dividends may be higher or lower than shown as a result of future changes in the company's experience, especially the interest rates earned on investments. A terminal dividend is payable upon surrender, lapse, or death, after at least 15 policy years, but only if declared by the company at such time, and is included in the total death benefit, in summary values for total cash value and total paid-up insurance, and in the interest-adjusted surrender cost index.
*Illustrated dividends assume no loans on policy. Policy loans will affect dividends.___29
30___ †The values shown in the ledger assume an annual mode of premium payment and a fixed policy loan interest rate of 8.00% applied in arrears, except in the case of a partial cash premium payment; then, a change to the automatic monthly premium mode has been assumed. The issuance of any policies or riders is subject to the company's regular underwriting practices. The amounts of coverage and premiums for any policies or riders, if issued, may differ from those illustrated.
#Summary values are calculated as of the end of the year.___31

Figure A-2. (*Continued*)

6. The initial amount of life insurance that will be payable to the named beneficiary upon the death of the insured.

7. Beginning-of-the-year ledger statement versus end-of-the-year ledger statement. Dividends, when paid, are not paid until the end of a specific year. If an end-of-the-year ledger statement is used, it would show dividends paid during the first year, which would be inaccurate.

8. The amount of premium to be paid each year.

9. The cash amount of premium to be paid each year. Here it is $2001 for the first 20 years. Starting in year 21, the cash amount payable is 0.

10. The cumulative guaranteed amount of reserve (guaranteed cash value) that has accumulated for each year.

11. The cumulative total amount of reserve (i.e., the guaranteed cash value), including the nonguaranteed cash value of the additional paid-up life insurance purchased each year, starting at the beginning of year 2, with the yearly declared paid dividend.

12. The yearly amount of increase in the total reserve (guaranteed cash value and the nonguaranteed cash value of the additional paid-upinsurance purchased each year).

13. The yearly difference between the gross premium of $2001 and the yearly guaranteed cash-value increase and the yearly increase of the nonguaranteed cash value of the additional paid-up life insurance purchased by the yearly declared paid dividend. A minus sign (−) means the combined yearly increase is less than the gross premium of $2001. A figure without a minus sign is mathematically correct, but it does not reflect the time value of money.

14. The amount of additional paid-up life insurance purchased by the declared paid dividend.

15. The yearly total death benefit including the projected additional paid-up life insurance purchased through the projected dividends. From year 16 on, the projected terminal dividend is included.

16. A statement indicating that dividends are used to purchase paid-up insurance. The gross premium of $2001 is paid during the first 20 years. Thereafter dividends are used to reduce the gross premium of $2001 and, if necessary, a portion of the paid-up insurance is surrendered to pay the balance of the gross premium. Looking at column 8 in year 21 reveals that this is unnecessary. The projected dividend in year 21 is $3984, more than the gross premium of $2001. When you see a minus sign (−) in this column, it means that amount of money that exceeds the gross premium. The statement, "Div. Adds Death Benefit reaches its lowest point in year 20," is a bug in the insurance company's ledger statement computer system, and should not be included for this ledger statement. Finally, from year 21 on, the dividend in excess of the gross premium is used to purchase additional paid-up life insurance. If desired, the death benefit could be frozen at $180,071 (year 20) and the dividend amount in excess of the gross premium than could be paid in cash.

17. The life expectancy of a 45-year-old male is 29 years—age 74.

18. Summary page values for this insurance company's ledger statement are different from the values shown on the nonsummary pages for two reasons. First, the yearly declared dividend is assumed to be paid at the end of the year. Second, the terminal dividend is included. The insurance company assumes for the summary page that the policy is surrendered for the years shown.

19. Cumulative amount of guaranteed cash value for the years shown.

20. Cumulative amount of total cash value for the years shown including the nonguaranteed cash value of additional paid-up insurance purchased through the dividends.

21. $2001 times the number of years shown.

22. The difference between column 21 and column 20. Although mathematically correct, it does not take into consideration the time value of money.

23. The amount of paid-up life insurance for the years shown that can be purchased by the guaranteed cash value. Once purchased, no additional premiums are required and the insurance company pays a paid-up dividend per $1000 of paid-up insurance.

24. The amount of paid-up life insurance for the years shown that can be purchased by the total cash value.

25. Terminal dividend, may be payable after the policy has been in force 15 years or longer.

26. Interest adjusted index. There is a bug in the insurance company's system. The numerical figures should be the same for 20 years and age 65. The year 20 figures are correct.

27. Premium information for various payment options, i.e., annual (once a year), semiannual (twice a year), quarterly (4 times a year), and preauthorized monthly payment through checking account (PAC). Cost is higher if not paid once a year. This is because of the expenses to send a premium notice more than once a year and the time value of money (the insurance company does not have the use of your money all at once).

28. Statement that dividends in any form are not guaranteed.

29. Statement that a loan against the reserve (cash value) will affect dividends.

30. Statement that the guaranteed fixed contractual interest rate charged for loans against the reserve is 8 percent payable in arrears, meaning that interest is due 1 year from the date of the loan.

31. Statement about the summary page calculations.

Ledger Statements Do Not Tell All.   You should be told either verbally or in writing the following additional information:

▪ You should be told on the ledger statement what the insurance company assumes it must earn on money coming in the store (premium payments) to warrant the dividends it projects. For the ledger statement you just read, the dividend interest assumption rate is 11.57 percent for the first year, graded up over a 20-year period to 11.73 percent.

▪ You should also be told on the ledger statement the investment strategy employed by the insurance company, which dictates the dividend interest assumption rate. For the ledger statement you just read, the investment strategy is a *weighted-average portfolio rate*. This means that 40 percent is weighted toward old money and 60 percent weighted toward new money. The insurance company, as part of its investment strategy, anticipates gains from real estate and common stock investments.

- You should be told on the ledger statement under what conditions your dividends will be reduced if you make a loan against the reserve (guaranteed cash value) of the policy. As stated in the ledger statement, the fixed guaranteed interest rate charged for loans against the reserve is 8 percent. Because the insurance company assumed that it must earn from 11.57 percent to 11.73 percent on money coming in, if only the fixed rate of 8 percent is paid, the dividend will be reduced because the insurance company is earning 3.57 to 3.73 percent less than it assumed.

- For example, in year 20, a maximum loan is made against the reserve (the guaranteed cash value) of $38,580. Ninety-two percent of $38,580 can be borrowed (less 8 percent interest) which is $35,493.60. One year later, interest of $2839.49 is due. The insurance company assumed it must earn 11.73 percent, which is $4163.40 (11.73 percent of $35,493.60). The difference between $4163.40 and $2839.49 is $1323.91. Therefore, in year 21 your dividend will be reduced by $1323.91. The projected dividend in year 21 will not be $3984 in excess of the gross premium of $2001; instead it would be $2660.09. The effect of the reduction in dividend results in loan interest of 12 percent, not 8 percent. Interest of $2839.49 plus loss of dividend of $1323.91 divided by the loan of $35,493.60 is 12 percent.

- Although not stated on the ledger statement, this particular insurance company gives the option of electing a variable loan rate versus the fixed loan rate. If the variable loan rate is equal to the dividend interest asssumption rate, the dividend will not be reduced. If the variable loan rate exceeds the dividend interest assumption rate, the dividend will be increased. At the time this book is being written, variable loan rates are in the range of 10.97 percent and 10.54 percent. This information should also be included on the ledger statement.

- The rate of return expressed in terms of compound interest should be given either on the ledger statement or by the life insurance agent. Ideally, it should be provided for each year. If the agent does not have the proper financial decisions software, it will be economically impossible to provide yearly rates of return. A financial decisions calculator (e.g., Hewlett-Packard 41C Series with the financial decisions module) can be used, however, on an economical basis to provide rates of return for various years (year 1, year 5, year 10, year 20, and to life expectancy).

■ The rate of return upon death for this policy for sequential years is as follows:

Year	Rate of return
1	4,897.50%
5	90.50
10	30.00
20	12.87
29 (life expectancy)	9.77

■ Once the rate of return upon death is known, then it can be determined what would have to be earned before taxes (it is assumed that the death benefit is considered life insurance proceeds and, as such, not subject to federal or state income taxes) in other financial services products (e.g., mutual funds, certificates of deposit, real estate, or commodities) to duplicate the tax-exempt rate of return provided by life insurance. The before-tax rate of return is determined by dividing the life insurance rate of return by the marginal tax bracket subtracted from 100 percent (for 15 percent, the factor is 0.85; for 28 percent, 0.72; for 33 percent, 0.67; and for 34 percent, 0.66). The result is as follows:

Year	15% taxpayer	28% taxpayer	33% taxpayer	34% taxpayer
1	5,761.76%	6,802.08%	7,309.70%	7,420.45%
5	106.47	125.69	135.07	137.12
10	35.29	41.67	44.78	45.45
20	15.14	17.88	19.21	19.50
29 (life expectancy)	11.49	13.57	14.58	14.80

■ The rate of return upon surrender should also be provided. When the rate of return upon surrender is positive, it means that taxes are due. Taxes are due on the difference between the cash-surrender value and the premiums paid. The result before taxes is as follows:

Year	Rate of return
1	− 100%
5	− 8.62
10	2.57
20	7.16
29 (life expectancy)	7.40

■ You should be reassured that the ledger statement is the official ledger statement produced by the computer service of the life insurance company. If it is not "bug-free," the bugs should be revealed to you.

Traditional Graded Premium Life Paying Dividends as Declared

How to Navigate Your Way through a Ledger Statement for Traditional Graded Premium Whole Life (Figure A-3)

1   20 PAY LIFE ILLUSTRATION

†PLAN: Graded PremiumLife___*2*___

*5*___BASIC ANNUAL PREMIUM 1ST POLICY YEAR: $622.00

CLASS: Preferred Standard___*3*___

THEREAFTER: See Page 5

Male Age 45___*4*

*6*___FACE AMOUNT: $100,000

7 Beg. Pol. Year	*8* Premium Payable*	*9* Cash Premium Payment*	*10* Guar. Cash Value	*11* Total Cash Value*	*12* Ann. Incr. in Total Cash Value*	*13* Total Cash Value Incr.(−) Cash Prem.*	*14* Div. Adds Death Benefit*	*15* Total Death Benefit*
1	$ 622	$ 622	$ 0	$ 0	$ 0	−$ 622	$ 0	$100,000
2	741	741	0	10	10	−731	35	100,035
3	860	860	422	463	453	−407	139	100,139
4	979	979	992	1,096	633	−346	337	100,337
5	1,098	1,098	1,676	1,891	795	−303	672	100,672
6	1,217	1,217	2,476	2,869	978	−239	1,186	101,186
7	1,336	1,336	3,390	4,050	1,181	−155	1,917	101,917
8	1,455	1,455	4,421	5,457	1,407	−48	2,902	102,902
9	1,574	1,574	5,568	7,116	1,659	85	4,182	104,182
10	1,693	1,693	6,984	9,205	2,089	396	5,791	105,791
11	1,812	1,812	8,343	11,429	2,224	412	7,770	107,770
12	1,931	1,931	9,820	13,994	2,565	634	10,158	110,158
13	2,050	2,050	11,414	16,937	2,943	893	12,997	112,997
14	2,169	2,169	13,125	20,249	3,312	1,143	16,219	116,219
15	2,288	2,288	14,954	23,961	3,712	1,424	19,856	119,856
16	2,407	2,407	16,899	28,108	4,147	1,740	23,942	124,129
17	2,526	2,526	18,963	32,722	4,614	2,088	28,495	128,884
18	2,645	2,645	21,148	37,907	5,185	2,540	33,676	134,311
19	2,764	2,764	23,455	43,720	5,813	3,049	39,543	140,474
20	2,883	2,883	25,888	50,151	6,431	3,548	46,005	147,283

16   *Dividends are used to purchase paid-up insurance in years 1 through 20. Thereafter, dividends are used to reduce premiums, and if necessary, a portion of the paid-up insurance is surrendered to pay the balance of the premium.
"Div. Adds Death Benefit" reaches its lowest point in year 20.

Figure A-3. Ledger statement for traditional graded premium life paying dividends as declared.

(Continued)

1. Length of time in years that the gross premium is to be paid.

2. Plan of life insurance. Here it is traditional graded premium whole life paying dividends as declared. Ordinary life and whole life are interchangeable terms having the same meaning or significance.

20 PAY LIFE ILLUSTRATION

Beg. Pol. Year	Premium Payable*	Cash Premium Payment*	Guar. Cash Value	Total Cash Value*	Ann. Incr. in Total Cash Value*	Total Cash Value Incr.(−) Cash Prem.*	Div. Adds Death Benefit*	Total Death Benefit*
21	$ −846	0	$28,448	$ 54,243	$ 4,092	$ 4,092	$ 47,564	$149,247
22	−1,153	0	30,986	58,643	4,400	4,400	49,633	151,482
23	−1,535	0	33,492	63,420	4,777	4,777	52,317	154,331
24	−1,960	0	35,957	68,615	5,195	5,195	55,658	157,835
25	−2,434	0	38,375	74,276	5,661	5,661	59,706	162,043
26	−2,940	0	40,744	80,438	6,162	6,162	64,482	166,976
27	−3,491	0	43,071	87,163	6,725	6,725	70,027	172,675
28	−4,073	0	45,361	94,496	7,333	7,333	76,357	179,157
29 _17_	−4,696	0	47,627	102,504	8,008	8,008	83,503	186,451
30	−5,350	0	49,873	111,235	8,731	8,731	91,480	194,576
31	−6,054	0	52,099	120,753	9,518	9,518	100,327	203,569
32	−6,830	0	54,297	131,132	10,379	10,379	110,115	213,501
33	−7,711	0	56,454	142,469	11,337	11,337	120,959	224,488
34	−8,678	0	58,552	154,835	12,366	12,366	132,942	236,612
35	−9,740	0	60,580	168,309	13,474	13,474	146,156	249,962
36	−10,881	0	62,530	182,958	14,649	14,649	160,673	264,611
37	−12,095	0	64,402	198,853	15,895	15,895	176,556	280,620
38	−13,365	0	66,201	216,054	17,201	17,201	193,844	298,030
39	−14,692	0	67,935	234,637	18,583	18,583	212,579	316,882
40	−16,091	0	69,615	254,691	20,054	20,054	232,821	337,237

Figure A-3. (*Continued*)

3. Insurability status—e.g., nonsmoker, smoker (would be standard) or rated (extra charge because of being a higher risk for medical or occupational reasons). Preferred risk for this company means nonsmoker, nonrated. It is the company's best insurability classification.

4. Gender and issue age—male, age 45.

5. Gross premium for the first year only (premium charged not taking dividends into consideration) not including any additional benefits provided by rider (e.g., waiver of premium).

6. The initial amount of life insurance that will be payable to the named beneficiary upon the death of the insured.

7. Beginning-of-the-year ledger statement versus end-of-the-year ledger statement. Dividends when paid are not paid until the end of a specific year. If an end-of-the-year ledger statement were used, it would show dividends paid during the first year, which would be inaccurate.

20 PAY LIFE ILLUSTRATION
Summary# Page ___18___

	19 ___ Guar. Cash Value	20 ___ Total Cash Value*	21 ___ Cash Premium Payments	22 ___ Total Cash Value Less Prem. Pymts.*	23 ___ Guar. Paid-up Insurance	24 ___ Total Paid-up Insurance*
5 years	$ 1,676	$ 2,069	$ 4,300	$ 2,231 –	$ 4,251	$ 5,249
10 years	6,984	10,070	11,575	1,505 –	15,206	21,924
15 years	14,954	26,350	21,825	4,525	28,318	49,898
20 years	25,888	56,368	35,050	21,318	43,283	94,244
Age 65	25,888	56,368	35,050	21,318	43,283	94,244

25 ___ Terminal dividend*   15th year: $187.00   20th year: $1683.00

Interest-adjusted indexes* based on a 5.00% interest rate, for basic policy only:

26 ___						
Life insurance net payment cost index	10 years:	$9.04	20 years:	$9.48	Age 65:	$9.44
Life insurance surrender cost index	10 years:	3.75	20 years:	1.54	Age 65:	1.36
Equivalent level annual dividend	10 years:	2.06	20 years:	6.14	Age 65:	6.59

Premium Page

Premium Information:	Annual	Semiannual	Quarterly	Pac.
Graded Premium (1st policy year)	$622.00	$318.96	$162.02	$54.20

27 ___ Annual Renewal Premiums: Graded Premium Life

2d year	$ 741.00	3d year	$ 860.00	4th year	$ 979.00	5th year	$1,098.00
6th	1,217.00	7th	1,336.00	8th	1,455.00	9th	1,574.00
10th	1,693.00	11th	1,812.00	12th	1,931.00	13th	2,050.00
14th	2,169.00	15th	2,288.00	16th	2,407.00	17th	2,526.00
18th	2,645.00	19th	2,764.00	20th	2,883.00	Thereafter	3,002.00

Figure A-3. (*Continued*)

8. The amount of premium to be paid each year.

9. The cash amount of premium to be paid each year (i.e., the gross premium for the first 20 years). Starting in year 21, the cash amount payable is 0.

10. The cumulative guaranteed amount of reserve (guaranteed cash value) that has accumulated for each year.

11. The cumulative total amount of reserve, ie., the guaranteed cash value including the nonguaranteed cash value of the additional

20 PAY LIFE ILLUSTRATION
Explanatory Notes

*Includes dividend values. Dividends are not guaranteed.___28_

Illustrated dividends are based on the company's current mortality, expense, and investment experience. Actual dividends may be higher or lower than shown as a result of future changes in the company's experience, especially the interest rates earned on investments. A terminal dividend is payable upon surrender, lapse, or death, after at least 15 policy years, but only if declared by the company at such time, and is included in the total death benefit, in summary values for total cash value and total paid-up insurance, and in the interest-adjusted surrender cost index.

*Illustrated dividends assume no loans on policy. Policy loans will affect dividends.___29_

_30_____†The values shown in the ledger assume an annual mode of premium payment and a fixed policy loan interest rate of 8.00% applied in arrears, except in the case of a partial cash premium payment; then, a change to the automatic monthly premium mode has been assumed. The issuance of any policies or riders is subject to the company's regular underwriting practices. The amounts of coverage and premiums for any policies or riders, if issued, may differ from those illustrated.

#Summary values are calculated as of the end of the year.___31_

Figure A-3. (Continued)

paid-up life insurance purchased each year, starting at the beginning of year 2, with the yearly declared paid dividend.

12. The yearly amount of increase in the total reserve (guaranteed cash value and nonguaranteed cash value of the additional paid-up insurance purchased each year).

13. The yearly difference between the gross premium paid each year and the yearly guaranteed cash-value increase and the yearly increase of the nonguaranteed cash value of the additional paid-up life insurance purchased by the yearly declared paid dividend. A minus sign (−) means the combined yearly increase is less than the gross premium paid in that year. A figure without a minus sign is mathematically correct, but it does not reflect the time value of money.

14. The amount of additional paid-up life insurance purchased by the declared paid dividend.

15. The yearly total death benefit including the projected additional paid-up life insurance purchased through the projected dividends. From year 16 on, the terminal dividend is included.

16. A statement indicating that dividends are used to purchase paid-up

insurance. The gross premium is paid during the first 20 years. Thereafter, dividends are used to reduce the gross premium and, if necessary, a portion of the paid-up insurance is surrendered to pay the balance of the gross premium. Looking at column 8 in year 21 reveals that this is unnecessary. The projected dividend in year 21 is $846, more than the ultimate graded premium life gross premium of $3002. When you see a minus sign (−) in this column, it means the amount of money that exceeds the gross premium. The statement, "Div. Adds Death Benefit reaches its lowest point in year 20" is a bug in the insurance company's ledger statement computer system, and should not be included for this ledger statement. Finally, from year 21 on, the dividend in excess of the ultimate gross premium of $3002 is used to purchase additional paid-up life insurance. If desired, the death benefit could be frozen at $147,283 (year 20) and the dividend amount in excess of the gross premium then could be paid in cash.

17. The life expectancy of a 45-year-old male is 29 years—age 74.

18. Summary page values for this insurance company's ledger statement are different from the values shown on the nonsummary pages for two reasons. First, the yearly declared dividend is assumed to be paid at the end of the year. Second, the terminal dividend is included. The insurance company assumes for the summary page that the policy is surrendered for the years shown.

19. Cumulative amount of guaranteed cash value for the years shown.

20. Cumulative amount of total cash value for the years shown including the nonguaranteed cash value of additional paid-up insurance purchased through the dividends.

21. The gross premium times the number of years shown.

22. The difference between column 21 and column 20. Although mathematically correct, it does not take into consideration the time value of money.

23. The amount of paid-up life insurance for the years shown that can be purchased by the guaranteed cash value. Once purchased, no additional premiums are required and the insurance company pays a paid-up dividend per $1000 of paid-up insurance.

24. The amount of paid-up life insurance for the years shown that can be purchased by the total cash value.

25. Terminal dividend, may be payable after the policy has been in force 15 years or longer.

26. Interest-adjusted index. There is a bug in the insurance company's system. The numerical figures should be the same for 20 years and age 65. The year 20 figures are correct.

27. Gross premium information for a graded premium whole life policy shown on an annual basis (payment once a year). Gross premium grades (increases each year) over a 20-year period, leveling off in year 21 at $3002. If the gross premium is not paid annually, the cost is higher. This is because the insurance company must send a bill more than once a year and the time value of money (the insurance company does not have the use of your money all at once).

28. Statement that dividends in any form are not guaranteed.

29. Statement that a loan against the reserve (cash value) will affect dividends.

30. Statement that the guaranteed fixed contractual interest rate charged for loans against the reserve is 8 percent payable in arrears, meaning that interest is due 1 year from the date of the loan.

31. Statement about the summary page calculations.

Ledger Statements Do Not Tell All.   You should be told either verbally or in writing the following additional information:

▪ What the insurance company assumes it must earn on money coming in the store (premium payments) to warrant the dividends projected. For the ledger statement you just read, the dividend interest assumption rate is 11.57 percent for the first year, graded up over a 20-year period to 11.73 percent.

▪ The investment strategy employed by the insurance company, which dictates the dividend interest assumption rate. For the ledger statement you just read, the investment strategy is a *weighted-average portfolio rate*. This means that 40 percent is weighted toward old money and 60 percent weighted toward new money. The insurance company, as part of its investment strategy, anticipates gains from real estate and common stock investments.

▪ Under what conditions your dividends will be reduced if you make a loan against the reserve (guaranteed cash value) of the policy. As stated in the ledger statement, the fixed guaranteed interest rate charged for loans against the reserve is 8 percent. Because the insurance company assumed that it must earn on money coming in from 11.57 percent to 11.73 percent, if only the fixed rate of 8 percent is paid, the dividend will be reduced because the insurance company is earning 3.57 to 3.73 percent less than it assumed.

▪ For example, in year 20, a maximum loan is made against the reserve (the guaranteed cash value) of $25,888. Ninety-two percent of $25,888 can be borrowed (less 8 percent interest) which is $23,816.96. One year later, interest of $1905.36 is due. The insurance company assumed it must earn 11.73 percent, which is $2793.73 (11.73 percent of $23,816.96). The difference between $2793.73 and $1905.36 is $888.37. Therefore, in year 21 your dividend will be reduced by $888.37. The projected dividend in year 21 will not be $846 in excess of the gross premium of $3002; instead it would fall $42.37 short. This means in year 21, $42.37 will have to be the cash payment, unless there still remains sufficient paid-up life insurance that can be surrendered.

▪ The effect of the reduction in dividend results in loan interest of 12 percent, not 8 percent. Interest of $1905.36 plus loss of dividend of $888.37 divided by the loan of $23,816.96 is 12 percent.

▪ Although not stated on the ledger statement, this particular insurance company gives the option of electing a variable loan rate versus the fixed loan rate. If the variable loan rate is equal to the dividend interest asssumption rate, the dividend will not be reduced. If the variable loan rate is in excess of the divdidend interest assumption rate, the dividend will be increased. At the time this book is being written, variable loan rates are in the range of 10.97 percent and 10.54 percent. This information should also be included on the ledger statement.

▪ The rate of return expressed in terms of compound interest should be given either on the ledger statement or by the life insurance agent. Ideally, it should be provided for each year. If the agent does not have the proper financial decisions software, it will be economically impossible to provide yearly rates of return. A financial decisions calculator (e.g., Hewlett-Packard 41C series with the financial decisions module) can be used, however, on an economical basis to provide rates of return for various years (year 1, year 5, year 10, year 20, and to life expectancy).

▪ The rate of return upon death for this policy for sequential years is as follows:

Year	Rate of return
1	15,977.17%
5	143.78
10	44.12
20	14.92
29 (life expectancy)	9.42

■ Once the rate of return upon death is known, then it can be determined what would have to be earned before taxes (it is assumed that the death benefit is considered life insurance proceeds and as such not subject to federal or state income taxes) in other financial services products (e.g., mutual funds, certificates of deposit, real estate, or commodities) to duplicate the tax-exempt rate of return provided by life insurance. The before-tax rate of return is determined by dividing the life insurance rate of return by the marginal tax bracket subtracted from 100 percent (for 15 percent, the factor is 0.85; for 28 percent, 0.72; for 33 percent, 0.67; and for 34 percent, 0.66). The result is as follows:

Year	15% taxpayer	28% taxpayer	33% taxpayer	34% taxpayer
1	18,796.67%	22,190.51%	23,846.52%	24,207.83%
5	169.15	199.69	214.60	217.85
10	51.91	61.28	65.85	66.85
20	17.55	20.72	22.27	22.61
29 (life expectancy)	11.08	13.08	14.06	14.27

■ The rate of return upon surrender should also be provided. When the rate of return upon surrender is positive, it means that taxes are due. Taxes are due on the difference between the cash-surrender value and the premiums paid. The result before taxes is as follows:

Year	Rate of return
1	− 100.00%
5	− 25.81
10	− 3.02
20	5.41
29 (life expectancy)	6.10

■ You should be reassured that the ledger statement is the official ledger statement produced by the computer service of the life insurance company. If it is not bug-free, the bugs should be revealed to you.

Interest-Sensitive Whole Life

How to Navigate Your Way through a Ledger Statement for Interest-Sensitive Whole Life (Figure A-4)

1. Base mandatory premium combined with a rider (similar to a paid-up additions rider for a traditional whole life policy) which accommodates additional money, resulting in an annual payment of $2001.

POLICY WITH ANNUAL PREMIUM SAVE PLUS   RIDER   _1_
PREFERRED CLASS   _2_

_3_ ISSUE AGE: 45 Male

_4_ Policy Year	_5_ Base Premium	_6_ Rider Premium	_7_ Total Premium	_8_ Total Death Benefit	_9_ Total Accumula-tion Account	_10_ Total Cash Value
1	$732.94	$1,268.06	$2,001.00	$103,674	$ 2,079	$ 1,298
2	732.94	1,268.06	2,001.00	107,435	4,310	3,282
3	732.94	1,268.06	2,001.00	111,317	6,441	5,359
4	732.94	1,268.06	2,001.00	115,331	8,744	7,700
5	732.94	1,268.06	2,001.00	119,490	11,237	10,300
6	732.94	1,268.06	2,001.00	123,807	13,938	13,119
7	732.94	1,268.06	2,001.00	128,297	16,862	16,078
8	732.94	1,268.06	2,001.00	132,978	20,029	19,279
9	732.94	1,268.06	2,001.00	137,867	23,456	22,740
10	732.94	1,268.06	2,001.00	142,977	27,153	26,470
11	732.94	1,268.06	2,001.00	148,325	31,136	30,522
12	732.94	1,268.06	2,001.00	153,927	35,426	34,880
13	732.94	1,268.06	2,001.00	159,797	40,038	39,561
14	732.94	1,268.06	2,001.00	165,951	44,991	44,582
15	732.94	1,268.06	2,001.00	172,404	50,299	49,958
16	732.94	1,268.06	2,001.00	179,170	55,973	55,700
17	732.94	1,268.06	2,001.00	186,305	62,081	61,877
18	732.94	1,268.06	2,001.00	193,838	68,650	68,514
19	732.94	1,268.06	2,001.00	201,800	75,707	75,639
20	732.94	1,268.06	2,001.00	210,226	83,281	83,282
21	732.94	−732.94	0.00	215,755	89,472	89,472
22	732.94	−732.94	0.00	221,679	96,098	96,098
23	732.94	−732.94	0.00	228,022	103,194	103,195
24	732.94	−732.94	0.00	234,818	110,804	110,804
25	732.94	−732.94	0.00	242,105	118,974	118,974
26	732.94	−732.94	0.00	249,924	127,739	127,740
27	732.94	−732.94	0.00	258,313	137,128	137,128
28	732.94	−732.94	0.00	267,331	147,179	147,180
29 _11_	732.94	−732.94	0.00	277,039	157,940	157,941
30	732.94	−732.94	0.00	287,491	169,455	169,455

Figure A-4. Ledger statement for interest-sensitive whole life.

2. Insurability classification for this company. Preferred means non-smoker and not rated extra because of medical and occupational reasons.

3. Gender and issue age—male, age 45.

4. This is an end-of-year ledger statement.

5. Base premium of $732.94 which must be paid each and every year that the policy is in force.

6. Rider premium of $1268.06 in addition to the mandatory base premium of $732.94. In year 21 and for every year thereafter, $732.94 is withdrawn [minus sign (−)] from the rider to pay the base premium of $732.94.

7. Total premium is $2001, consisting of $732.94 base premium and $1268 paid into the rider. $2001 is paid each year for 20 years. Starting in year 21 and every year thereafter, the premium outlay is 0. Base mandatory premium of $732.94 is paid by withdrawing $732.94 each year from the rider.

8. Total death benefit.

9. Accumulation account money.

10. Total cash value.

11. Life expectancy is 29 years for a 45-year-old, or to age 74.

Ledger Statements Do Not Tell All.   You should be told either verbally or in writing the following additional information:

■ The investment strategy employed by the life insurance company, (e.g., pure portfolio rate, modified portfolio rate, weighted-average portfolio rate, old money or new money) in order to warrant the current interest-rate assumption. Although not stated on the ledger statement, the current interest-rate assumption is 10.25 percent for 1 year and 9.5 percent thereafter. The guaranteed rate at all times is 5.5 percent. The actuarial department of the life insurance company was called and asked to state the investment strategy employed. The response was that it is classified information.

■ Although not stated on this ledger statement, other ledger statements from the same insurance company state "currently declared mortality." In addition to asking for the investment strategy employed, a definitive explanation of mortality charges as to the ratio of current charges to the maximum charges that can be imposed was asked for; again the response was that this is classified information.

■ What the interest rate is on the loan against the cash value. How much interest does the insurance company charge you? How much interest do they pay you on money you borrow? For this ledger statement, this information was revealed to me by calling the home office of the insurance company. They charge 7.41 percent in advance (most companies charge interest in arrears) and pay 6 percent on borrowed money (meaning that when you borrow out money you are not earning the current rate on the money). The interest-adjusted index is not indicated on this ledger statement. Make sure that this is provided on the ledger statement for insurance you purchase.

■ Total accumulation account value. This is the amount of money that is earning interest based on the current interest-rate assumption (i.e., 10.25 for 1 year and 9.5 percent thereafter). It is not, however, the amount of money you would receive if the policy is surrendered. It is also not the amount of money you can borrow against.

■ The total cash value includes the value of the rider plus the guaranteed reserve (cash value) of the policy. This is the amount of money that you receive if you surrender the policy and is the amount of money you can borrow against. For balance sheet purposes, this value must be used, not the total accumulation account value. These respective values become the same in year 20 (within a penny). They are different before year 20 because this is a 20-year rear-end-loaded contract. As such, there are penalties imposed if the policy is terminated before 20 years.

■ The rate of return expressed in terms of compound interest should be given either on the ledger statement or by the life insurance agent. Ideally, it should be provided for each year. If the agent does not have the proper financial decisions software, it will be economically impossible to provide yearly rates of return. A financial decisions calculator (e.g., Hewlett-Packard 41C Series with the financial decisions module) can be used, however, on an economical basis to provide rates of return for various years (year 1, year 5, year 10, year 20, and to life expectancy).

■ The rate of return upon death for this policy for sequential years is as follows:

Year	Rate of return
1	5,081.11%
5	98.20
10	34.46
20	14.10
29 (life expectancy)	9.66

■ Once the rate of return upon death is known, then it can be determined what would have to be earned before taxes (it is assumed that the death benefit is considered life insurance proceeds and as such not subject to federal or state income taxes) in other financial services products (e.g., mutual funds, certificates of deposit, real estate, or commodities) to duplicate the tax-exempt rate of return provided by life insurance. The before-tax rate of return is determined by dividing the life insurance rate of return by the marginal tax bracket subtracted from 100 percent—for 15 percent, the factor is 0.85; for 28 percent, 0.72; for 33 percent, 0.67; and for 34 percent, 0.66. The result is as follows:

Year	15% taxpayer	28% taxpayer	33% taxpayer	34% taxpayer
1	5,977.78%	7,057.10%	7,583.75%	7,698.65%
5	115.53	136.39	146.57	148.79
10	40.54	47.86	51.43	52.21
20	16.59	19.58	21.04	21.36
29 (life expectancy)	11.36	13.42	14.42	14.64

■ The rate of return upon surrender should also be provided. When the rate of return upon surrender is positive, it means that taxes are due. Taxes are due on the difference between the cash-surrender value and the premiums paid. The result before taxes is as follows:

Year	Rate of return
1	− 35.13%
5	0.97
10	5.03
20	6.56
29 (life expectancy)	6.89

■ The rate of return upon surrender even before taxes never equals the interest assumption of 10.25 percent for 1 year and 9.5 percent thereafter.

■ You should be reassured that the ledger statement is the official ledger statement produced by the computer service of the life insurance company. If it is not bug-free, the bugs should be revealed to you. In addition, make sure that the ledger statement contains the following information: guaranteed interest rate to be paid on the cash value, the current interest rate, mortality charges statement, interest-adjusted index, guaranteed fixed loan rate charged for loans made against the cash value, and interest paid on borrowed money.

Universal Life

How to Navigate Your Way through a Ledger Statement for Universal Life (Figure A-5)

1. Flexible premium adjustable life is the type of insurance. The generic name is universal life. "For use in Massachusetts" means the policy form has been approved by the Insurance Department of the Department of Banking and Insurance, Division of Insurance, Commonwealth of Massachusetts. "Approved" does not mean "recommended." It means that the policy form has met the require-

1 FLEXIBLE PREMIUM ADJUSTABLE LIFE FOR USE IN MASSACHUSETTS

PREMIUMS: FIRST YEAR: $2,001.00 *2*
INCREASING DEATH BENEFIT OPTION *3*
CLASSIFICATION: Preferred *4*

INSURANCE AGE: 45   SEX: Male *5*
THEREAFTER: Varying *6*
INITIAL FACE AMOUNT: $100000 *7*
PAYMENT MODE: Annual *8*

9 End of Year	Age	*10* Yearly Premium	*11* Annual Withdrawal	*12* Guaranteed Interest of 4.5%			*13* Assumed Interest of 8.00%		
				Cash Value	Net Cash Value	Death Benefit	Cash Value	Net Cash Value	Death Benefit
1	46	$2,001.00	$0	$ 1,749	$ 809	$101,749	$ 1,749	$ 809	$101,749
2	47	2,001.00	0	3,198	2,362	103,198	3,615	2,779	103,615
3	48	2,001.00	0	4,658	3,927	104,658	5,606	4,874	105,606
4	49	2,001.00	0	6,124	5,497	106,124	7,731	7,104	107,731
5	50	2,001.00	0	7,589	7,067	107,589	9,999	9,476	109,999
6	51	2,001.00	0	9,047	8,629	109,047	12,416	11,998	112,416
7	52	2,001.00	0	10,490	10,177	110,490	14,994	14,681	114,994
8	53	2,001.00	0	11,911	11,702	111,911	17,744	17,536	117,744
9	54	2,001.00	0	13,301	13,196	113,301	20,678	20,574	120,678
10	55	2,001.00	0	14,650	14,650	114,650	23,810	23,810	123,810
11	56	2,001.00	0	15,948	15,948	115,948	27,155	27,155	127,155
12	57	2,001.00	0	17,180	17,180	117,180	30,724	30,724	130,724
13	58	2,001.00	0	18,332	18,332	118,332	34,533	34,533	134,533
14	59	2,001.00	0	19,386	19,386	119,386	38,596	38,596	138,596
15	60	2,001.00	0	20,326	20,326	120,326	42,925	42,925	142,925
16	61	2,001.00	0	21,129	21,129	121,129	47,538	47,538	147,538
17	62	2,001.00	0	21,773	21,773	121,773	52,444	52,444	152,444
18	63	2,001.00	0	22,235	22,235	122,235	57,658	57,658	157,658
19	64	2,001.00	0	22,486	22,486	122,486	63,189	63,189	163,189
20	65	2,001.00	0	22,495	22,495	122,495	69,052	69,052	169,052

Assumed interest rates are for illustrative purposes only; actual rates may be more or less than those shown.

Figure A-5. Ledger statement for universal life.

ments of the Insurance Department and may be distributed for sale to residents of the Commonwealth of Massachusetts.

2. The premium is $2001.

3. The initial death benefit of $100,000 is increased each and every year by the cash-value amount of the policy. This is referred to as *universal life option II.*

4. Insurability status—e.g., nonsmoker or smoker (would be standard), or rated (extra charge because of being a higher risk for medical or occupational reasons). The preferred risk for this company means nonsmoker, nonrated. It is the company's best insurability classification.

FLEXIBLE PREMIUM ADJUSTABLE LIFE

End of Year	Age	Yearly Premium	Annual With-drawal	Guaranteed Interest of 4.5%			Assumed Interest of 8.00%		
				Cash Value	Net Cash Value	Death Benefit	Cash Value	Net Cash Value	Death Benefit
21	66	$0	$0	$20,262	$20,262	$120,262	$ 73,226	$ 73,226	$173,226
22	67	0	0	17,621	17,621	117,621	77,590	77,590	177,590
23	68	0	0	14,522	14,522	114,522	82,149	82,149	182,149
24	69	0	0	10,909	10,909	110,909	86,907	86,907	186,907
25	70	0	0	6,730	6,730	106,730	91,866	91,866	191,866
26	71	0	0	1,931	1,931	101,931	97,027	97,027	197,027
27	72	0	0	*******	*******	*******	102,393	102,393	202,393
28	73	0	0				107,962	107,962	207,962
14 29	74	0	0				113,730	113,730	213,730
30	75	0	0				119,691	119,691	219,691
31	76	0	0				125,835	125,835	225,835
32	77	0	0				132,128	132,128	232,128
33	78	0	0				138,495	138,495	238,495
34	79	0	0				144,836	144,836	244,836
35	80	0	0				150,981	150,981	250,981
36	81	0	0				156,756	156,756	256,756
37	82	0	0				162,020	162,020	262,020
38	83	0	0				166,526	166,526	266,526
39	84	0	0				170,032	170,032	270,032
40	85	0	0				172,170	172,170	272,170

Figure A-5. (*Continued*)

5. Gender and issue age—male, age 45.

6. A premium of $2001 is paid each year for 20 years. Starting in year 21, the premium is 0.

7. The initial face amount of life insurance payable to the named beneficiary is $100,000.

8. The premium is to be paid annually (once a year).

9. This is an end-of-the-year ledger statement.

10. A yearly premium of $2001 is paid once a year each and every year for the first 20 years.

11. The amount withdrawn from the cash value as a living benefit. For this ledger statement, there are no withdrawals.

12. Guaranteed interest of 4.5 percent column. This is the minimum percentage rate at which the insurance company will accumulate

FLEXIBLE PREMIUM ADJUSTABLE LIFE
Plan Summary Page___15___

Based on the Current Interest Rate

End of Year	(1) Total Premiums	(2) Total Withdrawals	(3) Net Cash Value	(4) Difference (1) (2) + (3)	(5) Cash Value	(6) Death Benefit
5	$10,005	$0	$ 9,593	$ 411	$10,116	$110,116
10	20,010	0	24,450	4,440−	24,450	124,450
15	30,015	0	45,445	15,430−	45,445	145,445
20	40,020	0	76,137	36,117−	76,137	176,137
Age 65	40,020	0	76,137	36,117−	76,137	176,137

Interest-Adjusted Indexes Based on a 5.00% Interest Rate for Basic Policy Only___16___

	Guaranteed Interest of 4.5%		Current		Assumed Interest of 8.00%	
	10 Years	20 Years	10 Years	20 Years	10 Years	20 Years
Surrender Cost	$ 8.39	$12.18	$ 1.38	$ 1.58−	$ 1.82	$ .10
Net Payment	18.84	18.01	18.41	16.46	18.44	16.60

Figure A-5. (*Continued*)

the reserve. Under this column are cash value, net cash value, and death benefit. The cash value is the amount of reserve earning interest. It is not, however, available to borrow against nor is it the amount received if the policy is surrendered. The net cash value is the amount of money in any given year that is available to borrow against and is the amount of money payable if the policy is surrendered. It is also the amount that must appear on the balance sheet when necessary. The death benefit is based on the current interest rate of 8.5 percent for the first year only. Thereafter, the guaranteed minimum rate of 4.5 percent applies. The current mortality charges are for the first year only. Thereafter, the maximum mortality charges can be imposed. Under these assumptions, if no further premiums are paid, the insurance will lapse at age 72. For assumption purposes, the guaranteed section is the worst possible scenario.

13. Assumed interest of 8 percent column (the current interest rate is 8.5 percent for the first 10 years and 9.1 percent thereafter) is 50 basis points (0.50 percent) for the first 10 years and 110 basis points (1.1 percent) *less* than the current rate. Cash value is predicated on

---

FLEXIBLE PREMIUM ADJUSTABLE LIFE
Explanatory Notes Page_____17

The current rate is 8.50% for the first 10 years and 9.10% thereafter._____18
Each premium is credited with interest at the current rate of the company. The rate for the policy reflects the weighted average of the rate on each premium. A portion of the cash value is reinvested at the end of each year at the then-current rate._____19

The interest rates shown are effective annual rates. Interest is credited after deduction of expense and cost of insurance charges._____20

A policy loan balance may not be credited with the full current interest rate, but the rate applied will not be less than the greater of 4.5% and 2% less than the policy loan interest rate._____21

The net cash value equals the cash value minus any policy loan balance minus any surrender charge._____22

Actual amounts may differ from those shown due to changes in: current interest rate, cost of insurance rate, face amount, timing or amount of premiums, or death benefit option._____23

It is unlikely that dividends will be paid on this policy. Dividends, if any, will be small and paid only in later policy years._____24

This illustration incorporates the company's interpretation of the Tax Reform Act of 1984 as it pertains to the definition of life insurance in general and universal life in particular. The company will comply with any IRS regulations issued regarding its interpretation of the definition of life insurance._____25

The "Current" column uses current mortality costs and current interest rate, which are not guaranteed beyond the first year._____26

The "Guaranteed" column uses the current mortality costs for the first year and the current interest rate guaranteed for the initial premium. Thereafter, this column uses the guaranteed minimum interest rate and guaranteed maximum mortality costs._____27

_____28_____A fixed policy loan interest rate of 8% applied in arrears will be charged on any policy loan balance.

Actual interest will be credited on a daily basis as of the date the payment is received at the company's home office._____29

Figure A-5. (*Continued*)

an 8 percent interest assumption. This is also true for the net cash value and the death benefit. The assumed rate of 8 percent was chosen by myself; this is an example of the range approach.

14. Life expectancy of a 45-year-old male is 29 years, or age 74.

15. Summary page indicates values based on the current interest rate, not the assumed rate. The assumed rate of 8 percent is less than the current rate, i.e., 8.5 percent for the first 10 years and 9.1 percent thereafter.

16. Interest adjusted index: guaranteed interest rate, current interest rate, and assumed rate.

17. Explanatory notes page.

18. Statement about the current interest rate at the time the ledger statement was printed.

19. Investment strategy of the insurance company.

20. Statement about how interest is credited.

21. Borrowed money does not earn current interest rate of 8.5 percent. Will earn either 4.5 percent or 2 percent less than the current rate, whichever is greater.

22. The net cash value and the cash value are different up to year 10. Prior to year 10, the cash value is less than the net cash value because of a rear-end load. There are penalties if the policy is surrendered prior to the end of year 10.

23. Variables due to changes in interest rates, mortality charges, how premiums are paid, or changes in the death benefit option, e.g., going from option II to option I.

24. Dividend statement.

25. Insurance company statement that the ledger statement conforms to the Tax Reform Act of 1984 and meets the various tests, i.e., the net single premium, cash-value accumulation, and corridor tests, as well as the guideline on annual premium for all policies issued on or after December 31, 1984.

26. Current column not used for this ledger statement. Guaranteed and assumed columns are used.

27. Guaranteed interest rate column statement.

28. Fixed contractual loan interest rate on loans against the reserve (net cash value) is 8 percent.

29. Interest statement.

Ledger Statements Do Not Tell All.   You should be told either verbally or in writing the following additional information:

▪ The investment strategy employed by the life insurance company is a modified portfolio rate, using a percentage rollover concept with investments having a maturity date of 6 to 8 years. Percentage rollover means that X percent of previously invested money plus interest earned on the reserve (the cash value) is rolled over each and every year into a new-money rate.

▪ The ratio of current mortality charges as used in the ledger statement to the maximum charges that can be imposed should be revealed. For this ledger statement, the ratio of current charges to maximum charges for sequential years is as follows. The charges are shown on an

annual basis (the actual mortality charges are deducted monthly) per
$1000 of insurance at risk.

Year	Age	Current	Maximum	Ratio
1	45	2.80	5.35	52%
5	50	3.72	7.60	49
10	55	5.37	11.91	45
15	60	7.69	18.62	41
20	65	11.93	29.11	41

■ This reveals that there is ample margin for the insurance company
to increase its mortality charges to cover itself against: unduly high rates
of mortality (such as that which occurs among AIDS sufferers), changes
in current tax law which governs how life insurance companies pay
taxes, and just about any other area that may increase the cost of doing
business.

■ This particular universal life product has been priced by the insurance company to make a profit or a contribution to surplus, essentially
through the investment spread.

■ If necessary, the insurance company by contract can and will de-
crease the current interest rate to as low as 4.5 percent and increase the
mortality charges to their maximum — if the cost of doing business so
dictates.

■ The rate of return expressed in terms of compound interest should
be given either on the ledger statement or by the life insurance agent.
Ideally, it should be provided for each year. If the agent does not have
the proper financial decisions software, it will be economically impossible
to provide yearly rates of return. A financial decisions calculator (e.g.,
Hewlett-Packard 41C Series with the financial decisions module) can be
used, however, on an economical basis to provide rates of return for various years (year 1, year 5, year 10, year 20, and to life expectancy).

■ The rate of return upon death for this policy for sequential years is
as follows:

Year	Rate of return
1	4,984.91%
5	94.28
10	31.93
20	12.37
29 (life expectancy)	8.38

■ Once the rate of return upon death is known, then it can be determined what would have to be earned before taxes (it is assumed that the
death benefit is considered life insurance proceeds and as such not subject to federal or state income taxes) in other financial services products

(e.g., mutual funds, certificates of deposit, real estate, or commodities) to duplicate the tax-exempt rate of return provided by life insurance. The before-tax rate of return is determined by dividing the life insurance rate of return by the marginal tax bracket subtracted from 100 percent (for 15 percent, the factor is 0.85; for 28 percent, 0.72; for 33 percent, 0.67; and for 34 percent, 0.66). The result is as follows:

Year	15% taxpayer	28% taxpayer	33% taxpayer	34% taxpayer
1	5,864.60%	6,923.49%	7,440.16%	7,552.89%
5	110.92	130.94	140.72	142.85
10	37.56	44.35	47.66	48.38
20	14.55	17.18	18.46	18.74
29 (life expectancy)	9.86	11.64	12.51	12.70

▪ The rate of return upon surrender should also be provided. When the rate of return upon surrender is positive, it means that taxes are due. Taxes are due on the difference between the cash-surrender value and the premiums paid. The result before taxes is as follows:

Year	Rate of return
1	− 59.57%
5	− 1.81
10	3.14
20	4.95
29 (life expectancy)	5.27

▪ The rate of return upon surrender even before taxes never equals the interest assumption of 8 percent.

▪ You should be reassured that the ledger statement is the official ledger statement produced by the computer service of the life insurance company. If it is not bug-free, the bugs should be revealed to you.

Variable Life

How to Navigate Your Way through a Ledger Statement for Variable Life (Figure A-6)

1. Initial death benfit is $100,000; plan of life insurance is variable life.

2. Gender and issue age — male, age 45.

3. $2394 is the annual premium.

4. Projected dividends are determined by mortality and expense factors used to purchase variable benefit paid-up life insurance. The projected dividends are small (e.g., at the beginning of the following years: $490, second; $592, fifth; $652, tenth; and $453, twentieth).

$100,000 Variable Whole Life Plan___*1*
For Age 45 Male___*2*
Annual Premium $2,394___*3*

4
Dividends Used to Purchase Paid-up Additions

5	*6*	*7*	*8*	*9*	*10*	*11*	*12*	*13*
		Premi-ums Accumu-lated	Death Benefit* Assumed Investment Returns			Cash Value* Assumed Investment Returns		
End of Year	Annual Premium	at 5%	0%	6%	12%	0%	6%	12%
1	$2,394	$ 2,514	$101,367	$101,391	$101,532	$ 1,103	$ 1,154	$ 1,205
2	2,394	5,153	102,707	102,880	103,510	3,145	3,372	3,606
3	2,394	7,924	104,024	104,471	105,962	5,164	5,700	6,268
4	2,394	10,834	105,304	106,157	108,904	7,156	8,137	9,216
5	2,394	13,890	106,549	107,941	112,382	9,201	10,776	12,572
6	2,394	17,098	107,749	109,818	116,420	11,214	13,536	16,286
7	2,394	20,467	108,910	111,797	121,060	13,190	16,422	20,395
8	2,394	24,004	110,023	113,872	126,335	15,126	19,434	24,935
9	2,394	27,717	111,088	116,046	132,287	17,013	22,573	29,949
10	2,394	31,617	112,107	118,327	138,968	18,853	25,845	35,485
11	2,394	35,712	113,068	120,705	146,416	20,634	29,248	41,591
12	2,394	40,011	113,961	123,176	154,678	22,351	32,782	48,320
13	2,394	44,525	114,772	125,729	163,796	23,999	36,451	55,733
14	2,394	49,265	115,490	128,357	173,818	25,570	40,255	63,896
15	2,394	54,242	116,104	131,052	184,800	27,055	44,192	72,874
16	2,394	59,468	116,604	133,808	196,801	28,444	48,262	82,743
17	2,394	64,955	116,984	136,624	209,890	29,727	52,460	93,580
18	2,394	70,716	117,238	139,502	224,146	30,891	56,784	105,469
19	2,394	76,766	117,359	142,443	239,654	31,923	61,230	118,496
20	2,394	83,118	117,334	145,442	256,496	32,806	65,790	132,756
@60	2,394	54,242	116,104	131,052	184,800	27,055	44,192	72,874
@65	2,394	83,118	117,334	145,442	256,496	32,806	65,790	132,756
@75	2,394	167,007	112,535	180,166	527,026	34,997	118,565	374,646

PREMIUMS   Annual   Mo. ISA
*14*___Insurance   2394.00   211.10
SUBJECT TO UNDERWRITING LIMITS___*15*
SELECT___*16*
*17*___*Dividends based on current scale—1988 issue. Not an estimate or guarantee of future results. Hypothetical investment results are illustrations only and should not be deemed representative of past or future investment results. Results illustrated assume no loans. 8% loan provision. This illustration must be preceded or accompanied by a current prospectus.

Figure A-6. Ledger statement for variable life.

5. End-of-year ledger statement. This means the initial death benefit of $100,000 is assumed to be paid at the beginning of the year; subsequent death benefit depending upon the interest assumption (e.g., 0 percent, 6 percent, and 12 percent) assumed to be paid at the end of the year. Cash values (the assumed values of the separate investment account — 0, 6, and 12 percent) are calculated as of the end of the year.

6. Out-of-pocket cash payment is $2394 each year, paid on an annual (once a year) basis.

7. 5 percent interest assumption column. The value of $2394 compounded at 5 percent if not used to purchase life insurance.

8. Death benefit increase because of the projected dividends purchasing additional paid-up life insurance. In the absence of dividends, the death benefit would not increase because the separate investment account must produce a rate of return in excess of 4 percent in order for the death benefit to increase.

9. Death benefit increases due to the projected dividends purchasing additional paid-up life insurance and the 6 percent interest assumption is 2 percent higher than 4 percent.

10. Death benefit increases due to projected dividends purchasing additional paid-up life insurance and 12 percent interest assumption is 8 percent higher than 4 percent.

11. This column has a value even at 0 percent interest assumption because not all of the premiums paid were required to meet the insurance company's expenses.

12. The projected value of the separate investment account (cash value) based on a net investment return (after expenses and deductions) of 6 percent.

13. The projected value of the separate investment account (cash value) based on a net investment return (after expenses and deductions) of 12 percent.

14. Annual premium for $100,000 variable life is $2394; the monthly premium by automatic deduction from checking account is $211.10.

15. The underwriting requirements (medical, social, and economic) of the insurance company must be met, in order for the insurance to be issued.

16. Insurability status — e.g., nonsmoker or smoker, or rated (extra charge because of being a higher risk for medical or occupational reasons).

Select for this company means nonsmoker, nonrated. It is the company's best insurability classification.

17. Statement about dividends, assumed investment returns (e.g., 6 percent and 12 percent) and loan interest of 8 percent. In addition, there is a statement pertaining to the prospectus which clearly indicates that variable life is considered a security and as such must be registered with the Securities and Exchange Commission (SEC).

Ledger Statements Do Not Tell All.   You should be told either verbally or in writing the following additional information:

■ The separate investment account—which is analogous to the reserve (cash value) of traditional whole life and graded premium life, interest sensitive, and universal life—is made up of four divisions: stock, bond, money market, and master (common stock, other equity securities, bonds, and money market instruments) portfolio. Inquire about what percentage of your net premium (after expenses and deductions) can go into each. In addition, find out how often you can change from one to the other.

■ There is an issue about various expenses and deductions, as to whether or not they are contractually guaranteed not to increase. For this company, variable life policy charges to the policy are: sales loads, policy fees, annual administrative charges, state premium tax, and risk charge. Charges to the separate investment account are: cost of insurance (mortality charges), mortality and risk expense, and management fees and expenses. Ask for a total disclosure of each.

■ The rate of return expressed in terms of compound interest should be given either on the ledger statement or by the life insurance agent. Ideally, it should be provided for each year. If the agent does not have the proper financial decisions software, it will be economically impossible to provide yearly rates of return. A financial decisions calculator (e.g., Hewlett-Packard 41C Series with the financial decisions module) can be used, however, on an economical basis to provide rates of return for various years (year 1, year 5, year 10, year 20, and to life expectancy).

■ The rate of return upon death for this policy for sequential years is as follows:

Year	Rate of return
1	4,141.10%
5	86.94
10	30.81
20	14.25

■ The above rates are based on a 12 percent interest assumption death benefit.

■ The rate of return upon death can be used when comparing various variable life policies among respected companies. (They can also be used for any life insurance policy.) Consider the following example:

Rate of return upon death in year 20	Cost per $1000 of life insurance per year for 20 years
14.25%	$ 9.34
14.23	9.36
13.25	10.59
13.00	10.93

■ How were these numbers determined? $1000 is the future value (death benefit) to be paid, 20 years is the time. Interest is known (14.25 percent, 12.23 percent, 13.25 percent, 13 percent). You then solve for payment—how much must be spent each year to accumulate $1000 in 20 years at the various interest rates?

■ Once the rate of return upon death is known, then it can be determined what would have to be earned before taxes (it is assumed that the death benefit is considered life insurance proceeds and as such not subject to federal or state income taxes) in other financial services products (e.g., mutual funds, certificates of deposit, real estate, or commodities) to duplicate the tax-exempt rate of return provided by life insurance. The before-tax rate of return is determined by dividing the life insurance rate of return by the marginal tax bracket subtracted from 100 percent (for 15 percent, the factor is 0.85; for 28 percent, 0.72; for 33 percent, 0.67; and for 34 percent, 0.66). The result is as follows:

Year	15% taxpayer	28% taxpayer	33% taxpayer	34% taxpayer
1	4,871.88%	5,751.53%	6,180.75%	6,274.39%
5	102.28	120.75	129.76	131.73
10	36.25	42.79	45.99	46.68
20	16.76	19.79	21.27	21.59

■ The rate of return upon surrender should also be provided. When the rate of return upon surrender is positive, it means that taxes are due. Taxes are due on the difference between the cash-surrender value and the premiums paid. The result before taxes is as follows:

Year	Rate of return
1	− 49.67%
5	1.64
10	7.05
20	8.95

■ The above rates of return are based on a 12 percent interest assumption separate investment account performance. The rate of return upon surrender even before taxes never equals the separate investment account investment performance of 12 percent.

■ The premiums accumulated at 5 percent column on the ledger statement replaces the Interest Adjusted Index. This is what your money would be worth at 5 percent net after taxes if not used to purchase life insurance. In order to net 5 percent after taxes, the before-tax rate of return in the following tax brackets is:

15% taxpayer	28% taxpayer	33% taxpayer	34% taxpayer
5.88%	6.94%	7.46%	7.58%

■ You should be reassured that the ledger statement is the official ledger statement produced by the computer service of the life insurance company. If it is not bug-free, the bugs should be revealed to you.

Policy Currently in Force

How to Navigate Your Way through a Ledger Statement for a Policy Currently in Force (Figure A-7)

1. Policy number for existing policy.
2. Ordinary life (whole life) plan of insurance.
3. Insurability classification. The insured is a nonsmoker having no medical or occupational reasons to pay more for life insurance. Preferred standard is this company's best insurability classification.
4. Insurance issued at age 31. Gender, male. Policy is now 6 years old.
5. Initial face amount payable to named beneficiary—$100,000.
6. Insured pays the premium on a semiannual (twice a year) basis of $713.20.
7. Annual premium (payable once a year) is $1391.
8. Beginning-of-the-year ledger statement. All values on the nonsummary pages are based on the beginning of the year, not the end of the year.
9. Annual premium to be paid. In year 1992, $329 to be paid because the dividend payable at the beginning of year 1992 is used to reduce the insurance premium. In 1996, the yearly paid dividend exceeds the gross premium of $1391 by $87. In this column, when you see a minus (−) sign, it means that the numerical figure exceeds

PREMIUM OFFSET ILLUSTRATION—POLICY NO. 12345678___1

†PLAN: Ordinary Life___2___
CLASS: Preferred Standard___3___
Male Issue Age 31___4___

5___Face Amount: $100,000
6___1988 Semiannual Premium: $713.20
7___1988 Total Annual Premium: $1,391.00

8 Year Beg. Prem. Anniv.	9 Annual Pre- mium Payable*	10 Cash Pre- mium Payment*	11 Div. Adds Death Benefit*	12 Div. Adds Cash Value*	13 Guar. Cash Value	14 Total Cash Value*	15 Ann. Incr. in Total Cash Value*	16 Total Cash Value Incr.(−) Prem Pymt.*	17 Total Death Benefit*
1988	$1,391	$1,391	$ 0	$ 0	$ 6,779	$ 6,779			$100,000
1989	1,391	1,391	2,040	609	8,161	8,770	$1,991	$ 600	102,040
1990	1,391	1,391	4,483	1,382	9,581	10,963	2,193	802	104,483
1991	1,391	1,391	7,310	2,327	11,036	13,363	2,400	1,009	107,310
1992	329	0	6,309	2,073	12,432	14,505	1,142	1,142	106,309
1993	242	0	5,595	1,898	13,859	15,757	1,251	1,251	105,595
1994	152	0	5,161	1,806	15,319	17,125	1,368	1,368	105,161
1995	39	0	5,052	1,824	16,810	18,634	1,508	1,508	105,052
1996	87−	0	5,286	1,968	18,332	20,300	1,666	1,666	105,286
1997	220−	0	5,860	2,248	19,883	22,131	1,832	1,832	105,970
1998	364−	0	6,782	2,682	21,463	24,145	2,013	2,013	107,005
1999	516−	0	8,050	3,279	23,069	26,348	2,203	2,203	108,402
2000	680−	0	9,671	4,057	24,700	28,757	2,408	2,408	110,169
2001	865−	0	11,675	5,041	26,354	31,395	2,638	2,638	112,337
2002	1,064−	0	14,070	6,250	28,029	34,279	2,885	2,885	114,913
2003	1,291−	0	16,895	7,719	29,725	37,444	3,165	3,165	117,803
2004	1,542−	0	20,179	9,478	31,439	40,917	3,473	3,473	121,154
2005	1,817−	0	23,945	11,556	33,170	44,726	3,809	3,809	124,989
2006	2,124−	0	28,230	13,993	34,917	48,910	4,184	4,184	129,345
2007	2,459−	0	33,062	16,824	36,677	53,501	4,591	4,591	134,249

Illustrated dividends* are used to purchase additional paid-up insurance years 1988 through 1991. Thereafter, dividends are used to reduce premiums, and if necessary, a portion of the ___18___ paid-up insurance is surrendered to pay the balance of the premium. Dividends illustrated are not guaranteed and will vary.
1988 Benefits/Coverages: Waiver___19___

Figure A-7. Ledger statement for policy currently in force.

(Continued)

The gross premium by that amount. For this ledger statement, when the dividend exceeds the gross premium, it is used to purchase additional paid-up life insurance.

10. Out-of-pocket expense paid by insured. From year 1992 on, it is 0 because the yearly dividend is used to reduce the gross premium of $1391. Any balance due (e.g., $329 in 1992; $242 in 1993; $152 in

PREMIUM OFFSET ILLUSTRATION—POLICY NO. 12345678

Year Beg. Prem. Anniv.		Annual Premium Payable*	Cash Premium Payment*	Div. Adds Death Benefit*	Div. Adds Cash Value*	Guar. Cash Value	Total Cash Value*	Ann. Incr. in Total Cash Value*	Total Cash Value Incr.(−) Prem. Pymt.*	Total Death Benefit*
2008		$ 2,824−	$0	$ 38,470	$ 20,087	$38,448	$ 58,535	$ 5,034	$ 5,034	$139,732
2009		3,224−	0	44,491	23,825	40,225	64,050	5,515	5,515	145,829
2010		3,668−	0	51,173	28,090	42,008	70,098	6,048	6,048	152,589
2011		4,156−	0	58,563	32,934	43,792	76,726	6,628	6,628	160,058
2012		4,694−	0	66,715	38,417	45,575	83,992	7,265	7,265	168,292
2013		5,288−	0	75,688	44,602	47,355	91,957	7,966	7,966	177,347
2014		5,937−	0	85,538	51,555	49,128	100,683	8,726	8,726	187,281
2015		6,651−	0	96,334	59,351	50,891	110,242	9,559	9,559	198,162
2016		7,476−	0	108,212	68,109	52,640	120,749	10,506	10,506	210,126
2017		8,346−	0	121,200	77,883	54,369	132,252	11,503	11,503	223,200
2018		9,322−	0	135,417	88,786	56,074	144,860	12,608	12,608	237,505
2019		10,397−	0	150,970	100,925	57,746	158,671	13,811	13,811	253,146
2020		11,593−	0	167,989	114,424	59,384	173,808	15,137	15,137	270,253
2021		12,910−	0	186,605	129,411	60,986	190,397	16,589	16,589	288,957
2022		14,359−	0	206,955	146,025	62,556	208,581	18,185	18,185	309,394
2023	20	15,946−	0	229,181	164,424	64,099	228,523	19,941	19,941	331,683
2024		17,674−	0	253,422	184,765	65,622	250,387	21,864	21,864	355,986
2025		19,554−	0	279,826	207,231	67,129	274,360	23,973	23,973	382,451
2026		21,607−	0	308,561	232,019	68,619	300,638	26,279	26,279	411,246
2027		23,867−	0	339,834	259,358	70,088	329,446	28,808	28,808	442,579
2028		26,400−	0	373,931	289,524	71,526	361,050	31,604	31,604	476,735
2029		29,203−	0	411,127	322,784	72,923	395,707	34,657	34,657	513,988
2030		32,300−	0	451,723	359,418	74,270	433,688	37,981	37,981	554,640
2031		35,687−	0	496,009	399,699	75,564	475,263	41,575	41,575	598,980
2032		39,363−	0	544,271	443,907	76,805	520,712	45,450	45,450	647,294
2033		43,343−	0	596,810	492,344	77,995	570,339	49,627	49,627	699,882
2034		47,639−	0	653,935	545,343	79,141	624,484	54,144	54,144	757,055
2035		52,270−	0	715,970	603,269	80,250	683,519	59,036	59,036	819,136
2036		57,280−	0	783,283	666,543	81,327	747,870	64,350	64,350	886,493
2037		62,734−	0	856,307	735,645	82,381	818,026	70,156	70,156	959,560

Dividends illustrated are not guaranteed and will vary.

Figure A-7. (Continued)

1994; $39 in 1995) is paid by surrendering a portion of paid-up life insurance purchased from years 1988 through 1991.

11. The cumulative amount of paid-up life insurance purchased by the projected dividends.

12. The cumulative cash value of the paid-up life insurance purchased by the dividends. Although mathematically correct, it does not take into consideration the time value of money.

PREMIUM OFFSET ILLUSTRATION—POLICY NO. 12345678
Summary Page___21___

22___Time Period	23___Guar. Cash Value	24___Total Cash Value*	25___Cash Premium Payments*	26___Total Cash Value Less Prem. Pymts.*
5 years	$12,432	$ 14,505	$5,564	$ 8,941
10 years	19,883	22,241	5,564	16,677
15 years	28,029	35,122	5,564	29,558
20 years	36,677	54,688	5,564	49,124
Age 65	52,640	122,663	5,564	117,099

27___Terminal dividend*   1997 $110.00   2002 $843.00   Age 65 $1,914.00

1988 Premium Information	Pd. up/Ren. Date	Annual	Semiannual
Ordinary life	Jan. 20, 2051	$1356.00	$695.26
Waiver	Jan. 20, 2016	$35.00	$17.94

Explanatory Notes

28___ *Includes dividend values. The dividend levels in this illustration are based on the company's current experience with respect to mortality, persistency, taxes, expenses, and investments. They are not guaranteed. The dividends actually paid will be determined by the company's future experience in these factors and will likely differ from those illustrated, being either higher or lower.

29___ Among these dividend factors, investment earnings are of major significance. The illustrated dividends assume continuation of the company's current investments experience. If all other dividend factors were to remain at current experience levels, future dividends would be higher or lower than those illustrated, depending upon future investment earnings.

30___ A terminal dividend may be payable on surrender, lapse, or death after at least 15 policy years if declared by the company, and is included in the ledger statement death benefit and summary page total cash value.

31___ †The values shown in the ledger statement assume an annual mode of premium payment.

Figure A-7. (*Continued*)

13. The cumulative guaranteed cash value (the reserve). Again, although mathematically correct, it does not take into consideration the time value of money.

14. The total cumulative cash value (cumulative guaranteed cash value—reserve—and nonguaranteed cash value of additional paid-up insurance purchased by the dividends). Although mathematically correct, it does not take into consideration the time value of money.

15. Yearly increase of total cash value. The time value of money is not taken into consideration.

16. The difference between the total cash value and the gross premium of $1391 on a yearly basis. Absence of a minus (−) sign after the

numerical figure means that the yearly total cash-value increase is in excess of the gross premium of $1391. The time value of money is not considered.

17. The initial death benefit of $100,000, increased by the purchase of additional paid-up life insurance purchased by the projected dividends, equals the yearly total death benefit. From 1998 on, the terminal dividend is included.

18. Statement about how the dividends are used to vanish the premium, starting in year 1992.

19. Additional accessories (benefits) provided by rider (here, waiver of premium). The cost is included in the gross premium of $1391.

20. The insured is now 37 years old. The life expectancy of a 37-year-old male is 36 years, which would be year 2023.

21. Summary page values shown on this page (guaranteed cash value, total cash value, cash premium payments, and total cash value less premium payments) are based on end-of-year values, not beginning-of-year.

22. Time period—5 years, 10 years, 15 years, 20 years, and age 65.

23. Cumulative guaranteed cash value.

24. Cumulative total cash value.

25. Cumulative cash premium payments only for the time period remaining payments are due on the ledger statement (e.g., $1391 for 1988, 1989, 1990, and 1991).

26. Difference between columns 24 and 25. Columns 23, 24, 25, and 26 do not take into consideration the time value of money.

27. Terminal dividend for the years shown.

28. Dividend footnote statement.

29. Investment aspect of the dividends statement.

30. Terminal dividend statement.

31. Premium assumption statement.

Ledger Statements Do Not Tell All.   You should be told either verbally or in writing the following additional information:

▪ You will note that the interest-adjusted index is not provided on the ledger statement. To provide it would be inaccurate because it would ignore the time period that has expired since the policy has been in force. A cash-flow analysis (also known as "traditional method of cost disclosure") would be misleading because it would not take into consideration the time value of money.

▪ The rate-of-return method (also known as "the Brownlie method") is the only method that can be used to measure the alleged compound interest return (based on the current in-force ledger statement, which is only a current snapshot in time) upon death and surrender.

▪ The investment strategy for this in-force policy, which dictates the projected dividends, is a weighted-average portfolio rate consisting of 60 percent for new money and 40 percent for old money.

▪ The investment strategy produces a dividend interest assumption rate of 11.57 percent grading up to 11.73 percent over a 20-year period. The insurance company also anticipates gains from real estate and common stocks.

▪ The procedure for determining the rate of return for an exisitng policy is as follows: the first-year payment is the current surrender value of the policy (i.e., $6107; furnished on a separate statement by the insurance company) and any remaining premium to be paid (i.e., $713.20) for a total first-year payment of $6820. The amount of $6107 as a payment compensates for the time period that has expired since the policy was issued. Subsequent premium payments as shown on the ledger statement are $1426.40 ($713.20 twice a year) for 1989, 1990, and 1991. From 1992 on, the projected out-of-pocket cash premium payment is 0. The future values to be paid as shown on the ledger statement are the total cash value (column 14) and total death benefit (column 17).

▪ The following present-value payments (premium payments) $6820, $1426.40, $1426.40, and $1426.40, and the following future values (total cash value and total death benefit), result in the following yearly rates of return shown in the next table.

▪ Rates of return upon surrender are before taxes. When the rate of return is positive, taxes are due. The difference between the total cash value and the sum of premiums paid is subject to marginal ordinary federal income tax.

▪ The total death benefit is assumed to be life insurance proceedsand as such is not subject to marginal ordinary federal income tax.

▪ In order to determine the before-tax rate of return which must be achieved in another financial services product (e.g., mutual funds, real estate, commodities) in order to duplicate the rate of return upon death provided by life insurance, subtract from 100 your own specific marginal ordinary federal income tax bracket—i.e., 15 percent, 28 percent, 33 percent, and 34 percent (corporate)—and divide the yearly rate of return upon death by the result.

Year	Total cash value	Rate of return	Total death benefit	Rate of return
1 (1988)	$ 6,779	− 0.60%	$100,000	1,366.23%
2 (1989)	8,770	3.42	102,040	276.48
3 (1990)	10,963	4.99	104,483	138.85
4 (1991)	13,363	5.85	107,310	90.37
5 (1992)	14,505	6.47	106,309	65.69
6 (1993)	15,757	6.88	105,595	51.31
7 (1994)	17,125	7.16	105,161	42.01
8 (1995)	18,634	7.39	105,052	35.54
9 (1996)	20,300	7.57	105,286	30.82
10 (1997)	22,131	7.73	105,970	27.26
11 (1998)	24,145	7.86	107,005	24.48
12 (1999)	26,348	7.97	108,402	22.26
13 (2000)	28,757	8.06	110,169	20.45
14 (2001)	31,395	8.15	112,337	18.97
15 (2002)	34,279	8.22	114,913	17.73
16 (2003)	37,444	8.29	117,803	16.68
17 (2004)	40,917	8.35	121,154	15.78
18 (2005)	44,726	8.40	124,989	15.01
19 (2006)	48,910	8.45	129,345	14.36
20 (2007)	53,501	8.50	134,249	13.79
21 (2008)	58,535	8.55	139,732	13.29
22 (2009)	64,050	8.59	145,829	12.85
23 (2010)	70,098	8.62	152,589	12.47
24 (2011)	76,726	8.66	160,058	12.14
25 (2012)	83,992	8.69	168,292	11.84
26 (2013)	91,957	8.72	177,347	11.58
27 (2014)	100,683	8.75	187,281	11.35
28 (2015)	110,242	8.78	198,162	11.14
29 (2016)	120,749	8.81	210,126	10.96
30 (2017)	132,252	8.83	223,200	10.79
31 (2018)	144,860	8.85	237,505	10.64
32 (2019)	158,671	8.88	253,146	10.51
33 (2020)	173,808	8.90	270,253	10.39
34 (2021)	190,397	8.92	288,957	10.29
35 (2022)	208,581	8.93	309,394	10.19
36 (2023)	228,523	8.95	331,683	10.11

■ Exactly the same procedure should be followed for the proposed replacement policy, including: being told the investment strategy, dividend interest assumption rate (if a dividend paying policy), current versus assumed rate of interest if universal or interest sensitive whole life, and the ratio of current to maximum mortality charges. If the policy is variable life, request total disclosure about all expenses and deductions. The rate of return upon death and surrender based on the ledger statement must then be compared to the yearly rates of return for the existing policy.

Bibliography

The works listed below, among many others, have been essential study and research material throughout my business career. Their value as an educational resource is indirectly reflected in this book.

Some materials have been taken directly from *Tax Facts I, 1987* and *Tax Facts I, 1988*. The materials are specific Internal Revenue Service statements, and their use is not an infringement of the rights of the National Underwriter Company. However, in the spirit of total disclosure, the National Underwriter Company has been informed of the intended usage, and has granted its written permission for use of the quoted materials.

Brownlie, William D., CLU, ChFC, CIP, LIA: *Life Insurance: Its Rate of Return*, The National Underwriter Company, Cincinnati, 1983.

The Financial Service Professional's Guide to the Tax Reform Act of 1986, The American College, Bryn Mawr, Pa., 1986.

Huebner, S. S., and Kenneth Black, Jr.: *Life Insurance*, 10th ed., Prentice-Hall, Englewood Cliffs, N.J., 1982.

Rose, Peter S.: *Money and Capital Markets*, special ed., Business Publications, Plano, Tex.,

Tax Facts I, 1987, and *Tax Facts I, 1988*, The National Underwriter Company, Cincinnati.

Welker, Ernest P.: *Life Insurance from the Buyer's Point of View,*, American Institute for Economic Research, Great Barrington, Mass., 1986.

White, Edwin H., and Herbert Chasman: *Business Insurance*, 5th ed., Prentice-Hall, Englewood Cliffs, N.J., 1987.

Index